A Brief and Practical Guide to EU Law

Third Edition

David Medhurst
Barrister, Temple

Blackwell
Science

© David Medhurst 1990, 1994, 2001

Blackwell Science Ltd
Editorial Offices:
Osney Mead, Oxford OX2 0EL
25 John Street, London WC1N 2BS
23 Ainslie Place, Edinburgh EH3 6AJ
350 Main Street, Malden
    MA 02148 5018, USA
54 University Street, Carlton
    Victoria 3053, Australia
10, rue Casimir Delavigne
    75006 Paris, France

Other Editorial Offices:

Blackwell Wissenschafts-Verlag GmbH
Kurfürstendamm 57
10707 Berlin, Germany

Blackwell Science KK
MG Kodenmacho Building
7–10 Kodenmacho Nihombashi
Chuo-ku, Tokyo 104, Japan

Iowa State University Press
A Blackwell Science Company
2121 S. State Avenue
Ames, Iowa 50014-8300, USA

First edition published 1990
Second edition published 1994
(1st & 2nd editions published under the title *A Brief
and Practical Guide to EC Law*)
Third edition (*A Brief and Practical Guide to EU Law*)
published 2001

Set in 10.5/12.5 pt Palatino
by DP Photosetting, Aylesbury, Bucks
Printed and bound in Great Britain by
MPG Books, Bodmin, Cornwall

DISTRIBUTORS

Marston Book Services Ltd
PO Box 269
Abingdon
Oxon OX14 4YN
(*Orders:*   Tel: 01235 465500
               Fax: 01235 465555)

USA
Blackwell Science, Inc.
Commerce Place
350 Main Street
Malden, MA 02148 5018
(*Orders:*   Tel: 800 759 6102
                   781 388 8250
           Fax: 781 388 8255)

Canada
Login Brothers Book Company
324 Saulteaux Crescent
Winnipeg, Manitoba R3J 3T2
(*Orders:*   Tel: 204 837-2987
               Fax: 204 837-3116)

Australia
Blackwell Science Pty Ltd
54 University Street
Carlton, Victoria 3053
(*Orders:*   Tel: 03 9347 0300
               Fax: 03 9347 5001)

A catalogue record for this title is available
from the British Library

ISBN 0-632-05184-1

Library of Congress
Cataloging-in-Publication Data
Medhurst, David.
    A brief and practical guide to EU law/David
Medhurst. — 3rd ed.
        p.   cm.
    Rev. ed. of: A brief and practical guide to EC
law. 2nd ed. c1994.
    Includes bibliographical references and index.
    ISBN 0-632-05184-1
    1. Law — European Union countries.
I. Medhurst, David. Brief and practical guide to
EC law.   II. Title.
KJE949 .M43   2001
341.242′2 — dc21
                                        00-052931

For further information on
Blackwell Science, visit our website:
www.blackwell-science.com

CONTENTS

Contents

Contents

Contents

Contents

PREFACE

In the third edition of this book I have maintained the aims of the first. I have written a book for lawyers who did not study European Union law as students, or who have since forgotten about it, and who need to familiarise themselves rapidly with the subject. For these the major textbooks are too fraught with new fangled jargon to approach without a simple introduction and practical guidance. I have therefore not tried to say anything grave and weighty, but have endeavoured to write something short and intelligible. To this end I have tried to leave out as much as I dared, rather than cram in as much as I could. I have written in plain English, explaining jargon wherever it appears, and avoiding acronyms.

A chapter on how to look up the law and read cases has been included, and there are answers to questions you dare not ask, such as: 'Where is the European Court?', 'How do I start an action?', 'What is the Advocate General?' or 'What kinds of document do I have to prepare?'.

Since the last edition of this book in 1994 there have been a number of developments that have made a new edition essential. The Amsterdam Treaty was not so profound a development as the Union Treaty, but it did result in a consolidation and renumbering of the tattered text of the Treaty of Rome. The Social Charter has been incorporated into the Treaty. A directive on parental leave, and the eradication of time limits instanced by the *Seymour-Smith* case are but some of the new terrors heaped on employers. In the area of free movement, the *Keck* case has put a gloss on the rule in *Dassonville*, and the *Silhouette* case has clarified the jurisprudence on trade mark protection. Competition law has been modernised, and this is reflected in a new single regulation on vertical agreements, and, at a domestic level, in the Competition Act 1998. The Agenda 2000 reforms have improved the Common Agricultural Policy. The *Factortame* saga has finally ended in the House of Lords, leaving us with clear guidance on when and how our national courts will award damages against the state if it fails to implement EU law.

I have not described every new development, but I have provided enough information for the reader to understand the significance of changes as they occur.

At the time of writing the European Union was preparing the final stages of its intergovernmental conference for the year 2000. The purpose of this conference will be to lay the foundations for the expansion of the European Union. There are 13 applicant countries, Bulgaria, Cyprus, Estonia, Hungary, Latvia, Malta, Lithuania, Poland, the Czech Republic, Romania, Slovenia, Slovakia and Turkey. The enlargement will take place in stages and it is possible the first new Member States may join as soon as 2003. The European Parliament is proposing changes in the institutional framework of the Union, in particular that the president of the Commission should be chosen by Parliament. It has also proposed a simplification of the Union Treaty, by dividing it into two parts, one dealing with the Union's objectives, fundamental rights, institutions and decision-making procedures, and the second concentrating on policies. This would be welcome, but irritating for lawyers who have barely become used to the Amsterdam consolidation. But, the main principles, the 'acquis' as the European lawyers would call it, will remain the same.

David Medhurst
July 2000

TABLE OF CASES

Table of Cases

Table of Cases

TABLE OF EC CASES

TABLE OF EC CONVENTIONS

TABLE OF EC DIRECTIVES

TABLE OF EC REGULATIONS

TABLE OF EC COMMISSION DECISIONS

TABLE OF UK STATUTES

TABLE OF UK STATUTES

TABLE OF UK STATUTORY INSTRUMENTS

TABLE OF UK STATUTORY INSTRUMENTS

TABLE OF EC COURT RULES AND PRACTICE NOTES

TABLE OF ENGLISH COURT RULES

TABLE OF EC COMMISSION NOTICES

ABBREVIATIONS

CAP	Common Agricultural Policy
CCBE	Comité Consultative des Barreaux Européens (the liaison body in the EC for the legal profession in Member States)
CCT	Common Customs Tariff
CELEX	Acronym for the Community law database
CMLR	Common Market Law Reports
COREPER	Committee of Permanent Representatives
EAGGF	European Agricultural Guidance and Guarantee Fund
EC	European Community
ECR	European Court Reports
ECSC	European Coal and Steel Community
ECU	European Currency Unit, now the Euro
EEC	European Economic Community
EEIG	European Economic Interest Grouping
EU	European Union
EURATOM	European Atomic Energy Community
EUROVOC	Acronym for a documentary language used by the Publications Office of the Europoean Communities as the basis for a thesaurus for indexing and retrieving information
FEOGA	European Agricultural Guidance and Guarantee Fund (Fonds Européen d'Orientation et de Garantie Agricole)
JO	Official Journal (Journal Officiel)
JOCE	Official Journal (Journal Officiel des Communautés Européennes)
MCA	Monetary Compensatory Amount
OJ	Official Journal
SCA	Special Committee on Agriculture
SME	Small or Medium Sized Enterprise

CHAPTER 1
THE TREATIES

1.1 Introduction

The United Kingdom joined the European Communities on 1 January 1973. To prepare for that event Parliament enacted the European Communities Act on 17 October 1972. In the title to the Act the word 'Communities' is used in the plural because there are three of them: the European Coal and Steel Community (ECSC), the European Atomic Energy Community (Euratom), and the European Community (EC); the latter used to be called the European Economic Community (EEC).

These Communities were created by three European Treaties. The first of these was the ECSC Treaty which was signed in 1951. It was followed by the EEC Treaty and the Euratom Treaty which were both signed in 1957. The 1951 Treaty is commonly known as the Treaty of Paris; the two latter Treaties are known as the Treaties of Rome. After undergoing various amendments the three European Treaties were incorporated into the Union Treaty, commonly known as the Maastrict Treaty, which was signed in 1991. The Union Treaty is now effectively the constitution of the European Union.

The system of law arising out of the Treaties was introduced to the United Kingdom by means of section 2(1) of the European Communities Act, which reads as follows:

> 'All such rights, powers, liabilities, obligations and restrictions from time to time created or arising by or under the Treaties, and all such remedies and procedures from time to time provided for by or under the Treaties, as in accordance with the Treaties are without further enactment to be given legal effect or used in the United Kingdom shall be recognised and available in law, and be enforced, allowed and followed accordingly ...'

The Act does not deliver Community law undiluted to the courts of the United Kingdom; it is more subtle than that. Only Community law which is 'without further enactment to be given legal effect' can automatically be used in the courts of the United Kingdom. Community legislation which confers rights in this way, so that those rights can be used directly in national courts, is said to be *directly applicable*. There are three main kinds of Community legislation: regulations, the Treaties themselves, and Directives. Regulations are usually directly applicable, and Treaty articles can sometimes have direct effect, but Directives are not usually directly effective.

Directives are directed to Member States, not individuals, and therefore must be made into United Kingdom law before they can be used. This process is dealt with by section 2(2) of the Act, which provides for the making of orders in council or regulations by ministers or departments in order to implement Community obligations. Generally Community law finds its way into domestic law by this process, but sometimes there will be an Act of Parliament which introduces an area of Community law in response to a Directive, such as the Consumer Protection Act 1987.

It used to be thought that a Directive never had direct effect, because a Directive is, in essence, an order directed to a Member State of the Community, and would appear not to concern the individual at all. But Member States have not always done their duty, and therefore the European Court, by its jurisprudence, has developed a principle that where a Member State does not implement a Directive it is nevertheless bound by it as against its citizens.

When dealing with Community law it is confusing, at first, to be told that there are three communities. For practical purposes, however, they have been merged into one, and provisions which occur in the EC Treaty are mirrored by parallel provisions in the ECSC and Euratom Treaties.

1.2 The Union

The European Communities form the foundation of the European Union. The Treaty on European Union came into effect in 1993 and incorporates four distinct treaties as follows:

(1) Treaty on European Union
- Title I – Common Provisions
- Title V – Common Foreign and Security Policy
- Title VI – Police and Judicial Cooperation in Criminal Matters
- Title VII – Closer Cooperation
- Title VII – Final Provisions

(2)   Title II – EC Treaty
(3)   Title III – ECSC Treaty
(4)   Title IV – Euratom

The European Union is a political concept and does not yet have legal personality; the European Community does have legal personality by virtue of article 281 [210] of the EC Treaty ([210] refers to the former article in the previous version). The full title of the EC Treaty is 'The Treaty Establishing the European Community', and it is the most important part of the Union Treaty. The EC Treaty, the regulations and Directives of the European Community, and the judgments of the European Court form the main body of European law. Therefore one properly speaks of European Community Law, rather than European Union Law, although the distinction is no longer very important.

In this book when we refer to 'the Treaty' we mean the EC Treaty, unless the context makes it clear that some other treaty is intended. The EC Treaty has been amended on many occasions since it was first made. At the time of writing the latest incarnation of the EC Treaty was that created by the Treaty of Amsterdam. The latter made few substantive changes, but the opportunity was taken to create a consolidated edition of the Union Treaty, deleting paragraphs that had become otiose, and renumbering all the articles. In this book the old numbering of the EC Treaty and of the Union Treaty is given in square brackets. The consolidated version of the Treaty on European Union is published in the *Official Journal of the European Communities* at OJ C340 10.11.97 p145, and is available from The Stationery Office. A table of equivalences, giving the old numbers and their replacements, is published at OJ C340 10.11.97 p85. The European Court has published guidance on the way in which the provisions of the various treaties are to be cited in Treaty Citation Note No 2 [1999] All ER (EC) 647. More details about this, and about how to find material in the Official Journal of the Communities, are set out in Chapter 4.

The chronology of the succession of treaties that have led to the Consolidated Union Treaty is as follows:

- ECSC Treaty (Treaty of Paris) April 1951
- EEC Treaty (Treaty of Rome) March 1957
- Euratom (Treaty of Rome) March 1957
- Merger Treaty 1965
- First Accession Treaty – UK 1972
- Second Accession Treaty – Greece 1979

- Third Accession – Spain and Portugal 1985
- The Union Treaty (Maastricht) 1992
- Fourth Accession – Sweden, Finland, Austria 1994
- Amsterdam Treaty 1997

There is a welter of annexes, protocols, and declarations attached to the treaties. These are set out in their present form at the end of the consolidated version of the Union Treaty. A protocol of particular interest to lawyers is the Statute of the Court of Justice of the European Community, which regulates the procedure and organisation of the European Court.

Apart from the treaties the European lawyer must be aware of several conventions made in the area of intergovernmental cooperation. The Brussels Convention deals with the reciprocal enforcement of judgments in civil and commercial matters, and the Rome Convention sets out the law applicable to contractual obligations; both of these conventions are summarised below. The Dublin Convention regulates the way in which refugees are dealt with, and conventions known collectively as the *Schengen Acquis* deal with arrangements for border control; these conventions are summarised in Chapter 10.

1.3   The ECSC Treaty – the Treaty of Paris

The Treaty Establishing the European Coal and Steel Community was signed on 18 April 1951 and has been in force since July 1952. The original signatories were Germany, Belgium, France, Italy, Luxembourg and the Netherlands. It is an institution which seeks to direct and control output, markets, supply, and demand in the limited area of coal and steel. Its days are numbered because it is due to expire on 23 July 2002, unlike the other treaties which have no limit. It served as a model for the EC Treaty and is a useful introduction to some of the jargon used in Community law. It is now a constituent of the Union Treaty.

After a brief and high sounding preamble about safeguarding world peace, and resolving age-old rivalries, the ECSC Treaty will be found to contain some 100 articles divided into four titles. Article 1 says that the ECSC is founded upon a common market, without actually defining what this is. Article 3 sets out the goals of the institutions of this Community. These include ensuring an orderly supply to the common market, ensuring that consumers have equal access to sources of production, and the promotion of international trade.

Article 4 lists those things which are incompatible with this common market, such as import and export duties, or charges having equivalent effect, quantitative restrictions on the movement of products, and state subsidies. The rather awkward phrases 'quantitative restriction' and 'equivalent effect' mean, in broad terms, quotas and taxes discriminating against imported goods. Such terms are encountered in Community law when the subject under discussion is free movement of goods within the Community.

Title Two of the Treaty is concerned with the institutions of the ECSC. There were originally four: a High Authority (now the Commission), a Common Assembly (now the European Parliament), a Special Council of Ministers, a Court of Justice, and a Court of Auditors. The Maastricht Treaty added the Court of Auditors to the list of institutions; its task is to audit the accounts of the ECSC. The five institutions have now all been merged with their counterparts in the other two Communities.

Title Three contains various economic and social provisions, including a provision in article 65 forbidding agreements tending to distort competition, such as those which fix prices. Title Four contains general and budgetary provisions.

There is a logical structure to the Treaty. First, the objects of the Community are set down: growth of employment, and a rising standard of living. These objects are to be attained by preventing practices which hamper free competition. Then, five institutions are created to carry this policy into effect. Finally, detailed economic and social provisions are made to achieve the aims of the Community. These include rules on prices, competition, production, wages, and movement of workers.

1.4   The EC Treaty – the Treaty of Rome

The Treaty Establishing the European Economic Community, commonly known as the Treaty of Rome, was signed at Rome on 25 March 1957. The original signatories were Belgium, Germany, France, Italy, Luxembourg, and the Netherlands. This is the Treaty with which one is generally concerned when considering Community law. It was amended in some important respects by a Treaty called the Single European Act, and was extensively remodelled by the Union Treaty (Maastricht). At Maastricht the title was amended to The Treaty Establishing the European Community, and in this book it is referred to as the EC Treaty or simply the Treaty. The term 'European Economic Community' was deleted throughout and replaced with the term 'European Community'. At each amendment the draftsmen tried to preserve the original numbering system of the articles, adding only a letter to an existing paragraph number. But by the time of the Amsterdam Treaty this arrangement had become too cumbersome, and consequently it was decided to simplify the text by adopting an entirely new numbering system, consolidating various amendments, and eliminating material that had become redundant.

The essential features to grasp about the EC Treaty are that it establishes four freedoms: the right to free movement of goods, persons, services and capital. It sets out common policies for agriculture, fisheries, transport, commerce and competition. The following is a summary of the contents of the consolidated EC Treaty, as it is after the amendments made by the Treaties of Maastricht and Amsterdam.

There is a preamble which speaks of laying the foundations for a closer union among the peoples of Europe, ensuring economic progress by action to eliminate barriers which divide Europe, improving living conditions, and abolishing restrictions on international trade. The preamble, though common lawyers may be tempted to ignore it, contains valuable guidance to the interpretation of the Treaty.

The Treaty is divided into six parts. Part One, consisting of articles 1 to 16 [1 to 7d], deals with general principles. According to article 2 [2] the Community has the task of promoting economic development, employment, social protection, equality between men and women, growth, competitiveness, the convergence of economic performance, an improved environment, the raising of the standard of living, and economic and social cohesion and solidarity among the Member States.

These objectives are to be achieved by establishing a common market and an economic and monetary union, and by implementing certain common policies or activities referred to in articles 3 [3] and 4 [3a] such as the prohibition, as between Member States, of customs duties and quantitative restrictions on the import and export of goods, a common commercial policy, an internal market characterised by the abolition of obstacles to freedom of movement, a common policy on agriculture and transport, and a system for ensuring that competition is not distorted.

6

Article 4 [3a] was inserted by the Maastricht Treaty. It states that the activities of the Member States are to include the irrevocable fixing of exchange rates so as to lead to the introduction of a single currency.

Article 7 [4] states that the tasks entrusted to the Community are to be carried out by five institutions:

- a European Parliament
- a Council
- a Commission
- a Court of Justice
- a Court of Auditors

The Court of Auditors is there to audit the accounts of the Community; it used not to feature in the above list but it was made a full institution by the Union Treaty (Maastricht). The Auditors are assisted by an Economic and Social Committee. This is a committee of representatives from such bodies as trade unions, employers' associations, and consumer groups throughout the Community. The European Parliament used to be called the European Assembly but it was renamed by the Single European Act in 1986.

Part Two, headed 'Citizenship of the Union', is an addition made by the Maastricht Treaty. Under article 17 [8] every person holding the nationality of a Member State becomes a citizen of the Union. Citizenship of the Union complements, but does not replace, national citizenship. Citizens of the Union have the right to move and reside freely within the territory of Member States, subject to limitations and conditions laid down in the Treaty. Under article 20 [8c] the right to petition the European Parliament is afforded to every citizen.

Part Three of the Treaty deals with Community policies. It is divided into 20 titles. Title I, articles 23 [9] to 31 [37], is concerned with free movement of goods. Actual customs barriers have long been eliminated. Of more enduring interest are disguised methods for restricting imports, such as special labelling or packaging requirements imposed on imported goods. Such conduct is forbidden by article 28 [30], which states that quantitative restrictions and all measures having equivalent effect are prohibited between Member States.

Title II of the third part of the Treaty is concerned with the common agricultural policy. In article 33 [39] the conflicting aims of the policy are set out, namely to increase productivity, to ensure a fair standard of living for the agricultural community, to stabilise markets, to ensure the availability of supplies and to ensure that supplies reach consumers at reasonable prices.

Title III deals with free movement. Article 39 [48] establishes the right of freedom of movement for workers in the Community. Article 43 [52] deals with the right of establishment of nationals of Member States within the territory of another Member State. Of interest to companies is article 48 [58] which treats companies in the same way as natural persons for the purposes of freedom of establishment. Article 49 [59] prohibits restrictions on the freedom to provide services within the Community. All restrictions on the movement of capital between Member States and between Member States and third countries are prohibited by article 56 [73b].

Title IV was added by the Treaty of Amsterdam. It is entitled 'Visas, Asylum, Immigration and Other Policies related to Free Movement of Persons'. The object of this title is to incorporate the Schengen Acquis into the EC Treaty. (The term '*Acquis*' means a developed area of law and jurisprudence.) The Schengen Acquis, consisting principally of two agreements signed in 1985 and 1990, provides for the gradual abolition of checks at the borders of signatory countries. The UK, Ireland and Denmark have obtained a derogation from the effects of Schengen. The derogation is contained in article 69 [73q] of the Treaty and states that the application of Title IV is subject to the provisions of a protocol. The protocol permits these three states to maintain border controls for the purpose of verifying the right of EC nationals to enter their territories, and for the purpose of deciding whether to grant permission to other nationals to enter.

Title V deals with transport. Article 70 [70] provides for matters within this Title to be governed by a common transport policy.

Title VI contains article 81 [85], which prohibits as incompatible with the common market, agreements which restrict or distort competition within the Community, and article 82 [86], which forbids the abuse by an undertaking of a dominant position within the common market; these provisions are likely to be mentioned whenever there is a problem in competition law. The Treaty of Amsterdam enables legislation to be made by qualified majority to implement rules on competition (unanimity was previously necessary). Article 92 [87] deals with state aid to industry, declaring aid which threatens to distort competition incompatible with the common market.

Title VII covers economic and monetary policy; this part of the Treaty was largely rewritten at Maastricht. The purpose of the economic and monetary policy is to provide a framework for an economic and monetary union that will lead to the establishment of a single currency. The unit of account used to be called the ECU (European Currency Unit), but the new currency is called the Euro. Transitional provisions with regard to achieving economic and monetary union are set out in articles 116 [109e] to 124 [109m].

Articles 105 [105] to 111 [109] contain provisions defining the tasks and powers of the European Central Bank (ECB) and the European System of Central Banks (ESCB), which were established by the Union Treaty. The ESCB is composed of the ECB and of the national central banks. Its primary objective is to maintain price stability. The ECB will have the exclusive right to authorise the issue of bank notes within the Community. Under article 110 [108a] the ECB may (within defined limits) make regulations, take decisions, make recommendations, and deliver opinions – in other words it has the power to make legislation and partake in the decision making processes of the Community.

Title VIII concerns employment. This title was added by the Treaty of Amsterdam with the object of developing a coordinated strategy for employment and in particular for promoting a skilled, trained and adaptable workforce in the Community.

Title IX deals with the common commercial policy of the Community.

Title X consists only of article 135 [116]. It was added by the Amsterdam Treaty and enables the Council to take measures to strengthen customs cooperation between Member States, and between the latter and the Commission.

Title XI covers social policy, education, vocational training and youth. Directives on equal pay and treatment, and various measures such as those enhancing the rights of workers on the transfer of undertakings, derive from this part of the Treaty. Article 141 [119] requires each Member State to ensure that the principle of equal pay for male and female workers for equal work or work of equal value is applied.

At Maastricht, the United Kingdom refused to agree to any changes in the social policy provisions of the Treaty, although the other Member States agreed to use the machinery of the Community in order to take measures to implement among themselves the policy set out in the European Social Charter. At Amsterdam the United Kingdom finally agreed to the changes that the other Member States had already settled on. The amendments enable the Council, in some cases by qualified majority, and under the co-decision procedure, to make new legislation in the social field. To understand the last sentence one has to know how legislation is made in the Community; the process is described in Chapter 2.

Title XII contains only article 151 [128]. This was added to the Treaty at Maastricht, and says that the Community will contribute to the flowering of cultures of the Member States. The Council has to act unanimously in order to adopt measures in this regard, so we may anticipate little fruit.

Titles to XIII to XX are additions, made by the Single European Act and expanded by the Maastricht and Amsterdam Treaties, dealing with public health, consumer protection, trans-European networks (for transport, telecommunications, and energy), industry, economic and social cohesion, research and technological development, the environment, and development cooperation.

Part Four of the Treaty concerns Member States agreeing to associate certain non-European countries with the Community. It is of political rather than legal interest.

Part Five deals with the institutions of the Community. Here are detailed provisions in articles 189 [137] to 248 [188c] about the powers and constitution of the European Parliament, Council of Ministers, Commission, Court of Justice, and Court of Auditors.

Article 249 [189] sets out the various subsidiary forms of legislation used by the Community, namely regulations, Directives, and decisions. Although it is by no means an exact analogy, the Treaty can be considered as a kind of constitution. Regulations and Directives are like our acts of Parliament. Regulations are directly applicable in all Member States. Directives are binding only as to the results to be achieved, and thus require implementing legislation in Member States before they can come into effect.

1.5   The Euratom Treaty

The Treaty Establishing the European Atomic Energy Community was signed at Rome on 25 March 1957. The original signatories were Belgium, Germany, France, Italy, Luxembourg and the Netherlands. The task of this Community is to contribute towards the raising of standards of living in Member States by creating the conditions necessary to the establishment and growth of nuclear industries. The architecture of the Euratom Treaty is similar to that of the Treaties which establish the other two communities. Articles 92 to 106 set up a nuclear common market.

1.6 The Merger Treaty and the Convention on Common Institutions

The foregoing Treaties having been made, it became clear that a tidying up operation was needed. There were three Communities, but each had its own institutions. The Convention on Certain Institutions Common to the European Communities was signed on 25 March 1957. Its effect was to merge the Assembly (now the European Parliament), the Court of Justice, and the Economic and Social Committee of the various communities. The Treaty Establishing a Single Council and a Single Commission of the European Communities was signed at Brussels on 8 April 1965 and came into force on 1 July 1967.

1.7 The First Accession Treaty

The Treaty Concerning the Accession of the Kingdom of Denmark, Ireland, the Kingdom of Norway, and the United Kingdom of Great Britain and Northern Ireland was signed on 22 January 1972. Norway backed out at the last moment. The United Kingdom deposited an instrument of ratification on 18 October 1972 and the Treaty entered into force, for the United Kingdom, on 1 January 1973.

From the date of accession the provisions of the original Treaties and the acts adopted by the institutions were made binding on the new Member States. There were various transitional provisions in the Treaty but the transitional period has now passed. For most purposes the law can be read as if the United Kingdom had belonged to the Community from its inception.

1.7.1 Gibraltar, the Channel Islands, Cyprus, Isle of Man

The EC Treaty, by virtue of article 299(4) [227(4)], applies to those European territories for whose external relations a Member State is responsible. Gibraltar is thus a part of the European Community, although it is not subject to the Community rules on the common agricultural policy and value added tax and is outside the customs union. By contrast, the sovereign base area of Cyprus does not come within the Community at all.

The Channel Islands and the Isle of Man have managed to have their cake and eat it. Their anomalous position is covered by the

Third Protocol to the First Accession Treaty. Under the provisions of this protocol only the Community rules on free movement of goods apply. They are included in the customs union, but are excluded from the common agricultural policy except as regards exports. Manxmen and Channel Islanders do not benefit from the Community rules on free movement of persons unless they have been ordinarily resident in the United Kingdom for five years.

1.8   The Second Accession Treaty

The Treaty Concerning the Accession of the Hellenic Republic was signed in Athens on 28 May 1979 and came into effect on 1 January 1981. It contained detailed transitional provisions, largely relating to agriculture. The Community provisions on free movement of workers came into effect on 1 January 1988.

1.9   The Third Accession Treaty

The Treaty Concerning the Accession of the Kingdom of Spain and the Portuguese Republic was signed in Lisbon and Madrid on 12 January 1985 and came into effect on 1 January 1986. Detailed transitional provisions were set out in the Treaty, but most of these interim arrangements were spent by January 1993, and Spanish workers now have full free movement rights within the Community.

1.10   The Single European Act

The Single European Act is a treaty that was signed in Luxembourg on 17 February 1986, and at the Hague on 28 February 1986. It came into force on 1 July 1987. It made extensive amendments to the other basic Community legislation and therefore should not be discussed in isolation. The full text can be found in the Common Market Law Reports [1987] 2 CMLR 741. It prepared the way for the Union Treaty.

The purpose of the Single Act, as evidenced by the first paragraph of the preamble, was to initiate a change in relations between the European States with a view to establishing a European Union. To this end article 2 created a European Council to bring together the heads of state of the European Communities at least twice a year. This formalised the regular meetings which were already taking place.

A number of amendments dealt with the machinery of Community institutions. A cooperation procedure was established, which gave the European Parliament greater influence over the legislative process. This procedure is now to be found in article 252 [189c] of the EC Treaty; it is complicated. Parliament can table amendments to legislation proposed by the Commission upon which the Council has adopted a common position. If Parliament rejects that common position the Council can adopt the act only by unanimity; in other words the Council can ignore Parliament if it wishes.

The Single European Act created the Court of First Instance, which is now attached to the European Court. At first it was concerned only with competition cases and the internal staff cases of the Community, but in 1993 its jurisdiction was extended to include all cases (save for referrals from national courts) brought by private litigants. Cases brought by Member States or institutions of the Community and referrals from national courts go directly to the European Court. Judgments of the Court of First Instance are subject to a right of appeal to the European Court on points of law only.

Articles in the EC Treaty dealing with economic and social cohesion, research and technological development, and the environment are the result of the Single European Act.

The Single European Act provided an accelerated programme for the creation of the internal market, described in article 14 [7a – formerly 8a] of the EC Treaty as an area without internal frontiers in which the free movement of goods, persons, services and capital is ensured. The date for the creation of the internal market was 31 December 1992.

An obstacle to the free movement of goods and services was the procurement policies of Member States. In order to prevent governments from unduly favouring their own nationals a series of Directives require large contracts for public works and public supplies to be subject to fair procedures for tendering. Legislation was introduced to enforce compliance with these Directives, and to extend their effect to water, energy, transport and telecommunications utilities. Another obstacle to free movement was the absence of legislation recognising the equivalence of professional qualifications. New legislation was introduced to make job relocation easier. The present state of this legislation is described in Chapter 10.

1.11   The Union Treaty

The Treaty on European Union was agreed on 11 December 1991 by the European leaders meeting at Maastricht. The Treaty was signed on 7 February 1992, and came into effect on 1 November 1993. The full text can be found in the Common Market Law Reports [1992] 1 CMLR 719, and in the *Official Journal of the European Community* (OJ C224 31.8.92 p1).

By this Treaty the twelve Member States of the Community resolved to form a European Union, founded on the existing European Communities. The Treaty of Rome was therefore altered, stitched, patched, and renamed the Treaty Establishing the European Community. The new European Community which was created by these amendments forms the first pillar of the Union.

The second pillar of the Union is a common foreign and security policy; its provisions are set out in Title V of the Union Treaty. It stands outside the scope of the EC Treaty and it is based on inter-governmental cooperation.

The third pillar, also based on intergovernmental cooperation, is set out in Title VI of the Union Treaty, headed 'Police and Judicial Co-operation in Criminal Matters'. Prior to the Amsterdam Treaty, the formulation of common policies on asylum was the province of this part of the Union Treaty, but asylum now falls within Title IV of the EC Treaty. Article 29 [K1] of the Union Treaty states that the Union's objective is to provide an area of freedom security and justice. Under article 34 [K6] the Council can adopt a common position, adopt framework decisions for the purpose of approximation of laws, or adopt decisions for any purpose consistent with the objectives of this part of the Union Treaty. These measures do not entail direct effect, although Member States can afford the European Court jurisdiction to give rulings on their validity and interpretation.

Amendments made to the EC Treaty increased the powers of the European Parliament. A procedure for making legislation between Parliament and the Council, known as co-decision, was created and this is now set out in article 251 [189b] of the EC Treaty. Under this procedure Parliament can reject certain kinds of proposed legislation, unless the difference between Parliament and the Council over the proposal can be resolved in a conciliation committee.

1.12 The Fourth Accession Treaty

The Treaty of Accession of Norway, Austria, Finland and Sweden was signed on 24 June 1994. Norway never ratified the Treaty. It came into force for the other signatories on 1 January 1995. Some transitional provisions are still extant. The current members of the European Community are therefore: Belgium, Denmark, Germany, Greece, Spain, France, Ireland, Italy, Luxembourg, Netherlands, Portugal, United Kingdom, Austria, Finland, and Sweden (15 Member States).

1.13 The Amsterdam Treaty

At the European Council meeting in Amsterdam on 16 and 17 June 1997 the heads of state agreed a draft treaty. The treaty was signed on 2 October 1997. Like the other treaties it had to be ratified by the legislature of each Member State and this process was completed on 1 May 1999.

Although the Amsterdam Treaty modified both the Union Treaty and the EC Treaty it did not make any radical changes. As a result of the Amsterdam Treaty, the Union Treaty declares in article 6 [F] that it is founded on the principles of liberty, democracy, respect for human rights and fundamental freedoms, and the rule of law, principles which are common to the Member States. The Union will 'respect fundamental rights' as guaranteed by the European Convention on Human Rights – the Convention is thus indirectly incorporated into EC law. The Council (if the European Parliament assents) may suspend the rights, including the right to vote, of a Member State that breaches the fundamental rights upon which the Union is founded: see article 7 [F1] of the Union Treaty, and article 309 [236] of the EC Treaty. A new article 13 [6a] of the EC Treaty enables the Council to take measures to combat discrimination based on sex, racial or ethnic origins, religion or belief, disability, age or sexual orientation. The salient features of the Amsterdam Treaty were as follows:

- *Security and justice:* An objective of the Union is: 'to maintain and develop the Union as an area of freedom, security and justice in which the free movement of persons is assured in conjunction with appropriate measures with respect to external borders, immigration, asylum and the prevention and combating of crime'. With this objective in mind the Council was given powers to make new legislation on asylum, illegal immigration, crossborder service of judicial and extrajudicial documents, and so on. Certain exemptions apply to the UK and Ireland with respect to the common travel area and the need for the UK to continue its system of border controls. The position of Denmark is also taken into account. There were measures to strengthen the Schengen Acquis.

- *Employment:* A new title on employment was inserted into the EC Treaty. Article 125 [109n] of this new title states that: 'Member States and the Community shall, according to this title, work towards developing a coordinated strategy for employment'.

- *Social policy:* The change here was that the Social Agreement which was formerly annexed to the Treaty and applied to Member States other than the UK was incorporated into the Treaty. Measures relating to equal treatment of men and women can be taken under the co-decision procedure. One of the first changes to come about as a result of these alterations was the implementation of the Parental Leave Directive. We must expect future Directives relating to working conditions, health and safety, consultation of workers, social security, protection on termination of contract, collective bargaining, and third country nationals.

- *Environment:* Changes were made to the Union Treaty and the EC Treaty with a view to achieving the integration of environmental protection into all sectoral policies. Member States can adopt a broad range of higher environmental measures than those agreed at Community level.

- *Public Health:* Amendments to article 152 [129] of the EC Treaty permit the Council to adopt various new measures concerning public health in the Community.

- *Consumer protection:* Amendments to article 153 [129a] of the EC Treaty enable the Council to take measures to promote the interests of consumers and to ensure a high level of consumer protection.

- *Other Community policies:* Amendments and various protocols and declaration were made in relation to citizenship, cultural activities, sport, fraud affecting the financial interests of the Community, customs, outermost regions, island regions, services of general economic interest, public service broadcasting, public credit institutions in Germany and voluntary services activities, animal welfare, trans-European networks and statistics.

- *Subsidiarity:* A protocol was annexed to the EC Treaty for the purpose of defining 'subsidiarity'.

- *Transparency:* A new article 255 [191a] was inserted into the EC Treaty guaranteeing the right, subject to limitations determined by the Council, for citizens to have access to EC documents.

- *Quality of Legislation:* The Conference declared that the Commission ought to 'establish by common accord guidelines for improving the quality of the drafting of Community legislation'. (Well, we shall see.) The first outcome was the preparation of the consolidated version of the Union Treaty.

1.14   The Brussels Convention

Article 293 [220] of the EC Treaty states that Member States are to enter into negotiations with each other to obtain agreement on the simplification of formalities governing the reciprocal enforcement and recognition of judgments. It was in pursuance of this article that the Convention on Jurisdiction and Enforcement of Judgments in Civil and Commercial Matters of 27 September 1968, commonly known as the Brussels Convention, was drawn up. An Accession Convention of 9 October 1978 took account of the enlargement of the Community when Britain joined in 1973. In 1982 a convention was signed to provide for the accession of Greece. A further convention made in 1989 provided for the accession of Spain and Portugal, and at the same time an opportunity was taken to amend the Convention. On 26 November 1996 the EC Member States signed the Convention on the Accession of Austria, Finland and Sweden. It thus extends to all the Member States of the Community (see OJ C15 15.1.97 p1). A consolidated version of the text is to be found at OJ C27 26.1.98 p1.

Questions relating to the interpretation of the Brussels Convention are referred to the European Court in the same way as questions arising under the EC Treaty, save that a reference may not be taken at first instance. The Convention was incorporated into British law by the Civil Jurisdiction and Judgments Act 1982, which entered into force on 1 January 1987.

The text of the Convention is appended to the Act. It provides a complete code as to how and when it is possible to sue and enforce judgments in the courts of Member States. A knowledge of the methods of interpretation used by the European Court is essential in order to understand it, and a knowledge of the procedure used by that Court is necessary if any question of interpretation arises.

A consideration of the terms of the Convention is beyond the scope of this book, but the basic rule, subject to a number of specific exceptions, is that persons domiciled in a *contracting state* may be sued in the courts of that state, whatever their nationality. The old rule that once enabled the English courts to assume jurisdiction simply by reason of the service of a writ within the jurisdiction has gone. Persons domiciled in another contracting state may be sued there only by virtue of the rules set out in articles 2 to 6 of the Convention. These exceptions may be summarised as follows:

- *Special Jurisdiction:* A person domiciled in a contracting state may be sued in contract in the courts for the place of performance, under employment contracts in the courts for the place where the employee habitually carries out his work, in tort in the courts for the place where the harmful event occurred, for maintenance in the courts for the place of domicile or habitual residence of the maintenance creditor, (see article 5 – there are other exceptions).

- *Insurance:* An insurer domiciled in a contracting state may be sued in the courts of the state where he is domiciled, or where the policy holder is domiciled (articles 7 to 12 contain other exceptions).

- *Consumer contracts:* A consumer may bring proceedings either in his own courts or in the courts for the state where the other party is domiciled.

- *Exclusive jurisdiction:* In certain cases a court will have exclusive jurisidiction regardless of domicile – as in proceedings which have as their object rights *in rem*, nullity or dissolution of companies, validity of entries in registers, registration or validity of patents, trade marks and designs, proceedings concerned with the enforcement of judgments, *etc.*

• *Prorogation of jurisdiction:* Agreements as to jurisdiction may be made between parties one or more of whom is domiciled in a contracting state.

As to prorogation of jurisdiction, such agreements must be in writing, or in form which accords with practices which the parties have established between themselves (i.e. a course of dealing) in accordance with article 17 as amended by the 1989 Accession Convention. But an agreement as to place of performance will have the incidental effect of conferring jurisdiction on the courts of the place of performance although it need not be in writing. In C-106/95 *Mainschiffahrts-Genossenschaft eG (MSG)* v *Les Gravières Rhenanes Sarl* [1997] ECR I-911, [1997] All ER (EC) 385, however, the European Court ruled that if there is a deliberate choice of place of performance with the object of designating jurisdiction, the agreement must comply with the formalities of article 17.

The Convention is limited to civil and commercial matters. It does not extend to revenue, customs or administrative matters, and does not apply, *inter alia*, to matrimonial property, bankruptcy proceedings and social security. It does extend, however, to matters relating to maintenance; a maintenance creditor can sue in the courts where he or she is domiciled.

The Lugano Convention of 16 September 1988 was made between the European Community and the European Free Trade Association (EFTA). It is closely modelled on the Brussels Convention, and allows for the enforcement and recognition of judgments between EFTA states and the Community, but it does not provide any system of appeals to the European Court. It was introduced into English law by the Civil Jurisdiction and Judgments Act 1991. On 26 November 1996 the EC Member States signed the Convention on the Accession of Austria, Finland and Sweden to the Brussels Convention, these states having joined the European Community. Norway, Switzerland and Iceland are subject only to the Lugano Convention.

1.15   *The Rome Convention*

The Convention on the Law Applicable to Contractual Obligations, commonly known as the Rome Convention, was introduced into

English law by the Contracts (Applicable Law) Act 1990 and came into effect on 1 April 1990. It provides a complete code as to the law which is to apply to contractual obligations in any situation where there is a choice between the laws of different countries. It differs from the Brussels Convention in that there was no specific provision of the EC Treaty under which it could be enacted, but the preamble speaks of a desire to continue in the field of private international law the work of unification of law which has already been done within the Community. Appeals lie to the European Court of Justice on questions of interpretation, but not from a court of first instance.

The Convention does not apply to questions of status or legal capacity, wills and succession, rights arising out of matrimonial or family relationships, bills of exchange, arbitration agreements, trusts, or certain insurance contracts.

The application of the Convention is not limited to cases where the law of a Member State is applicable, so that a Japanese, for example, will find that the same rules on choice of law apply no matter which forum he uses within the Community.

1.16   *The European Economic Area Treaty*

The European Economic Area Treaty was signed on 2 May 1992 and was intended to spread the gospel of the single market to the former EFTA countries. It was made between the European Community, then consisting of 12 states, on the one hand, and on the other hand Austria, Finland, Iceland, Liechtenstein, Norway, Switzerland and Sweden. Switzerland had a referendum in December 1992 and opted out. Liechtenstein became a member of the EEA on 1 May 1995. Austria, Sweden and Finland have now joined the European Community so that the scope of this treaty is limited to Iceland, Liechtenstein, and Norway. Freedom of movement for goods, persons, capital, and services applies throughout the EEA, which adopts most of the EC single market legislation. The EC rules on competition and state aids have been transposed almost word for word into the treaty, and the EC rules on public purchasing are applied. There is no automatic referral of cases to the European Court, but the EFTA states can implement a protocol whereby a court in those states may refer a case to the European Court, if it considers it necessary to ask a question on the interpretation of the EEA Treaty or acts adopted in pursuance thereof. An EFTA Court, which gives advisory opinions, was set up in 1992, originally with five judges, but since June 1995 it has comprised three judges appointed by Iceland, Liechtenstein and Norway.

1.17   *The Dublin Convention*

The Convention Determining the State Responsible for Examining Applications for Asylum Lodged in One of the Member States of the European Communities was signed at Dublin on 15 June 1990. It was ratified by all the Member States on 1 September 1997. It is designed to deal with the unseemly prospect of orbiting refugees and requires applications for asylum to be examined by one Member State. The terms of the Dublin Convention are examined in more detail in Chapter 10.

1.18   *The European Convention on Human Rights*

The European Convention for the Protection of Human Rights and Fundamental Freedoms was signed in Rome in 1950. The system of law arising from the European Convention on Human Rights is quite separate from the the European Union. All the Member States are bound by the Convention, but it extends to other European states who are part of the Council of Europe but not in the European Community. Human rights cases go only to the European Court of Human Rights at Strasbourg.

The Court of Justice of the European Communities, which sits in Luxembourg, has developed a jurisprudence which purports to incorporate Convention rights into European Community Law, but only as an interpretative principle; the position is discussed under the heading of legal principles and interpretation in Chapter 4. Article 2 [B] of the Union Treaty states that the Union has, as one of its objectives, the devlopment of an 'area of freedom, security and justice', and under article 6 [F] it must respect the fundamental rights guaranteed by the Convention. The absence of any statement of fundamental rights for citizens of the European Community has led to suggestions that a charter of such rights should be incorporated into the Treaty, an idea resisted by the UK government on account of the duplication that this would involve.

The UK's Human Rights Act received the Royal Assent on 9 November 1998. This Act is outside the scope of this book but we will touch on its provisions since it is likely that EC points will overlap with questions under the Convention. The two systems are very different. The Human Rights Act incorporates into UK law articles 2 to 12 and 14 of the European Convention on Human Rights, and articles 1 to 3 of the First Protocol to the Convention. Article 1 of the Convention secures the rights and freedoms set out in the rest of the Convention, and article 13 assures an effective remedy. These were the object of the Act and so there was no need to set them out in terms.

The Act enables questions on human rights to be raised in domestic proceedings in the UK. The main features of the Act are as follows. Primary and subordinate legislation must be read and given effect in a way which is compatible with Convention rights (this provision applies to any court). The High Court, the Court of Appeal and the House of Lords have power to make a 'declaration of incompatibility'. The Crown is entitled to notice if the court is contemplating such an order. Under section 6 of the Act it is unlawful for a public authority to act in a way which is incompatible with a Convention right. A person who claims that a public authority has acted (or proposes to act) in a way which is made unlawful by section 6 may bring proceedings against the authority or rely on the Convention right in any legal proceedings, but only if he is 'a victim of the unlawful act'. The court may, in relation to any act or proposed act of a public authority which it finds unlawful, grant such relief or remedy, or make such order, within its jurisdiction as it considers just and appropriate, but damages may be awarded only by a court which has power to award damages in civil proceedings. If a court has made a declaration of incompatibility, a minister of the Crown or her Majesty in Council can make amendments to legislation, known as 'remedial orders', to remove the offending part.

If all domestic remedies have been exhausted there remains a right to apply to the European Court of Human Rights. Until November 1998 there were two stages to an application. An applicant who had exhausted all domestic remedies applied in the first instance to the European Commission of Human Rights. This body established whether the complaint was admissible (whether it fell within the Convention, within the six months time limit, and whether domestic remedies have been exhausted). It endeavoured to reach a friendly settlement. If that failed it produced a report which expresses an opinion. The case might then be referred to the Court by the Commission or by the respondent state. In the case of the UK there was no individual right of petition.

On 1 November 1998 a new system was introduced, as set out in Protocol 11 to the Convention. This Protocol abolished the old system of Commission and Court and replaced them with a single Court which sits at Strasbourg. The new Court accepts individual petitions (see article 34 of the Convention as amended). The Court will only deal with a matter 'after all domestic remedies have been exhausted according to generally recognised rules of international law and within a period of 6 months from the date on which the final decision was taken'. If the Court declares the application admissible it must first examine the case and place itself at the disposal of the parties with a view to securing a friendly settlement. If a friendly settlement is effected the Court has power to strike out the case by means of a decision 'which shall be confined to a brief statement of the facts and of the solution reached'. If no settlement is reached the Court can proceed to make a determination. The Court sits in Chambers, and in a Grand Chamber. Usually cases are to be dealt with by a Chamber initially. Within a period of three months from the date of judgment any party can request the removal of the case to the Grand Chamber, and the Grand Chamber 'shall accept the case if a serious question affecting the interpretation or application of the Convention ... or a serious issue of general importance' is raised.

The Court gives a judgment which a ratifying state is bound to observe, and can award a sum of money as compensation and to cover legal costs and expenses.

CHAPTER 2
THE INSTITUTIONS

2.1 Introduction

The main institutions of the Community are the European Parliament, the Commission, the Council, the Court of Justice, and the Court of Auditors. The Court of Auditors has the task of examining Community accounts and making sure that they are kept regular and legal, but its activities are of little practical interest to lawyers. Important ancillary institutions are the Economic and Social Committee, consisting of representatives of the various categories of economic and social activity, and the Committee of the Regions. These institutions must be consulted when certain kinds of legislation are made. The Council of Europe is the name given to the periodic meetings of heads of state during which major political decisions are made. In this chapter we shall consider the nature and powers of these various institutions.

2.2 The European Parliament

The European Parliament has its seat at Strasbourg. It does not deserve to be called a parliament, for it neither proposes nor makes laws: the Commission proposes legislation, and the Council of Ministers makes laws. A proposal from the Commission is rather like a bill in the UK Parliament, but the extent to which the European Parliament may influence the process of making it into law depends upon the nature of the proposal. There are four procedures by which the European Parliament may become involved in the legislative process: consultation, co-operation, co-decision, and assent.

The EC Treaty sometimes requires that Parliament be consulted before the Council adopts a binding measure. In addition to these mandatory consultations the Commission will normally seek the opinion of Parliament on a wide range of measures. Due consultation of the Parliament in cases provided for by the Treaty consititutes 'an essential formality disregard of which renders the measure void': C-138/79 *Roquette* v. *Council* [1980] ECR 3333.

The Single European Act introduced the cooperation procedure whereby the European Parliament could amend, reject, or approve a common position adopted by the Council. The procedure as now modified is set out in article 252 [189c] of the EC Treaty. It enables Parliament to propose amendments to a proposal by the Commission. The Council must take the opinion of Parliament into account before voting, but the last word still lies with the Council which can unanimously ignore Parliament if it wishes. The procedure was never a success and is now confined mainly to aspects of Economic and Monetary Policy (see articles 99(5), 101, 103, 106 and 300(3) of the EC Treaty).

The Maastricht Treaty (the Union Treaty) introduced a procedure called co-decision. It is set out in article 251 [189b] of the EC Treaty. Under the co-decision machinery the last word, though a negative one, is with Parliament. If Parliament and the Council are unable to resolve their differences the President of the Council and the President of the European Parliament must convene a conciliation committee. If this fails to reach a compromise, Parliament can, in the last resort, reject the proposed legislation. This procedure applies to a wide range of measures, for example those involving equal treatment in matters of employment (article 141 [119]), freedom of movement (article 18 [8a]), and sea and air transport (article 80 [84]).

The accession of new states to the Union depends on the assent of Parliament (see article 46 Title VIII [article L Title VII]). Certain major international agreements that have major financial implications, or require amendment of acts adopted under co-decision, come under the assent procedure (see article 300(3) [228]). The assent of Parliament is required before the Council can suspend the rights of a Member State in consequence of a serious breach of the principles of liberty, democracy, human rights, and the rule of law upon which the Union is founded: see Title I article 7 [F1]. Certain legislation concerning the uniform electoral system, citizenship, the role of the Central Bank, and structural funds also comes under this procedure.

The worst that the Parliament can do is to pass a motion of censure on the activities of the Commission. If such a motion is passed the Commission must resign as a body: see article 201 [144] of the Treaty. Parliament has certain budgetary powers under article 272 [203]. It can set up a committee of enquiry to investigate alleged maladministration, under article 193 [138c]. It can appoint an ombudsman to receive complaints about maladministration, and any citizen can petition Parliament: see articles 194 and 195 [138d and e]. It can also bring an action in the European Court against the Commission or Council under article 232 [175], for failure to act, as was done in Case 13/83 *European Parliament* v. *EC Council* [1985] ECR 1513, [1986] 1 CMLR 138, on account of the failure of the Council to legislate for freedom to provide transport services.

The result of having little democracy at the heart of the Community is that it is run by civil servants. We must look at the powers of the Council and, more importantly, the Commission to see what really matters.

2.3 The Council of Ministers

The Council of Ministers, which has its headquarters in Brussels, is as near as the Community comes to a legislative body. (Do not confuse it with either the Council of Europe, which is the organisation that was responsible for the European Convention on Human Rights, or the European Council which is mentioned below.) It is a Council of ministers of the various Member States of the Community. Thus, if it were discussing agriculture it would be a meeting of ministers of agriculture; if economics of economics ministers, and so on. Meetings are usually convened by the Member State holding the presidency of the Union.

Most decisions are taken by qualified majority, which means that the votes of the various members are weighted; for example, the United Kingdom scores 10 whilst Belgium scores 5. Because ministers are usually employed elsewhere, the day to day work of the Council is done by Council Working Groups of officials taken from the Member States, who assist the Committee of Permanent Representatives of Member States, known as COREPER (Comité des Représentants Permanents). The latter consists of representatives from Member States with ambassadorial rank. In fact there is more than one COREPER and various other committees; agriculture, for example, is dealt with separately by the Special Committee on Agriculture (SCA) but this need not concern mere lawyers.

The Council puts the seal on, but does not propose, Community legislation. The Commission proposes legislation which it submits to the Council. The latter must consult the European Parliament and, depending on the terms of the Treaty article concerned, the Economic and Social Committee or the Committee of the Regions. A failure to observe the terms of the consultation procedure will render a measure invalid and liable to be annulled by the Court of Justice. The procedure is modified where co-decision, cooperation or assent procedures are involved.

2.4   *The European Council*

The heads of state or of government of the Community and the President of the Commission meet regularly as a body which is known as the European Council: see Title I article 4 [D]. The European Council has evolved from the regular summit meetings which have taken place between heads of government. The heads of state are obliged to meet at least twice a year, so as to provide the European Union with the necessary political impetus. The European Council is not the same as the Council of Ministers but can be regarded as an extension of the latter.

2.5 *The European Commission*

The Commission has its headquarters in Brussels and Luxembourg. It proposes Community policy and legislation which is then passed on to the Council for discussion and implementation. The Commission carries out decisions taken by the Council. It is divided administratively into various Directorates General; DG IV, for example, is responsible for competition policy.

It is confusing to find that both the Commission and the Council have powers to make legislation. Both can make regulations and directives, but that does not mean that the Commission acts other than in an executive fashion. For example, the Community law relating to the common agricultural policy consists of a series of basic Council regulations, each of which establishes a common organisation of the market for a particular product. But detailed rules for the implementation of these policies are made by the Commission.

In Case 25/70 *Köster* [1970] ECR 1161, [1972] CMLR 255, an attempt was made to say that a Commission regulation was invalid because, it was contended, the power to make the regulation lay with the Council and not the Commission. It was said that the

Council should have gone through the procedure set out in article 37 [43] of the Treaty. This required the Council to act only on a proposal from the Commission and after consulting the European Parliament. The European Court held that since the Commission did not go beyond the implementation of the basic regulation the Commission regulation was valid. Thus, implementing legislation could be made either by the Commission or by the Council without going through the full procedure of article 37 [43].

The duties and powers of the Commission are set out in article 211 [155] of the EC Treaty, namely: to ensure that the provisions of the Treaty and measures taken by the institutions are applied; to formulate recommendations or deliver opinions on matters dealt with in the Treaty; to have its own power of decision and participate in the shaping of measures taken by the Council and the European Parliament; and, to exercise the powers conferred on it by the Council for the implementation of the rules laid down by the Council.

The members of the Commission are Community civil servants. They are supposed to act in the general interest of the Community, and are completely independent. Article 213 [157] of the Treaty states that they shall neither seek nor take instructions from any Government or any other body. The larger Member States appoint two commissioners: the smaller states have one each. The Commission itself is entitled to appoint one or two vice presidents from among its own members (see article 217 [161]).

In article 256 [192] of the EC Treaty we find that the Commission has, amongst other powers, the capacity to impose fines. These fines can be very large, and there are only two months in which to appeal, with no extensions of time. It can also take interim measures, which are rather like an interlocutory injunction. For the uninitiated it is surprising to find an institution which is not a court, but can impose fines and, in effect, grant injunctions. Such a surprising idea perhaps merits a little diversion to look at an example.

Commission Decision (EEC) 87/500, *Brass Band Instruments Ltd* (OJ L286 9.10.87 p36) [1988] 4 CMLR 67, is a decision of the Commission which we will look at again when we examine the Community rules on competition. In this case Boosey & Hawkes, the well known brass band instrument manufacturer, had managed to gain a dominant position in its market, and was therefore in a position to stifle competition. This Goliath of the euphonium was challenged by a David called Brass Band Instruments Ltd.

Brass Band Instruments Ltd had been set up by former employees of Boosey & Hawkes plc and hoped to compete in the market by manufacturing and selling instruments directly to brass bands. The company complained to the Commission saying that Boosey & Hawkes plc were trying to nip the enterprise in the bud by, amongst other things, refusing to supply parts to its young competitor and withdrawing credit facilities. Such conduct is prohibited by article 82 [86] of the EC Treaty.

In the days before the Competition Act 1998 English domestic law did not provide any obvious or ready remedy to challenge the conduct of Boosey & Hawkes. The Commission therefore adopted an interim decision which required Boosey & Hawkes plc to supply the parts. The decision went on to say that if they failed to do so they would become liable to a penalty of 1000 ECUs per day. (The ECU was the European Currency Unit, a unit of account which has now evolved into a currency, the euro.)

The advantage of using the Commission in this way is that it provides a remedy in circumstances where a common law action might be inappropriate. A mere complaint to the Commission costs nothing. Another lesson to be learned is that this is not only law for Goliaths but can be used by Davids too. The disadvantage is that the Commission tends to be slow, and much prefers private litigants to use national courts if they can; it will only intervene if a point of principle is at stake.

Where, however, it is the conduct of a Member State that is in issue there is every reason to complain to the Commission. In some circumstances an individual can sue a Member State for damages occasioned by a failure to implement European law, but the circumstances in which this can be done are limited (see Chapters 6 and 7). The Commission, however, is responsible for the initiation of proceedings against Member States for the breach of Community law. Under article 226 [169] of the Treaty, the Commission will begin by delivering a reasoned opinion. If the Member State does not comply with the opinion the Commission can bring the matter before the European Court. If the Member State does not obey the order of the Court, the Commission can initiate proceedings under article 228 [171] which will result in a fine being imposed.

2.6   *The Court of Auditors*

The Court of Auditors is not a court, but an examiner of the accounts of the Community. At the end of each financial year it must draw up an annual report which is published in the *Official Journal*. It was made a full Community institution by the Union Treaty (see now article 7 [4] of the EC Treaty).

2.7 *The Economic and Social Committee*

The Economic and Social Committee has an advisory status. It consists of representatives of the various categories of economic and social activity in the Community, appointed by the Council, in particular representatives of producers, farmers, carriers, workers, dealers, craftsmen, professional occupations and representatives of the general public (see article 257 [193] of the Treaty). The Council and the Commission must consult the Committee when the Treaty so provides; the Court of Justice could annul the act of one of these institutions if the consultation has not taken place.

2.8 *The Committee of the Regions*

Under article 265 [198c] of the Treaty the Council or the Commission must consult the Committee of the Regions where the Treaty so provides and in all other cases, in particular those which concern cross-border cooperation, in which one of these two institutions considers it appropriate. The Committee members are appointed by the Council and consist of respresentatives of regional and local bodies. The idea is that local communities should be able to influence the Community institutions.

CHAPTER 3
LEGISLATION

3.1 Introduction

In order to carry out their tasks the Council, the Commission, and Parliament jointly with the Council, make regulations, issue directives, take decisions, make recommendations, and deliver opinions. The Union Treaty is a kind of constitution, and regulations and directives, though sometimes misleadingly called secondary legislation, are analagous to our acts of Parliament. They are to be found in large quantities in the *Official Journal*. This is the Community's official gazette; those who are new to Community law will find it difficult to use. Ways of finding your law are discussed in Chapter 4. Article 249 [189] of the EC Treaty explains the nature of the above measures:

- A *regulation* is of general application. It is binding in its entirety and directly applicable in all Member States.
- A *directive* is binding, as to the result to be achieved, upon each Member State to which it is addressed, but leaves to the national authorities the choice of form and methods.
- A *decision* is binding in its entirety upon those to whom it is addressed.
- *Recommendations* and *opinions* shall have no binding force.

Under article 254 [191] of the Treaty, regulations and directives must be published in the *Official Journal*; they come into force on the date specified in them or, if no date is specified, 20 days after publication. Decisions must be notified to those to whom they are addressed and take effect upon notification.

Though recommendations and opinions are of no binding force they may be used as an aid to interpretation, and the preamble to a directive or regulation will usually refer to such material.

Directives are directed to Member States. They do not confer rights on individuals, but impose obligations on Member States to bring about changes in their domestic laws or administrative procedures. Therefore, as a general rule, directives have no direct effect on the individual. Regulations, by contrast, require no implementing legislation; they are directly applicable law.

The Treaty itself contains some directly applicable law. In a series of decisions the European Court has said that certain articles of the Treaty have direct effect.

Confusion sometimes arises because the ECSC Treaty uses a specialised vocabulary. Under article 14 of the ECSC Treaty there is a power to make decisions and recommendations. Decisions are binding in their entirety and can be either general or individual in effect. Recommendations are binding as to the aims to be pursued, but leave the choice of methods to the person to whom they are addressed. Therefore, an EC regulation is much the same as an ECSC general decision; an EC directive is similar to an ECSC recommendation; and, an EC decision is similar to an ECSC individual decision.

3.2 Direct applicability

If some directly applicable law is available to the litigant he may rely upon it in his domestic court as surely as he might rest his case on a domestic statute. *Garden Cottage Foods Ltd* v. *Milk Marketing Board* [1983] 3 CMLR 43, [1984] AC 130, was an early case in which a question about the application of European law arose in the UK. The plaintiff was a little company, effectively a husband and wife team. They relied on the competition law of the Community. The Milk Marketing Board had refused to supply them with butter because it preferred to use large distributors. This conduct was contrary to article 82 [86] of the EC Treaty, a directly applicable article. They obtained an interlocutory injunction, and the Court then had to consider whether damages would be an alternative. Lord Diplock said that damages would be available in English law because a breach of the duty imposed by article 82 [86] not to abuse a dominant position in the common market could be categorised as a breach of a statutory duty.

Damages and injunctions, even an injunction suspending the operation of an Act of Parliament, may be obtained in a public law context. Case C213/89 *Regina* v. *Secretary of State for Transport* ex parte *Factortame Ltd and others (No 2)* [1990] ECR I-2433, [1990] 3 CMLR 375, [1991] 1 AC 603, concerned some Spanish fishermen, prone to fishing for Dover sole to serve up as *lenguado* in the tapas bars of Bilbao, who were obliged to challenge the legality of the Merchant Shipping Act 1988, because it prevented them from registering their vessels to fish in British waters. They complained that the law was discriminatory, contrary to article 294 [221], and interfered with their right to freedom of establishment as guaranteed by article 43 [52] of the Treaty.

The European Court said that they were entitled to an interim injunction suspending the operation of the English law until their rights in the matter were determined. In due course the European Court determined that the UK had acted unlawfully (see C221/89 *R v. Secretary of State for Transport* ex parte *Factortame* [1991] ECR I 3095 and C246/89 *Commission v. UK* [1989] ECR 3125). Finally, in joined cases C46&48/93 *Brasserie du Pêcheur SA v. Germany, R v. Secretary of State for Transport* ex parte *Factortame* [1996] ECR I-1029, [1996] 1 CMLR 889, the European Court ruled that the state was obliged to pay damages to the fishermen. As to the circumstances in which damages may be awarded and the manner of calculation see Chapter 7.

If the Community law is not clear, any court or tribunal (including, for example, an employment tribunal or an immigration tribunal) can refer a question to the European Court. Under article 234 [177] of the Treaty, the latter can give preliminary rulings on the interpretation of the Treaty or the validity and interpretation of acts of institutions of the Community. Where the question is raised before a court or tribunal against whose decisions there is no judicial remedy under our law, that is to say a court from which there is no appeal, that court or tribunal must bring the matter before the European Court.

3.3   Direct effect

Most Community law is made in the form of Directives. This is because it is designed to be absorbed in an indirect way. Community legislation sometimes finds its way into UK law by means of a statute. For example, the Consumer Protection Act 1987 implements the product liability Directive, Council Directive 85/374/EEC (OJ L210 7.8.85 p29). But Community law usually enters by the back door by way of a statutory instrument. Section 2(2) of the European Communities Act enables ministers or departments to make regulations for the purpose of implementing any Community obligation. This extends to any such provision as might be made by Act of

Parliament: for example, the Sex Discrimination Act 1975 (Application to Armed Forces etc.) Regulations 1994 amended section 85 of the Sex Discrimination Act 1975 so as to accord with obligations arising under Council Directive 76/207/EEC (OJ L39 14.2.76 p40) in relation to the armed forces of the Crown. Before this amendment the Act did not apply to service in the armed forces.

Section 2(2) of the European Communities Act does not, however, include the power to make any provision imposing or increasing taxation, or to make any provision taking effect from a date earlier than that of the making of the instrument containing the provision, or to confer any power to legislate by means of subordinate instruments (other than rules of procedure for courts or tribunals), or to create any new criminal offence punishable with imprisonment for more than two years (see Schedule 2 of the Act).

It used to be thought that Directives could never have direct effect. But, a problem arose when it was found that member states were not implementing Directives in the way they should. Case 148/78 *Pubblico Ministero* v. *Ratti* [1979] ECR 1629, [1980] 1 CMLR 96, was a case where Italy had been tardy in making legislation to give effect to some Council Directives. The Community legislation was designed to eliminate the obstacles to trade between Member States that were caused by different technical requirements over the labelling of chemicals.

Signor Ratti decided to label some of his solvents in accordance with the Community Directives. The old Italian law was still in force and he was prosecuted by the Pubblico Ministero for infringement of the Italian law. The Italian court referred the matter to the European Court which ruled that after the expiration of the period fixed for the implementation of a Directive a member state may not apply its internal law to a person who has complied with the requirements of the Directive. Even if it is provided with penal sanctions, a national law which has not yet been adapted in compliance with the Directive could not be enforced.

Thus, Directives can have direct effect, at least as between an individual and the state. But, it is not in every such case that a Directive will have direct effect. One has to look at the general scheme and wording of the Directive to see if it imposes clear, complete and precise obligations on the Member State, does not lay down any conditions other than precisely defined ones, and does not leave the Member State any margin of discretion in the performance of its obligations.

The effect of a Directive which has become directly applicable is said to be 'vertical'. In other words, it can be used, by a sort of estoppel, against the state. It cannot be used horizontally against another private individual.

Just to confuse matters, not all regulations are directly effective. It is a matter of interpretation. Not every regulation will be drafted in such a way as to give rights to individuals. It follows that one must examine any Community legislation to see if it passes the test for direct effect.

If the legislation in question is a Directive it is necessary to look first for any national laws which implement the Directive. If there is a national law available then it may not be necessary to look further. If there is no national law, or if the national law does not come up to expectation, it becomes necessary to consider whether the date for implementation of the Directive has passed. This date will usually be about a year after the Directive was published; the date will be clearly set out in the text. If that date has passed the Directive may confer individual rights, but it can only be used against the state.

Those curious to know how far horizontal effect has advanced may begin by reading Case 152/84 *Marshall* v. *Southampton and South West Hampshire Area Health Authority* [1986] ECR 723, [1986] 1 CMLR 688, where Miss Marshall complained that, contrary to the Council Directive (EEC) 76/207 (OJ L39 14.2.76 p40) on equal treatment, she was required to retire at 60 instead of 65. Against a private employer she would have been unsuccessful because the Directive did not have horizontal effect but she was able to recover damages against her employer because the Health Authority was an emanation of the state. The European Court said that:

> 'Wherever the provisions of a directive appear, as far as their subject matter is concerned, to be sufficiently precise, those provisions may be relied on by an individual against the State where the State fails to implement the directive in national law by the end of the period prescribed or where it fails to implement the directive correctly.'

In Case C-188/89 *Foster* v. *British Gas plc* [1990] ECR I 3313, [1990] 2 CMLR 833, the European Court was not even discouraged to find that the defendant was a private employer. Unlike her male colleagues Mrs Foster was obliged to retire at 60 and, like Miss Marshall, she relied on Directive 76/207 when she sued British Gas plc. She was met by the argument that the defendant was not a state authority, but the Court of Justice held that, nevertheless, British

Gas plc had been made responsible by the state for providing a public service under the control of the state, and had special powers beyond those which result from the normal rules applicable in relations between individuals. It followed that Mrs Foster could rely on the direct effect of Community legislation.

The outer limits of horizontal direct effect were seen in *Doughty* v. *Rolls Royce plc* (*The Times*, 14 January 1992). In this case the plaintiff was in the same situation as Mrs Foster, and argued that her employer provided a service, particularly in the area of defence, under the control of the state, but she was unable to persuade the Court of Appeal that Rolls Royce exercised any special powers of the type enjoyed by British Gas.

Academic lawyers, sensible that horizontal direct effect will go no further, have divined a principle called useful effect, or the interpretive principle, or simply sympathetic interpretation. Case C-106/89 *Marleasing SA* v. *La Comercial Internacional de Alimentacion SA* [1992] 1 CMLR 305 arose out of a dispute between Marleasing SA and a number of defendants, including La Comercial. The plaintiffs contended that La Comercial was incorporated for no reason other than to put the assets of another defendant out of their reach, and that by the law of Spain, which was sensitive to such stratagems, La Comercial did not exist. La Comercial protested that in the First Company Law Directive, Council Directive of 9 March 1968 (EEC) 68/151 (OJ L65 14.3.68 p8), there was an exhaustive list of the only circumstances, none applying to La Comercial, in which a company, by the law of the Community, might be declared to be a nullity. The problem for La Comercial was that the Directive had not been implemented in Spanish law, and, since Marleasing SA was not an emanation of the state, it was not possible to rely upon the doctrine of direct effect. But the European Court rescued La Comercial, by pronouncing that it was for the Spanish court to interpret its law in the light of the wording and purpose of the Directive, in order to preclude a declaration of nullity on a ground other than those listed in Article 11 of the Directive. Thus, La Comercial was able to make use of the Directive, which had a useful effect, though it was not directly effective.

The European Court is not bound by its own decisions, but nevertheless it develops a consistent jurisprudence. A study of the above cases will illustrate how the jurisprudence of the Court evolves, and how it is possible to predict with tolerable certainty the outcome of a case.

3.4 *Direct applicability of the Treaty*

Regulations are directly applicable, but what about the Treaty itself? Clearly it would be a nonsense if the Treaty provisions which give rise to regulations were not directly effective whilst the regulations were. In a series of decisions the European Court has said that certain articles of the Treaty are of direct effect; but not all. Some articles are obviously not of direct effect because they are not designed to give individuals rights. Articles 1 [1] to 4 [3a], for example, set out the broad general principles of the Community and one would hardly expect them to confer individual rights. Others have been held to be capable of conferring individual rights.

Case 41/74 *Van Duyn* v. *Home Office* [1974] ECR 1337, [1975] 1 CMLR 1, is one of the leading cases on the principles relating to direct effect. It arose out of article 39 [48] of the Treaty which has to do with freedom of movement for workers in the Community; the article was held to be of direct effect. Before a provision can be of direct effect it must be *justiciable*; in other words, it must be appropriate to be enforced by a court. It must impose a clear, precise, and unconditional obligation, and should not leave a substantial discretion to the Member State. It can be seen that whether it is a directive, a Treaty provision, or a regulation the test is the same. In Case 43/75 *Defrenne* v. *SABENA* [1976] ECR 455, [1976] 2 CMLR 98, Advocate General Trabucchi described the test as follows:

> 'Under the criterion established by the case law of the European Court a Community provision produces direct effects so as to confer on individuals the right to enforce it in the courts, provided that it is clear and sufficiently precise in its content, does not contain any reservation and is complete in itself in the sense that its application by national courts does not require the adoption of any subsequent measure of implementation either by the States or the Community'.

An important point to note, in the *Defrenne* case, is that Miss Defrenne was suing not the state, but a company. Treaty articles are capable of having direct effect, not only between an individual and the state, but also between private individuals. Therefore, if a Directive does not provide any directly enforceable rights, the litigant may still be able to pray in aid a Treaty article upon which the Directive is based.

Sometimes it may be possible to use a Directive as aid to the interpretation of the Treaty article, and thus achieve the desired direct effect by a circuitous route. This is a method which has been used in some English cases on employment law. Article 141 [119] of the Treaty is of direct effect, and confers the right for men and women to receive equal pay for equal work. Council Directive 75/117 (OJ L45 19.2.75 p19) implements this principle but, in itself, is not directly applicable, except against the state. In *Pickstone* v. *Freemans plc* [1987] 3 WLR 811, [1987] 3 All ER 756, the Court of Appeal so interpreted article 141 [119] in the light of the Directive as, effectively, to give the plaintiff the rights she would have had if the Directive had had direct effect. The decision was later affirmed in the House of Lords but on other grounds.

The task of discovering whether an Article in the Treaty is of direct effect is not too arduous. The major text books contain lists of the articles with the relevant cases. Any case concerning an article of the Treaty will inevitably refer to the question of its direct effect. To add some unnecessary complexity there is academic argument over the difference between 'direct applicability' as used in article 249 [189] and the 'direct effect' which arises because of the criteria established by the case law of the European Court. The Court itself does not always make a distinction.

CHAPTER 4
INTERPRETATION AND RESEARCH

4.1 Introduction

Two practical problems face the tyro Community lawyer: how to find his law, and how to interpret it. Not only must he master a new set of research skills, but also acquire the continental manner of interpretation. In this chapter a description is given, with some practical examples, of how to research Community law. But simply finding the law is not enough. A common lawyer will have a list of common law and equity principles which he applies, almost instinctively, whenever he reads a statute or a case. He will not need to be reminded that equity treats as done that which ought to be done, that statutes are read literally, or that the ratio of the case is binding. Some of these ideas relate to mere interpretation, some to the common law and its philosophy of the freedom of the individual. Community law substitutes its own notions of how legislation should be interpreted, and what basic principles of law and justice should apply. It interprets legislation by reference to what it considers the legislator has intended, and as basic principles it applies law which is common to all the Member States; equality, certainty, proportionality, natural justice, and fundamental rights are the words used to express these basic principles.

4.2 Research

The first place to look for Community law is in one of the standard practitioners' encyclopaedias. It is worth mentioning this because the apoplexy brought on by the realisation that a question of Community law has arisen sometimes prevents a lawyer from looking in the obvious place.

Harvey on Industrial Relations and Employment Law (Butterworths) contains a comprehensive section on Community law, including the full text of the Council Directives on equal treatment. *Muir Watt &*

Moss on Agricultural Holdings (Sweet and Maxwell) contains a chapter on milk quotas. The *Encyclopaedia of Competition Law* (Sweet & Maxwell) contains a constantly updated section containing EC legislation, proposals and other materials. *Butterworths Immigration Law Service* contains all of the Directives on free movement together with a selection of Treaty material and extracts from the leading European cases. *Digings and Bennett on EC Procurement Law and Practice* (Sweet & Maxwell) contains European and international law materials. The *Product Liability and Safety Encyclopaedia* (Butterworths) contains all the relevant texts, as do *Palmer's Company Law* (Sweet & Maxwell, W Green), *Gore-Browne on Companies* (Jordans) and *Garner's Environmental Law* (Butterworths).

Volumes 51 and 52 of *Halsbury's Laws* contain a narrative on Community law and have the advantage of a regular update. *Atkin's Court Forms* contains a volume devoted to procedure in the European Court, together with various precedents. The Digest contains a volume on Community law, and thus provides a means to research case law in a way familiar to the English lawyer. The *Encyclopaedia of European Union Law* (Sweet & Maxwell) contains the text of all the various treaties and a wealth of other material.

A large French encyclopaedia, the *Recueils Practiques du Droit des Affaires dans les Pays du Marché Commun* (Jupiter) contains the Treaty in the five main Community languages. It contains a general introduction to the law relating to each article, and also the texts of the most important regulations and directives. Cases are arranged by Treaty article. It also contains a summary of the relevant national laws. It is therefore a source of information of a kind which it is difficult to find elsewhere.

4.3   Citation of the Treaty

For practical purposes one uses the Amsterdam consolidation when citing Treaty articles, but the need to distinguish between references to the Treaties as they stood and as they now stand may lead to confusion. The European Court has therefore issued a statement with regard to the correct method of citation as used in its judgments (Treaty Citation Note No 2 [1999] All ER (EC) 647).

Where reference is made to an article as it stands after 1 May 1999 the number of the article is immediately followed by two letters indicating the Treaty concerned:

- EU for the Treaty on European Union
- EC for the EC Treaty
- CS for the ECSC Treaty
- EA for the Euratom Treaty

Thus, 'art 234 EC' means the article of that Treaty as it stands after 1 May 1999. Where, on the other hand, reference is made to an article as it stood before 1 May 1999, the number of the article is followed by the words 'of the Treaty on European Union', 'of the EC (or EEC) Treaty', or 'of the EAEC Treaty', as the case may be. Therefore 'art 85 of the EC Treaty' refers to article 85 of the Treaty before 1 May 1999.

In addition, as regards the EC Treaty and the Treaty on European Union, again where reference is made to an article of a Treaty as it stood before 1 May 1999, the initial citation of the article in a text is followed by a reference in brackets to the corresponding provision of the same Treaty as it stands after 1 May 1999, as follows:

- 'Article 85 of the EC Treaty (now art 81 EC)', where the article has not been amended by the Treaty of Amsterdam
- 'Article 51 of the EC Treaty (now, after amendment, art 42 EC)', where the article has been amended by the Treaty of Amsterdam
- 'Article 53 of the EC Treaty (repealed by the Treaty of Amsterdam)', where the article has been repealed by the Treaty of Amsterdam.

By way of exception to the latter rule, the initial citation of the former articles 117 to 120 of the EC Treaty, which have been replaced *en bloc* by the Treaty of Amsterdam, is followed by the following wording in brackets: '(arts 117 to 120 of the EC Treaty have been replaced by arts 136 EC to 143 EC)'. For example:

'Article 119 of the EC Treaty (arts 117 to 120 of the EC Treaty have been replaced by arts 136 EC to 143 EC)'

The same applies to Articles J to J.11 and K to K.9 of the Treaty on European Union. For example:

'Article J.2 of the Treaty on European Unon (arts J to J.11 of the Treaty on European Union have been replaced by arts 11 EU to 28 EU).

4.4 *Looking up directives and regulations*

No equivalent to *Halsbury's Statutes* exists as a research aid into Community legislation. Regulations, directives, and decisions, sometimes inaccurately called secondary legislation, are to be found in the *Official Journal* (OJ), sometimes referred to by its French initials (JO or JOCE). This is the Communities' official gazette. It is published daily and contains not only the official texts of Community legislation but also draft legislation, official announcements, written questions to the European Parliament, the formal parts of judgments by the European Court, and a variety of other documents.

4.4.1   The Special Edition

The *Official Journal* began in 1958 and was published in the languages of the original Member States. When the United Kingdom joined the Community in 1972 a Special Edition of the Official Journal was prepared. The Special Edition is a translation into English of the Community legislation that was still in force when the United Kingdom joined. For this reason the pagination is rather curious. It contains the page numbers of the original publication in the *Official Journal*, but, since not all of the original material is reproduced, there are occasional breaks in continuity. It also has its own continuous pagination. The latter is not supposed to be used for citations, but in practice the page number of the Special Edition is often given.

The Special Edition covers the years 1952 to 1972. When it was prepared the opportunity was also taken to prepare a compilation organised by subject matter. This Subject Edition was a useful reference tool, but unfortunately it is now out of date. From time to time, however, the Commission publishes compilations of legislation on particular subjects.

4.4.2   'L' and 'C' series.

Since 1968 the *Official Journal* has been published in two series. The 'L' series contains legislation. The 'C' series contains information, draft legislation, and various notices. Proceedings in the European Parliament are published in an Annex and certain notices to do with public works contracts are contained in a supplement. Until June 1967 the pagination of the *Official Journal* started afresh each year but since that date each daily issue has started with page 1.

4.5   *Identifying legislation*

From 1958 to 1962 regulations were numbered in a single sequence, from number 1 onwards, continuous throughout those five years. So we find that the well known Regulation 17 is referred to as follows:

Council Reg. 17 of 6 February 1962/EEC

From 1963 to 1967 the numbers of regulations begin afresh each year, for example:

Council Reg. 183/64/EEC

Until 1968 Euratom regulations were numbered in the same way as above but in their own sequence. From 1968 onwards all regulations, both of the EC and Euratom, are numbered in a single sequence, the name of the relevant community preceding the number:

Council Reg. (EEC) 4087/88
Council Reg. (Euratom) 1372/72

Directives and decisions before 1962 were not numbered and are referred to simply by the date:

Council Directive of 11 May 1960 (EEC)

From 1963 to 1967 both the EEC and Euratom numbered their Directives and decisions in separate sequences beginning at 1 for each year:

Council Dir. 63/226/EEC
Council Dir. 63/27/Euratom

From 1968 both Communities used the same series beginning at 1 for each year:

Council Dir. 77/312/EEC

Carefully note the order in which Community legislation is cited. In the case of a regulation the number precedes the year. In the case of a Directive the year precedes the number.

It is wise to note that the Community should always be mentioned when legislation is cited or confusion may result. The ECSC uses its own terminology for legislation. The ECSC takes decisions and makes recommendations or delivers opinions. An opinion is not binding and does not count as legislation. An ECSC general

decision is similar to an EC regulation. An ECSC individual decision is similar to an EC decision. An ECSC recommendation is
similar to an EC Directive.

4.5.1 COM documents

Commission working documents consist of reports on implementation of policy, broad policy documents, and proposals for
legislation, which go through various drafts as they pass from
committee to committee. In the early stages these documents are not
published, though they may sometimes circulate in *samizdat*. They
are cited as follows:

COM document	Year	Number	
COM	92	345	FINAL

The example given was a Proposal for a Council Directive
amending Directive 71/305/EEC concerning the coordination of
procedures for the award of public works contracts, and was ultimately published in the *Official Journal* at OJ C225 1.9.92 p13.

4.5.2 A practical example

Let us suppose that the reader wishes to find an item of legislation
relating to the free movement of workers. He will find in the library,
at the end of the impressive purple row of volumes of the *Official
Journal*, a cumulative index. This index is published every six
months. It is in two parts. Volume 1 is called the 'Analytical
Register'. Volume 2 is the 'Chronological and Alphabetical Index'. It
is an index of legislation which is in force. It does not include
repealed legislation.

To his dismay the reader will find that the Alphabetical Index is
barely alphabetical and hardly an index. It is based on the
EUROVOC thesaurus of Community terminology and consists of
broad topics rather than detailed entries. In this it is, however, no
different in spirit from Community law which always proceeds
from the general to the particular.

Finding the entry for free movement is quite easy, but a particular
entry, for hairdressers or dentists for example, will not be found.
The entry in the alphabetical index will enable the reader to turn up
the relevant page in the analytical register. In the analytical register

the titles of all the legislation for a particular topic are grouped together. An item might be listed as follows:

68/360/EEC: Council Directive of 15 October 1968 on the abolition of restrictions on movement and residence within the Community for workers of Member States and their families.

Below this entry will be found the *Official Journal* reference and a series of obscure codes which indicate the extent to which the Directive has been amended. The key to these codes is in the introduction to the index.

The number of an item of Community legislation is unique and serves to identify it, but it does not enable one to find it immediately in the *Official Journal*. If the number is all that is available, one must discover how to use it to find the *Official Journal* reference. The place to look is in the chronological index, which in turn gives the page in the analytical register. The entry in the chronological index, for the above directive, would be as follows:

3	68	L	0360
Code for secondary legislation	Year	Code for Directives	Number of Directive

A final check on the state of the legislation has to be done rather laboriously by looking through the monthly indexes which are published with the *Official Journal*. The monthly indexes accumulate into a yearly index and are in two parts: an alphabetical index, and a methodological table. The methodological table contains lists of the various kinds of legislation which have been published.

The *Official Journal* reference gives the part number, date, and page at which the directive begins:

OJ	L257	19.10.68	p13
Official Journal	Part number	Date of publication	Page on which Directive begins

Because the above reference relates to a pre-1972 Directive it will be found in the Special Edition in the volume for 1968, part (II). The reference to the Special Edition is written as follows:

Sp edn	1968	(II)	p485
Special Edition	Year	Part	Page number for Special Edition

There is no cumulative index to the 'C' series. In order to find proposed legislation and other similar documents by hand it is necessary to look through each of the annual indexes. It is at this point that it is easier to go to a computer database.

4.5.3 Databases

The official legal database of the European Union is called CELEX. The CELEX database contains both Community legislation and the judgments of the European Court. Further information can be obtained from the Office of Official Publications of the European Communities, 2 rue Mercier, L-2985 Luxembourg. CELEX is available on CD-ROM in the JUSTIS version available from Context Electronic Publishers, Grand Union House, 20 Kentish Town Road, London NW1 9NR. Those with adequate funds will be able to use LEXIS-NEXIS, the computer database operated by Butterworths. This contains the EURCOM, EUROPE and INTLAW libraries including Community case law in English.

The Court of Justice has an internet site (www.curia.eu.int). There are other sites, for the Commission, Parliament, and Council. The last 45 days of the Official Journal and recent European Court of Justice judgments are available free (europa.eu.int/eur-lex). There are many other useful addresses, and not a few useless ones, but as they change from time to time there is no point in listing them. They can be found easily enough by using any search engine.

4.5.4 Interpretation

At last the Directive has been found. Now the problem is how to interpret it. The common lawyer will, at first, find Community legislation infuriatingly vague. This vagueness is the first barrier to making use of Community law in the English courts.

The secret is that the draftsman proceeds from the general to the particular. If one continues to take Council Directive 68/360 as an example, it will be seen that it begins with a long preamble. The first paragraph of the preamble states that one is to have regard to the Treaty establishing the EEC and in particular article 40 [49]. A glance at article 40 [49] will show that it has to do with measures required to bring about freedom of movement for workers as defined in article 39 [48]. With this firmly in mind it would be very

surprising to find anything in the Directive that contradicted article
39 [48] or 40 [49] of the Treaty.

What is more, if there were some gap that needed to be filled a
court would clearly be guided by the purpose which was so clearly
and conveniently set out in the Treaty. More help is given by the
subsequent paragraphs of the preamble. In the event of a conflict
between the wording of the regulation itself and the preamble it is
the preamble which will prevail.

4.5.5   Teleological and contextual interpretation

The approach to interpretation which is now favoured by the Court,
known as *teleological* or purposive, is to look at the broad purpose or
object of the text. This is quite a natural and obvious method to use,
given the way in which Community law is written. It means that
literal interpretation does not have the same importance as it does in
English law. The Court will, of course, begin with the plain meaning
of the words, but where that conflicts with the general scheme and
context of the legislation it is the latter which will prevail. The 'plain
meaning', moreover, is not the same as the 'literal' meaning.

The Court favours a contextual interpretation. In other words, it
will not take an individual article of the Treaty out of context but
will have regard to the whole scheme of the Treaty. The Court is not
often given to pronouncements upon its methods of interpretation,
but in Case 6/64 *Costa* v. *ENEL* [1964] ECR 585, [1964] CMLR 425, a
case which is important because it helped to establish the principle
of the supremacy of Community law, the contextual method is seen
in operation. One of the articles of the Treaty which was considered
in this case was article 43 [52], which prevents Member States from
introducing restrictions on the right of establishment. The Court
said that article had to be 'considered in the context of the Chapter
relating to the right of establishment in which it occurs'. Considered
in this way, it was clear that it was capable of creating direct effects
between the individual and the state.

An irritation for English lawyers is the frequent absence of a
definition section. Partly this is a consequence of the influence of
continental legal systems, but there are obviously practical difficulties when Community legislation is written in several languages,
each one of which has equal weight when it comes to interpretation.
In the search for meaning it is often useful to look at the French
version – although all the languages of the Community are equal,

French is more equal than others. Legislation will certainly have been prepared, in its early stages, in French. If all else fails one has to look for those cases where the Court has given its interpretation.

4.6   Travaux préparatoires

An abiding fear for the English lawyer is that in search of the meaning of Community legislation he may have to go rooting amongst some obscure bundle of *travaux préparatoires*. It is true that in one instance, Case 6/60 *Humblet* v. *Belgium* [1960] ECR 559, the European Court referred to the opinion of governments put forward during parliamentary debates preparatory to the ECSC Treaty, but it is truly rare for the Court to go to such inordinate lengths.

For practical purposes the problem of deciding what to look at is solved by reference to the preamble. In the preamble to Directive 68/360, for example, it states that the Council had regard to the Opinion of the European Parliament and the Opinion of the Economic and Social Committee and the references to these documents are conveniently given at the foot of the title page of the Directive. Sometimes a directive will refer to the Commission White Paper on 'Completing the Internal Market' or some similar document, or to other directives or regulations; the *Official Journal* reference will usually be given.

4.7   *General principles*

Another problem to cope with at an early stage is the question of what background law the Court will apply. The Court will, of course, look first to the Treaties themselves, and the Community legislation made under the provisions of the Treaties. It will also refer to its own case law: for example, the concept of direct effect of directives is law which has been created entirely by the jurisprudence of the Court. Where there are gaps to be filled the Court will look to the fundamental principles of Community law as expressed in the Treaty, such as the right to freedom of movement in article 39 [48] of the Treaty, or to equal treatment in article 141 [119], or the principle of subsidiarity set out in article 5 [3b]. But, the Court goes further than looking mechanically at the Treaty. It will also refer to general principles common to the laws of Member States.

The most frequently mentioned interpretive principles are

- legal certainty
- non-retroactivity
- the protection of legitimate expectations
- proportionality
- equality
- subsidiarity
- natural justice
- fundamental human rights

It is in accordance with these principles that the Court interprets the express provisions of Community law and the legality of Community acts. The terms used are unfamiliar to a common lawyer.

4.7.1 Legal certainty

This means that the effect of a provision must be clear, and capable of being predicted. For example, the time limit for bringing proceedings to annul a decision of the Commission is only two months. The time limit may not be extended by the Court even if there is agreement between the parties. The object is that the legal situation should be clear. A striking example of the use of the principle of legal certainty is provided by Case 43/75 *Defrenne* v. *SA Belge de Navigation Aérienne (SABENA)* [1976] ECR 455, [1976] 2 CMLR 98. In this well known case an air hostess was able to show that, under the Treaty articles relating to equal pay, she was entitled to parity with male cabin staff. That meant that she was able to claim back-pay. Fearful for the economic consequences, however, the Court limited its judgment in such a way that, except for the plaintiff, it was not retroactive. She could claim her back-pay, but for others the right to claim damages for discrimination dated only from the day of the judgment. The principle of legal certainty enabled the Court to *fiat justitia* without *ruat caelum*; justice might be done without risk to the firmament.

4.7.2 Protection of legitimate expectation

This concept is an aspect of the principle of legal certainty. It does not have the ineffectual meaning that English courts would attach to the term. Where the conduct of an institution has led an individual to have a reasonable expectation that a certain course will be pursued he may rely upon that expectation. It is a kind of estoppel.

In Case 120/86 *Mulder* v. *Minister van Landbouw en Visserij* [1988] ECR 2321, [1989] 2 CMLR 1, a dairy farmer had been persuaded to give up the production of milk for a year because of a Council regulation designed to encourage farmers to suspend production. In the meantime the Council introduced a system of milk quotas. To his dismay, Mr Mulder found that when he wanted to recommence production he could not obtain a milk quota. This was because he had given up production during the reference period upon which the quota was based. The European Court held that, because he had been encouraged to give up production for a limited period, he could legitimately expect not to be subject to restrictions when he resumed production. The Commission regulation which affected him was held to be invalid, in so far as it did not allocate a quota to him.

4.7.3   Non-retroactivity

Like legitimate expectation, this is also related to legal certainty. Legislation is presumed not to be retroactive, unless there is some clear provision which would justify an alternative view. But it is not an absolute principle. Where the principle of legitimate expectation is not infringed, and where it is necessary to attain its objective a measure may be retroactive. In Case 63/83 *R* v. *Kent Kirk* [1984] ECR 2689 there was no such expectation. What happened was that Captain Kirk, a Danish fisherman, was caught fishing off North Shields on 6 January 1983. English law imposed penalties for fishing within 12 miles of the coast and he was fined £30 000 at North Shields magistrates court. He appealed on the ground that on 31 December 1982 the transitional rules about fishing, made in the 1972 Act of Accession when the UK joined the Community, had expired. The prosecutor relied on a Council regulation made on 26 January 1983 that extended the UK restrictions on fishing in order to preserve fish stocks. The European Court held, however, that it was not possible to rely on retroactive EC measures as a means of validating national measures that were void at the time.

4.7.4   Proportionality

Proportionality involves the idea that the means used to achieve an end should be no more than what is appropriate and necessary to attain that end. Case 118/75 *State* v. *Watson and Belmann* [1976] ECR 1185, [1976] 2 CMLR 552, is a simple specimen of the use of this principle. Italian law at that time required foreigners to register with the police within three days of entering Italy. This, in itself, was not incompatible with the right to free movement conferred by Article 48 of the Treaty; but the Italian legislation also imposed penalties of large fines and, in addition, the possibility of deportation. It was held that Italy was not entitled to impose a penalty so disproportionate to the gravity of the crime that it became an obstacle to the free movement of persons.

4.7.5 Equality

The principle of equality is fundamental to Community law. Its most obvious manifestation is in Article 141 [119] of the Treaty which states that men and women should receive equal pay for equal work. It is not, however, confined to discrimination cases, but embraces the general tenet that similar situations must not be treated differently by the law and burdens imposed by the law must be borne equally. In *Pastoors* v. *Belgium* [1997] ECR I 258, [1997] 2 CMLR 457, a German lorry driver was stopped by some conscientious Belgian policemen on his way through Antwerp. They found some 11 infringements of Netherlands legislation concerning recording equipment in road transport and related matters. The Netherlands legislation was designed to implement various EC regulations. After a tedious conversation Mr Pastoors was given a choice. He could pay a fixed penalty of Bfr 10 000 for each offence, in which case no more would be said, or he could dispute the charges. In the latter event, seeing that he was not resident in Belgium, he had to lodge a deposit of Bfr 15 000 per offence, pending the decision of the Belgian court. His employers decided that this game was not worth the candle and coughed up the penalty, but in proceedings against the Belgian state they asked for their money back.

The argument of the lorry driver and his employers was that a requirement to pay a deposit was contrary to article 12 [6] of the Treaty, because Belgian residents did not have to provide one. Article 12 is a specific expression of the general principle of equality in European law, prohibiting any discrimination on grounds of nationality. Belgium argued that the difference could be objectively justified because there was no convention between Belgium and Germany for the enforcement of judgments in criminal cases.

The European Court pointed out that European law forbids not only overt discrimination by reason of nationality, but also all covert forms of discrimination which, by application of other criteria of differentiation, lead to the same result. The regulations afforded a discretion to Belgium as to the kind of penalty to be imposed, but where a Member State had such a discretion the penalty had to be effective, dissausive, and proportionate; and, it had to be appropriate and necessary. The deposit was, however, excessive because, although it was designed to cover costs of proceedings, it was charged on each offence. There was only one set of proceedings, and the costs would not appreciably differ if there was one rather than many infringements.

4.7.6 Subsidiarity

Article 5 [3b] of the Maastricht Treaty defines subsidiarity, which was developed at the same time. It is a species of proportionality, connoting that the institutions of the Community should not go beyond what is necessary to achieve the objectives of the Treaty.

4.7.7 Natural justice

In European law, this does not differ significantly from the common law concept. It involves the right to be heard, to examine evidence, and to be legally represented. Case 17/74 *Transocean Marine Paint Association* v. *EC Commission* [1974] ECR 1063, [1974] 2 CMLR 459, is a case where, although there was no specific legislative provision which could be said to render the decision invalid, the European Court annulled a decision of the Commission in a competition case. Onerous conditions had been imposed on the plaintiffs. In the long correspondence that led up to the decision the Commission had never mentioned that it proposed to impose such conditions. There was a failure of natural justice because the plaintiffs never had an opportunity to express their point of view.

4.7.8 Fundamental human rights

Closely allied to the principle of natural justice is the idea of respect for fundamental human rights; there is no catalogue of human rights, but they include sexual equality, freedom of religion and the right to a fair hearing. One of the objectives set out in the Union is to maintain and develop the Union as an area of freedom, security and justice. In Case 4/73 *Nold KG* v. *Commission* [1974] ECR 491, [1974] 2 CMLR 338, it was accepted that reference could be made to international treaties which the Member States have signed, as well as the constitutional traditions of Member States. This principle has now found expression in article 6 [F] of the Union Treaty, which states that the Union is

> 'founded on the principles of liberty, democracy, respect for human rights and fundamental freedoms, and the rule of law, principles which are common to the Member States',

and that the Union

> 'shall respect fundamental rights, as guaranteed by the European Convention on Human Rights and Fundamental Freedoms ..., and as they result from the constitutional traditions common to the Member States, as general principles of Community law.'

In Case 36/75 *Rutili* v. *Minister for the Interior* [1975] ECR 1219, [1976] 1 CMLR 140, it was said, of the human rights enshrined in the Convention, that no restrictions in the interests of national security or public safety might be placed on such fundamental rights unless they are necessary for the protection of those interests in a democratic society.

The interrelationship between the law of human rights in the European Convention and the Union Treaty is not without problems. In Case 147/86 *Commission* v. *Greece* [1988] ECR 1637, [1989] 2 CMLR 845, an English couple were refused the right to open an English school. This was contrary to the Treaty right to establishment. They obtained orders in the Greek courts, but these orders remained unexecuted. They had to bring a separate action in the European Court of Human Rights for violation of article 6 of the Convention before they could obtain an award of damages.

The above case should be compared with C-299/95 *Kremzow* v. *Austria* [1997] ECR I-2629, [1997] 3 CMLR 1289. Mr Kremzow, a retired judge, murdered an Austrian lawyer. His argument was that since article 8a [18] of the EC Treaty entitled him to freedom of movement he ought not to be locked up. His argument involved some excursion into the European Convention, under which he claimed damages for unlawful detention under article 5(5). The European Court of Justice ruled that it had no power to say whether national legislation was in conformity with the European Convention where that legislation did not fall within the field of application of Community law.

4.8   *Case law*

Community law has no doctrine of *stare decisis*. This does not mean, however, that it is not possible to see the development of clear lines of authority. A principle, such as direct effect or the rule in *Dassonville* (see Chapter 9), becomes, by constant repetition, predictable; but no rule is immutable.

The jurisprudence of the European Court is published in an official report known as the European Court Reports (ECR). These reports contain all the judgments of the European Court, and they are published not only in English, but also in the other languages of the Community. The page numbers are the same whether the version used is in English or in another Community language; this makes for great ease of reference.

The European Court Reports are full reports that include the submissions of the litigants, but there are great delays in publication. A further disadvantage of the official reports is that they contain only the judgments of the European Court; decisions by the Commission are not included, nor are the judgments of the courts of Member States. The Common Market Law Reports (CMLR) are not an official set of reports but they have the advantage of prompt publication, contain judgments of the courts of Member States, and also contain some Commission decisions and legislative material. *Butterworths* publish a series of selected European cases in the All England Law Reports (European Cases), but this series only began in 1995.

In competition cases the Commission conducts hearings before a so-called hearing officer and the decisions of the Commission in such cases, coming at the end of a convoluted process involving consultation with the companies concerned, are almost as important as the judgments of a court. The official texts of these decisions appear in the *Official Journal*.

Citations of cases before the European Court are preceded by the case number, and since the creation of the Court of First Instance by a 'C' if the case was before the Court of Justice, and by a 'T' (from the French 'Tribunal') if it was before the Court of First Instance.

4.8.1 Reading cases

To a common lawyer the report of a case in the European Court is bizarre. The judgment is terse, the reasoning sparse and formal. The first thing to read is not the judgment, but the opinion of the Advocate General. In the European Court Reports his opinion used to be printed at the end of the report; nowadays it is printed in its logical place, at the beginning. It reads rather like a judgment of a common law judge, but one must not mistake it for the judgment.

The function of the Advocate General is discussed in the next chapter; he is there to make a reasoned and impartial submission to the Court, in order to assist it in coming to the right conclusion. His opinion is to be read as if it were the submission of a particularly impartial barrister, instructed as *amicus curiae*. By reading his opinion one may come to a fair understanding of the issues in the case.

The Advocate General is not a judge, though he is of equal status with the judges. His opinion may have great authority. If what he says is the only authority on a point it may be treated as one would the *obiter dicta* of a judge in the common law system. If the judges disagree with him there is still the possiblity of arguing that they were wrong. If the judges follow his opinion there is scope for explaining and strengthening the judgment by reference to the opinion. The opinion of the Advocate General is often the best place to begin reading a report because it gives the overall background to the case.

The formal judgment of the Court will begin by reciting the facts, the background law, and the submissions. Before the oral hearing one of the judges, who is referred to as the reporting judge or *juge rapporteur*, will have prepared a report for the Court summarising the main issues. It is from this report, the *rapport d'audience*, that the opening part of the judgment is prepared. In the next part of the judgment the grounds are given, followed by the formal ruling that constitutes the operative part of the judgment. The logic of this exercise is that, by a gradual process, the issues are distilled to a minimum. The final order therefore impinges precisely on the question in issue.

CHAPTER 5
THE COURT

5.1 Development of the Court

The Court of Justice of the European Communities sits in Luxembourg. There is one judge for each Member State and they usually sit in chambers of three or five judges, unless a Member State or Community institution which is party to the proceedings requests it to sit in plenary session. Under article 220 [164] of the EC Treaty the Court has the duty to ensure that in the interpretation and application of the Treaty the law is observed.

A Court of First Instance was created in 1989, by Council Decision (ECSC,EEC,Euratom) 88/591 (OJ L319 25.11.88, corrected by OJ L241 17.8.89 p1, and codified by OJ C215 21.8.89 p1). Its jurisdiction now extends, by virtue of Council Decision (Euratom ECSC EEC) 93/350 of 8 June 1993 (OJ L144 16.6.93 p21), to all actions by natural and legal persons brought under articles 230 [173], 232 [175], 235 [178], and 238 [181] of the EC Treaty (and to equivalent proceedings under the ECSC and Euratom Treaties). This means that all private direct actions, as opposed to actions by Member States and Institutions of the Community, begin in the Court of First Instance. Appeals lie to the Court of Justice on points of law only. All referrals from national courts still go direct to the Court of Justice. The judges of the Court of First Instance usually sit in chambers of three or five judges, depending on the complexity of the case, but the rules of procedure permit a single judge to hear the less complex cases (see OJ L135 29.5.99 p92). Article 225 [168a] of the EC Treaty was amended by the Maastricht Treaty so as to give authority to the Council to extend the jurisdiction of the Court of First Instance to such classes of cases as it may determine after a request by the Court of Justice.

In this chapter we shall consider the structure of the European Court, the kinds of action which may be brought before it, and the way in which judgments are enforced. In the next chapter we will consider the rules of procedure.

5.2   *The Advocate General*

To an English lawyer a curious feature of the European Court is the role played by the Advocate General. Under article 222 [166] of the Treaty the Court of Justice is assisted by nine Advocates General whose duty it is to make reasoned submissions on cases brought before the Court. They act with complete impartiality and independence. During hearings the Advocate General sits with the judges, but to the side of the Court. After the parties have addressed the Court he delivers an opinion which he reads out to the Court. It is prepared, rather like a reserved judgment, after an adjournment. The parties cannot comment on what he says.

His opinion will be found printed alongside the Court's judgment in the law reports. It is rather similar in style to the judgment of an English judge. As we have seen already, its practical use to lawyers is as a means to divine the likely reasoning of the Court. When reading a judgment of the Court it is best to begin with the opinion of the Advocate General in order to obtain an idea of the issues in the case. The opinion of the Advocate General can be used as authority if the Court agrees with him. If the Court does not disagree with him then what he says may be of persuasive authority. If it disagrees with him his opinion is useful in any attempt to show that the Court was wrong.

The Court of First Instance does not have a body of Advocates General, but if it is considered that a case is of particular legal or factual complexity the President will appoint one of the judges to perform that function.

5.3   *The* juge rapporteur

The *juge rapporteur* will be appointed by the President of the Court as soon as the papers arrive. His task is to see the case through the Court. Initially only the *juge rapporteur* will study the papers. He will prepare a preliminary report dealing mainly with procedural issues, such as whether a preliminary inquiry may be necessary. By the time of the hearing he will have prepared a full report which will contain a resumé of the facts and submissions of the parties.

On the day of the hearing the Court will already have read this report. There is no need for the advocate for the claimant to open the case in the way in which counsel would begin in an English court; opening the case is a function performed by the *juge rapporteur*.

5.4   Types of action

Actions brought before the Court are essentially of two kinds: *direct actions*, where Member States, or Community institutions bring actions against each other; and *references* under article 234 [177] of the Treaty that arise when national courts ask the Court of Justice to decide on the interpretation of Community law.

The scope for private parties to bring direct actions is limited. A private litigant can only bring a direct action against a Community institution if it has made a decision which is of direct and individual concern to him. In certain circumstances it is possible to sue a Community institution for damages, but it is not possible for one private individual to sue another in the Court of Justice. If a private litigant wishes to raise a point of Community law against another person, he must first bring an action in his national court, and then ask that court to refer the question to the European Court for its ruling.

The jurisdiction of the Court of Justice is mainly confined to the judicial review of the acts of Community institutions, and the interpretation of the Treaty. We shall now examine the various types of action which can be brought before the Court.

5.4.1   Actions against Member States

If the Commission considers that a Member State has failed to fulfil an obligation under the Treaty it has a duty, under article 226 [169] of the Treaty, to deliver a reasoned opinion on the matter, after giving the State concerned the opportunity to submit its observations. If the State concerned does not comply with the opinion the Commission may bring the matter before the Court of Justice. The hearing before the Court is not simply a review of the Commission's opinion, but a hearing on all the issues.

An example of the application of article 226 [169] is the well known 'German Beer Case', Case 178/84 *EC Commission* v. *Germany* [1987] ECR 1227, [1988] 1 CMLR 780. In Germany the marketing of foreign beers was prohibited, unless they met strict German beer purity laws. The Commission was successful in bringing an action against Germany for failure to fulfil obligations under article 28 [30] of the Treaty, which prohibits measures having an equivalent effect to restrictions on imports.

If a Member State considers that another Member State has failed to fulfil an obligation under the Treaty it may bring the issue before the Court, under article 227 [170] of the Treaty. Before a Member State brings such an action it has to bring the matter before the Commission. The Commission has to deliver a reasoned opinion, after each of the States concerned has been given an opportunity to submit its own case. If the Commission has not delivered an opinion within three months, the absence of an opinion does not prevent the matter from being brought before the Court.

The judgment of the Court in proceedings under articles 226 [169] and 227 [170] used to be merely declaratory. But now, under article 228 [171] as amended by the Maastricht Treaty, there is a power to impose fines on Member States. The procedure is as follows. If the Commission considers that a Member State has not complied with a judgment of the Court it must, after giving the State an opportunity to submit its observations, issue a reasoned opinion specifying the points on which the Member State has not complied. The Commission may bring the case before the Court of Justice if the Member State fails to take the measures necessary to comply with the judgment. The Court can then impose a lump sum or penalty payment.

Under article 88 [93] there is an infringement procedure in relation to state aid. If, after giving notice to the parties concerned to submit their comments, the Commission finds that aid granted by a Member State is not compatible with the common market (because it distorts competition or is being misused) it has to decide that the State concerned shall abolish or alter the aid within a period determined by the Commission. If the State does not comply, the Commission or any interested State may refer the matter to the Court (this is in derogation from articles 226 [169] and 227 [170]). There is no administrative stage during which the Commission delivers an opinion as there is in articles 226 and 227.

5.4.2   Actions for annulment

The acts of Community institutions are subject to judicial review. Under article 230 [173] of the EC Treaty the Court has the duty to review the legality of the following: acts adopted jointly by the European Parliament and the Council; acts of the Council, of the Commission and of the European Central Bank, other than recommendations and opinions and acts of the European Parliament intended to produce legal effects vis-à-vis third parties. This jurisdiction is given to the Court in cases brought by Member States, the Council, or the Commission on the following grounds: lack of competence, infringement of an essential procedural requirement, infringement of the Treaty or any rule of law relating to its application, or misuse of power. The Court has jurisdiction under the same conditions in actions brought by the European Parliament and by the Central Bank for the purpose of protecting their prerogatives.

'Lack of competence' means absence of the legal power to adopt an act, and is, by its nature, a rare ground. Note that the infringement of a procedural requirement must be of an essential requirement; minor infringements will not be sufficient.

Article 230 [173] includes within in its scope principles analogous to *audi alteram partem* and *ultra vires*. It is wide enough to cover general principles of law which the Court applies, including proportionality (that the end should justify the means), the principle of legal certainty, and equality. The principle of *audi alteram partem* applies even where there is no specific legislative provision: in Case 17/74 *Transocean Marine Paint Association* v. *EC Commission* [1974] ECR 1063, [1974] 2 CMLR 459, part of a decision of the Commission was annulled because, although it contained onerous conditions, no opportunity had been given to the plaintiffs to deal with them in any of the antecedent correspondence.

Any natural or legal person can bring proceedings under article 230 [173], but there are limitations to this jurisdiction. The action can be brought against a decision addressed to the plaintiff. The decision must, however, amount to a legally binding measure. A mere letter from the Commission can be sufficient, provided that it can be shown to bring about a distinct change in the plaintiff's legal position; but, preparatory steps to making a decision cannot be challenged.

Under article 230 [173] an action can also be brought against a decision which, although in the form of a regulation or decision addressed to another person, is of direct and individual concern to the plaintiff. Thus, Community institutions cannot, merely by choosing the form of a regulation, prevent an application by an individual to annul a decision of direct and individual concern to him; the choice of form does not alter the nature of a measure.

A decision will be of direct concern if it does not involve the discretion of some other person. Case 66/69 *Alcan Aluminium Raeran SA* v. *EC Commission* [1970] ECR 385, [1970] CMLR 337, concerned tariff quotas for aluminium. The Belgian government had asked the Commission to open a tariff quota for 1968 under certain provisions derived from the ECSC Treaty. The Commission refused. The question that came before the Court was whether that decision directly concerned three metal importers. The Commission's powers were not unlimited because the Member States kept a large discretionary power. They had a discretion whether to request the quota, and whether or not to open it when it was granted. So the origin of the legal position of the plaintiffs lay not in the decision of the Commission, but in the act of the Member State. It was held that therefore the decision did not directly concern the plaintiff.

The problem of whether a decision was of individual concern was discussed in the 'Clementines case', so called because it concerned an importer of that fruit: Case 25/62 *Plaumann & Co v. EEC Commission* [1963] ECR 95 at 107, [1964] CMLR 29. It was said that, in order for a measure to be of individual concern to persons other than those to whom it is addressed, it must affect their legal position because of a factual situation which differentiates them individually in the same way as a person to whom it is addressed.

The time limit for bringing proceedings is short: they must be instituted within two months. The period of two months runs from the date of publication of the measure, or notification to the claimant. If there is no publication or notification, it is a period of two months from the day on which the measure came to the knowledge of the claimant. There is an extension of time on account of the distance between the Court and the applicant's place of residence which, in the case of the United Kingdom, is 10 days. It is not possible to apply for extensions of time, nor is it possible for litigants to agree an extension of time. Although the period for bringing actions is extremely short it is unlikely in practice that the litigant will have been unaware that a decision was about to be made. In competition cases, for example, a statement of objections is sent by the Commission, and an opportunity is given for the party to put its case to the Commission before any decision is taken.

If the Court finds that an action under article 230 [173] is well founded, it will declare the act concerned void. In the case of a regulation, however, the Court must, if it considers it necessary, state which of the effects of the regulation which it has declared void shall be considered definitive.

5.4.3 The article 241 [184] exception

The short time limit and the limited *locus standi* under article 230 [173] is mitigated to some extent by article 241 [184] of the Treaty, which enables persons affected by a regulation to challenge it indirectly in proceedings where the regulation is in issue. In French texts this right is referred to as *exception d'illégalité*. There is really no comparable doctrine in English law; it spoils the fruit but does not strike at the root. It might be used in a case where a person was unable to challenge a regulation because he was not directly and individually concerned, but found that he was made the subject of a later decision based upon the regulation. In such a case, he might plead that the regulation was inapplicable on the ground of infringement of an essential procedural requirement, or one of the other grounds set out in article 230 [173]. Article 241 [184] (as amended) reads as follows:

> 'Notwithstanding the expiry of the period laid down in the fifth paragraph of article 230, any party may, in proceedings in which a regulation adopted jointly by the European Parliament and the Council, or a regulation of the Council, of the Commission, or of the ECB is at issue, plead the grounds specified in the second paragraph of article 230 in order to invoke before the Court of Justice the inapplicability of that regulation.'

The object of article 241 [184] is to protect an interested party from the application of an illegal regulation, without calling in issue the regulation itself. It cannot, therefore, be used as an action to annul. In the context of the national court it might be raised as an indirect means to challenge Community legislation. The national court would then have to refer the matter to the Court of Justice for a ruling.

In Case 92/78 *Simmenthal* v. *Commission* [1979] ECR 777, [1980] CMLR 25, there is a description of the way in which the remedy works. A number of regulations provided for the common organisation of the market in beef and veal, by controlling the price of frozen beef. The plaintiff lacked the *locus standi* to complain about the original regulations because they were not directed to any particular individual. The Commission, acting under these regulations, made a decision fixing the minimum price for frozen beef. The plaintiff was able to challenge the decision on the basis that the enabling legislation was inapplicable.

5.4.4 Actions for failing to act

Article 232 [175] of the Treaty, as amended, provides that should the European Parliament, Council or Commission, in infringement of the Treaty, fail to act, the Member States and other institutions of the Community may bring an action. This kind of action is only admissible if the institution has first been called upon to act. If, within two months, the institution has not defined its position the action can be brought within a further period of two months. The Court regards this remedy as complementary to article 230 [173]. In Case 13/83 *European Parliament* v. *EC Council* [1985] ECR 1513, [1986] 1 CMLR 138, the European Parliament brought an action against the Commission on account of the failure of the latter to legislate for freedom to provide transport services, but there are few examples of similar actions.

Article 232 [175] allows any natural or legal person to complain to the Court where an institution of the Community has failed to act. This might appear to provide a fruitful avenue for private individuals, but in fact the jurisdiction in this case is very circumscribed. It only applies where the institution concerned has failed to address an act other than a recommendation or an opinion to the litigant. A regulation is of general effect and would not come within article 232 [175], nor would a Directive addressed to a Member State.

5.4.5 Compensation for damage

Under article 215 [159] of the Treaty the contractual liability of the Community is governed by the law applicable to the contract. Article 235 [178] provides, however, that in disputes relating to non-contractual liability the Court of Justice shall have jurisdiction. Use of this jurisdiction is rare, but an interesting case where the plaintiff was able to recover substantial damages from the Commission is Case 145/83 & 53/84 *Adams* v. *EC Commission* [1985] ECR 3539, [1986] 1 CMLR 506.

In order to understand by what fate Mr Adams was driven to sue the Commission in the European Court it is necessary to refer to an earlier litigation. In 1979 the European Court had given its judgment in Case 85/76 *Hoffman LaRoche* v. *Commission* [1979] ECR 461, [1979] 3 CMLR 211. The Commission had alleged that Hoffman LaRoche had abused a dominant position in the market, contrary to Article [82] of the Treaty. The Court recognised that the Swiss multinational's conduct in the market in vitamins could adversely affect both competition and intra-Community trade. The judgment contributed not a little to the liberation of the European market in vitamins.

Mr Adams had been the informant. He had enabled the Commission to uncover the anticompetitive practices of Hoffman LaRoche. The Commission was bound to keep his identity secret. But, owing to the negligence of the Commission's officials, Mr Adams's identity was not kept secret for very long. He was arrested at the Swiss border and, on the basis of a complaint by Roche, charged with the criminal offences under Swiss law of disclosure of business information and breach of business confidentiality. He was granted bail, but was ultimately sentenced to a year's imprisonment. The sentenced was suspended. In the European Court he claimed damages for negligence in relation to the breach of confidence by the Commission staff, and an award was made in his favour. Another example of the use of article 235 [178] is Case C104/89 and C37/90 *Mulder* v. *EC Council and EC Commission* [1992] ECR I-3061. This case is explained in Chapter 15.

5.4.6   Staff cases

Article 236 [179] of the Treaty states that the Court shall have jurisdiction in disputes between the Community and its servants under the conditions laid down in the staff regulations or conditions of employment. The Court of First Instance deals with these disputes.

5.4.7   Appeals against penalties

By virtue of article 229 [172] of the Treaty the Court has unlimited jurisdiction in relation to penalties provided for in regulations made by the Council or jointly by the Council and Parliament. 'Unlimited jurisdiction' in this context means that the Court has the power not only to annul a penalty but to substitute another. The same unlimited jurisdiction is given to the Court in staff cases and actions for damages. The court is able to go further than merely quashing the matter appealed against. The term does not have the same meaning as the English concept of the unlimited powers, or inherent jurisdiction of the High Court.

5.4.8   Arbitrations

The Court of Justice has power under article 238 [181] of the Treaty to give judgment pursuant to any arbitration clause in a contract concluded by the Community. It also has jurisdiction in disputes between Member States relating to the Treaty which are submitted to the Court under a special agreement. This area of jurisdiction is little used.

5.4.9   Interim measures

Interim measures are prescribed by the Court under article 243 [186]. Such orders are effectively interim injunctions. Article 242 [185] states that actions brought before the Court do not have any suspensory effect. The Court may, however, if it considers that circumstances so require, order the application of the contested act to be suspended.

5.4.10   Referrals

Article 234 [177] of the Treaty states that the Court of Justice is to have jurisdiction to give preliminary rulings concerning the following: the interpretation of the Treaty; the validity and interpretation of acts of the institutions of the Community and of the European Central Bank and the interpretation of the statutes of bodies established by an act of the Council, where those statutes so provide. Where such a question is raised before any court or tribunal of a Member State, that court or tribunal may, if it considers that a decision on the question is necessary to enable it to give judgment, request the Court of Justice to give a ruling. Where, however, any such question is raised in a case pending before a court or tribunal of a Member State against whose decisions there is no judicial remedy under national law, that court or tribunal must bring the matter before the Court of Justice.

A referral will usually be the method for the private litigant to bring a case before the Court of Justice. In Case 30/77 *R* v. *Bouchereau* [1977] ECR 1999, [1977] 2 CMLR 800, it was a magistrates court which made the reference. Case 41/74 *Yvonne Van Duyn* v. *Home Office* [1974] ECR 1337, [1975] 1 CMLR 1, is well known because it was the first case in which the United Kingdom courts referred a case. Miss Van Duyn asked for a declaration in the Chancery Division that she was entitled under Community law to enter the United Kingdom, and so obtained a reference to the Court of Justice.

A point to note is that when a Court has given judgment it is too late to ask for a reference. Difficulties may arise in the Court of Appeal in this regard because of the need to ask for leave, either of the Court of Appeal or the House of Lords, in order to appeal to the latter court. It is only a court or tribunal against whose decisions there is no appeal that must refer the question to the Court of Justice. It would appear that, where leave is required for an appeal to the House of Lords, it is the Court of Appeal that must make a reference. There is some academic argument over this, but the practical advice is to get your reference as early as possible.

5.4.11 *Acte claire*

It is not unusual to find resistance on the part of the national court to the idea of a reference. Lord Denning, in *Bulmer* v. *Bollinger* [1974] Ch 401, [1974] 3 WLR 202, tried to lay down guidelines with regard to those cases where it might be appropriate to ask the Court of Justice for a preliminary ruling. He said that unless the point was really difficult or important it would seem better for the English judge to decide it for himself. This view is very unsatisfactory when seen from a European perspective because it would lead to the development of different approaches to Community law in different jurisdictions.

The European Court has, in two cases, given some support to the idea that it is not always obligatory for a court to make a reference. In Cases 28–30/62 *Da Costa* [1963] ECR 31, [1963] CMLR 224, it was said to be unnecessary where the point had already been decided in a previous case. In Case 283/81 *CILFIT Srl* v. *Ministry of Health* [1982] ECR 3415, [1983] 1 CMLR 472, the Court went further and said that it was not necessary to make a reference where the point was so obvious as to leave no scope for any reasonable doubt. A reading of these cases will show that the Court is none too enthusiastic about this doctrine which has come to be known as *acte claire*.

5.4.12 Enforcement of judgments

A judgment given against a Member State used to be merely declaratory. When Member States refused to obey the Court the quarrel had to be resolved politically. During the so-called lamb war, lorry loads of English lamb were being hijacked by irate French farmers. The French placed a ban on the import of mutton and lamb from the United Kingdom. Proceedings were brought against France under article 226 [169] of the Treaty and, indeed, France was held to have infringed articles 25 [12] and 28 [30] of the Treaty (Case 232/78 *EC Commission* v. *France* [1979] ECR 2729, [1980] 1 CMLR 418). The French, unabashed, simply refused to comply. A second action was commenced by the Commission, based upon the infringement of article 228 [171] of the Treaty.

Article 228 [171] states that, if the Court of Justice finds that a Member State has failed to fulfil an obligation under the Treaty, the State shall be required to take the necessary measures to comply with the judgment of the Court. But, at that time, there was no power to impose any penalty, and it was a Council compromise in the form of a sheep meat regime which finally ended the litigation.

The position now is different. Article 228 [171], as amended by the Maastricht Treaty, states that if the Commission considers that the Member State concerned has not taken the measures necessary to comply with the judgment of the Court it shall, after giving that State the opportunity to submit its observations, issue a reasoned opinion specifying the points on which the Member State concerned has not complied with the judgment of the Court.

If the Member State concerned fails to take the necessary measures to comply with the Court's judgment within the time limit laid down by the Commission, the latter may bring the case before the Court of Justice. In doing so the Commission has to specify the amount of the lump sum or penalty payment to be paid by the Member State which it considers appropriate.

If the Court of Justice finds that the Member State concerned has not complied with its judgment it may impose a lump sum or penalty payment. At the time of writing (July 2000) the Commission had commenced proceedings on account of the reluctance of the French to eat British beef, and one waits with interest to find whether this litigation will end in a fine or a compromise.

Where a judgment is given in an article 234 [177] case, on a reference to the Court, there is no problem of enforcement. The judgment is simply a step in the proceedings in the court of the Member State and will be enforced automatically in those proceedings.

Actions against Community institutions do not raise practical problems of enforcement. Usually the judgment will be one which results in the annulment of a decision or a regulation, and thus takes effect without the need for further proceedings.

Sometimes proceedings brought by an institution against an individual or a company will result in a money obligation. Article 244 [187] of the Treaty states that judgments of the Court of Justice shall be enforceable under the conditions laid down in article 256 [192]. Article 256 [192] states that enforcement is governed by the rules of civil procedure in force in the State where the judgment is carried out. The order for enforcement

> 'shall be appended to the decision, without other formality than verification of the authenticity of the decision, by the national authority which the Government of each Member State shall designate for this purpose'.

In the United Kingdom the application to append the order for enforcement to a judgment is made to the Secretary of State. The High Court is then obliged to register the judgment on application. The procedure is governed by the European Communities (Enforcement of Community Judgments) Order 1972 (SI 1972 No 1590, and RSC Ord. 71 rr. 15–24 in Schedule 1 of the Civil Procedure Rules).

The application to register a Community judgment for enforcement is made, without notice and must be supported by a witness statement or affidavit exhibiting the Community judgment, and the order for its enforcement. Execution may not issue without the permission of the High Court until 28 days have expired. During that time an application may be made to vary or cancel registration on the grounds that judgment has been wholly or partly satisfied. If the European Court decides to suspend the enforcement of a Community judgment an application can be made to register that order.

In practice the Community judgment most likely to be registered is not an order of the European Court at all, but a decision by the Commission imposing a monetary penalty. Such decisions arise in competition cases. They can be registered by the Commission and enforced like a judgment. If, however, the debtor appeals to the European Court against the Commission's decision, and is unsuccessful, it is the order of the European Court which will be registered for enforcement.

CHAPTER 6
PROCEDURE

6.1 Introduction

There are three procedures by which, according to the circumstances, European law may be invoked: complaining to the Commission, bringing a direct action in the European Court, and bringing an action in a national court from whence a referral may be taken to the European Court.

A complaint to the Commission need take no particular form. If the complaint concerns the conduct of a Member State it may result in action by the Commission against the Member State. The only circumstance in which a complaint can be made against a private individual is when it involves competition law. A special procedure ensues. When Brass Band Instruments complained, as described in Chapter 2, about the refusal of Boosey and Hawkes to supply their factory with certain vital components for their euphoniums the result was that the Commission made its Decision ((EEC) 87/500, *Brass Band Instruments* (OJ L286 9.10.87 p36); [1988] 4 CMLR 67). Brass Band Instruments was a small company that was complaining about the anticompetitive conduct of its larger competitor. The latter had obtained a dominant position in the market for brass band instruments. Brass Band Instruments applied to the Commission, alleging an infringement of article 82 [86] of the EC Treaty. The complaint was that Boosey and Hawkes had refused to supply them with parts. Before the implementation of the Competition Act 1998 there was no convenient method of obtaining a remedy in the UK. The Commission was prevailed upon to adopt a decision, as an interim measure, ordering Boosey and Hawkes to supply the parts under pain of a penalty of 1000 ECUs per day. In competition cases the Commission has been driven to issue a Notice on Co-operation between National Courts and the Commission in Applying Articles 81 [85] and 82 [86] (OJ C39 13.2.93 p.6). In this notice the Commission has pointed out the advantages of using national courts, namely that the Commission cannot award damages, that national courts can adopt interim measures more rapidly, that national courts can combine Community and national law claims, and that the Commission cannot award costs. The Commission, for its part, intends in future to devote itself to proceedings which have particular political, economic or legal significance. For a more detailed description of this notice the reader should refer to Chapter 12 of this book. In the UK the Competition Act 1998 now provides a remedy in the national context which can be conveniently combined with an action for breach of Community law, the national law being a mirror image of the Community law.

A direct action against a Community institution typically involves an action for annulment brought under article 230 [173]; any natural or legal person can bring such an action against a decision of direct and individual concern to him. But if a Community institution is accused of failing to act the proceedings must be brought under article 232 [175]; the Court then has power to order the institution to take the necessary measures. An irregular decision by the Commission is always susceptible to challenge by a person directly and individually concerned. On the other hand, regulations and directives, because they do not usually directly concern any particular individual, are not easily challenged under article 230 [173]; considerable ingenuity is needed to find the *locus standi* for a direct action.

There are two matters worth remembering in connection with articles 230 [173] and 232 [175]: a decision does not have to be a formal document and the words 'failure to act' in article 232 [175] have a very restricted meaning. Both matters were considered in Cases 166 & 220/86 *Irish Cement Limited* v. *EC Commission* [1988] ECR 6473, [1989] 2 CMLR 57. The plaintiff had received some aid from the Irish government towards the capital cost of increasing production at its cement works in Limerick. A rival company was awarded a more generous grant to build a cement plant. The plaintiff therefore asked the Commission to institute proceedings against the Irish authorities, on the grounds that the money paid to its rival was unlawful state aid and would distort competition. In a letter to the plaintiffs the Commission refused so to do. The plaintiffs contended that the Commission had failed to act.

The Court disagreed. It said that the letter constituted a sufficient action to obviate proceedings under article 232 [175]. This was because article 232 [175] refers to a failure to act in the sense of a failure to take a decision or define a position; it does not refer to the adoption of a measure which happens to differ from the one desired by the plaintiff. The Court nevertheless remarked that the letter was a decision against which an action to annul might have been brought under article 230 [173]. This was not a crumb of comfort to the plaintiff who, alas, had not acted within the two months time limit allowed for bringing annulment proceedings. Thus, the case shows the merits of acting quickly when a direct action is involved, and the narrow scope of an action brought under article 230 [175].

When action is brought in the national court, claiming a breach of some directly applicable provision of Community law, the national court is bound to refer any question of interpretation of Community law to the European Court under article 234 [177] of the Treaty. This was the method used by Miss Marshall in Case 152/84 *Marshall* v. *Southampton and South West Hampshire Area Health Authority* [1986] 1 CMLR 688, [1986] ECR 723, when she complained that she had suffered unlawful discrimination, contrary to a Directive which was designed to afford men and women the right to equal treatment in employment.

A problem that arises when an advocate asks an English court to refer a question to the European Court is that an English judge is prone to regard the whole idea as cumbersome and unnecessary. It is only when a question is raised before a court against whose decisions there is no judicial remedy under national law that a court is obliged to bring the matter before the European Court. A judge at first instance is therefore likely to be reluctant to refer a matter, particularly if he considers the answer to the question is obvious. Indeed, the whole ethos of an English court is to decide the matter then and there. The advocate must be prepared to counter these tendencies. When the action brought depends upon national legislation which has been created in order to implement a directive it might appear to be purely domestic in scope, but it will often be found that national legislation does not accurately reflect the requirements of the relevant directive. If the directive is directly applicable it may be possible to rely on it, and ignore the national law; but, where the claimant is not suing the state, he will be driven to the different tactic of persuading the court to adopt a sympathetic approach to the interpretation of national law, in the light of the underlying Community measure. The problems that arise when Community law is used in an English court are considered in Chapter 7.

We shall now consider the rules of procedure governing complaints to the Commission, direct actions, and referrals. We will then consider costs, legal aid, and rights of audience. The final topic of this chapter will be the procedural requirements of the Court of First Instance.

6.2   Complaining to the Commission

Complaints to the Commission are dealt with in a relatively informal way. As an aid to complainants, however, the Commission has issued a standard complaint form which is obtainable from any of the Commission's information offices. It is also published in the *Official Journal* (OJ C26 1.2.89 p6). The form requires certain information, namely the name of the complainant, his nationality, his address or registered office, his sphere of activity, the identity of the Member State (or body or undertaking) which has failed to comply with Community law, the subject matter of the complaint and damage suffered, if any, the steps taken before national or Community authorities, both administrative and by way of proceedings before courts or tribunals and finally any documentary evidence in support of the complaint.

Any individual may lodge a complaint with the Commission. The complaint may either be sent direct to the Commission in Brussels or handed in at one of the Commission's information offices. An acknowledgement of receipt is sent to the complainant, as soon as the complaint is registered. The complainant is informed of the action taken on his complaint. He is also informed of any infringement proceedings that the Commission intends to institute against a Member State, as a result of the complaint, and of any legal action it intends to take against an undertaking. If proceedings have already been instituted he may, where appropriate, be informed about them.

The Commission will respect confidences; as we have seen: in Case 145/83 *Adams* v. *EC Commission* [1985] ECR 3539, [1986] 1 CMLR 506, an action lay against the Commission for the negligence of its servants in revealing their source of information.

6.3   Competition cases

In competition cases the procedure is governed by article 19 of Council Regulation 17 (OJ L13 21.2.62 p204, Sp edn 1959–62 p.87) and by Commission Regulation (EC) 2841/98 (OJ L354 30.12.98 p18). Article 3 of Regulation 17 states that those entitled to make application to the Commission are Member States, and natural or legal persons who claim a legitimate interest; but the Commission can also act of its own initiative, so that those unable to show strictly that they have a legitimate interest can still complain, and hope that the Commission will take up the cudgels on their behalf.

In competition cases a complaint might be, for example, that there is an agreement or cartel which distorts competition in the Community, or that a company has abused a dominant position in the common market. The complaint does not have to take any particular form; a letter will do. As a general rule, however, the complaint will identify the parties, give details of the infringements of the Treaty, show that the complainant has a legitimate interest, contain any evidence and documents relied on, state what steps have been taken to bring the infringement to an end, and declare that the contents are correct.

The party against whom a complaint is made will receive a statement of objections from the Commission identifying the issues. At the same time the Commission fixes the time limit in which the company has an opportunity to reply. The time limit may not be less than two weeks, and may be extended. The Commission will usually inform the company of the contents of its file by means of an annex attached to the statement of objections, although certain documents may be withheld on the grounds of confidentiality. The Commission is obliged to have regard to the legitimate interests of undertakings in the protection of business secrets and other confidential information and it will set a date by which parties may indicate parts of the objections which contain such information.

In its reply the company may set out all the matters relevant to its defence, and attach any relevant documents in proof of the facts relied on. If it so requests, in its written comments, the company is entitled in appropriate cases to have an oral hearing before the Commission. The hearing is informal, before a hearing officer appointed for the purpose, and the public are not admitted; the hearing is an administrative one, an opportunity for the company to be heard. Statements by each person heard must be recorded on tape. Persons appearing before the Commission may be assisted by lawyers. Third parties may be heard, if they have a sufficient interest. The outcome of this procedure will be a decision by the Commission. Appeals against such decisions lie to the Court of First Instance.

In Chapter 12 we will return to regulation 17 in order to examine two other kinds of procedure: for negative clearance, and exemption from the effects of article 81 [85] of the Treaty. These procedures are used where parties have entered into agreements and wish to obtain either an exemption from the competition rules, or an assurance that their agreements do not breach the rules.

6.4   Direct actions

Before the Court of Justice of the Community the procedure has two phases: one written, one oral. The written stage consists in the exchange of written pleadings (*mémoires*) between the parties. This stage is concluded by the preparation of a report by the *juge rapporteur*. The oral stage permits direct contact between the judges and the parties. During this stage the advocates will make submissions in open court and answer questions put to them by the Court. The Advocate General then delivers his opinion, in open court, to the judges. The judges deliberate in private. Finally a single judgment is delivered.

If the Court feels that there is insufficient evidence in the file it may, before the oral stage, order a preliminary enquiry (*instruction*) which may include the examination of witnesses, the production of documents, or the preparation of experts' reports. In practice, the European Court prefers to put questions in writing for written reply, rather than relying on answers given at an oral hearing.

6.5   Rules of procedure

Certain procedural provisions are to be found in the Statute of the Court of Justice – this is in a protocol to the Treaty – and, under article 245 [188] of the Treaty, the Court has adopted its own rules of procedure which are published in the Official Journal (OJ L176 4.7.91 p7). The rules have been variously amended and a codified version incorporating all the amendments and corrections appears at OJ C65 6.3.99 p1. There is a detailed Practice Note: [1999] All ER (EC) 545.

6.5.1   The written procedure

An action is begun by sending a written application, known as a *requête*, to the Registrar at The European Court of Justice, in Luxembourg. Natural or legal persons, that is to say private litigants, will begin their actions in the Court of First Instance (as to which see below) but the rules of procedure there do not differ in any material way. Service is effected by the Court. The *requête* is referred to in the English version of the rules as a pleading, but it is wider in scope than that word would imply. Unlike English particulars of claim it is prepared for the benefit of both the Court and the other parties. It does not have to take any particular form but, under article 19 of the Statute, and article 38 of the Rules of Procedure, the *requête* has to contain the following:

• the name and address of the applicant
• the designation of the party against whom the application is made
• the subject matter of the proceedings and a summary of the pleas in law on which the application is based
• the form of order sought by the applicant
• where appropriate, the nature of any evidence offered in support

The 'form of order', meaning a summary of what precisely the litigant is asking the court to do, and what orders he proposes it should make, is not an entirely happy translation of the French word *conclusions*. The *conclusions* are an essential part of the pleadings. Generally they will be found at the end of the pleading, but the European Court is not given to excessive formalism, so they can be placed elsewhere in the pleadings. They must be sufficiently precise. It is important to ask for costs in the conclusions – it is too late to ask for them during the oral procedure.

No new plea in law may be raised at a later stage in the proceedings. The application therefore delimits the grounds of the claim. But there is no objection to raising, at any stage, new arguments in support of the original pleas in law. Guidance as to what the pleadings should contain is given in Case 4/69 *Lütticke* v. *Commission* [1971] ECR 325, in which the Court said that the pleadings must 'give all the details necessary to establish with certainty the subject matter of the dispute and the legal scope of the grounds invoked in support of the submissions'.

One should note that sometimes problems arise when terms are translated from the French. *Conclusions* is sometimes translated as 'submissions' as well as 'form of order'. The French word *plaidoirie* is sometimes translated as 'pleadings' but is confined to oral submissions.

For the purposes of the proceedings, the applicant has to state an address for service at the place where the Court has its seat (in Luxembourg), and the name of a person who is authorised and has expressed willingness to accept service. The application must be accompanied by the decision it is sought to annul. The lawyer acting for a party has to lodge at the Registry a certificate that he is entitled to practise before a court of a Member State; this certificate can be obtained from the Law Society or the Bar Council.

'A legal person governed by private law', in other words a company, has to lodge with the application some proof of its existence at law. The documents lodged with the application must also contain proof that the authority granted to the applicant's lawyer has been properly conferred on him. If the applicant does not manage to comply with these requirements the Registrar prescribes a reasonable period within which he has to comply; if the applicant fails to comply, the Court, after hearing the Advocate General, will decide whether to reject the application.

Every pleading must be signed by the party's agent or lawyer; only Member States or institutions of the Community will have an agent. If an application is not signed by a lawyer the Court will simply declare it inadmissible. All pleadings have to bear a date, but time runs from lodgment in the Registry. The original pleading, accompanied by all the annexes referred to in the pleading, and five copies plus a copy for every other party, have to be lodged with the Court. Copies have to be certified by the party lodging them. The annexes will consist of a file containing the documentary evidence relied on in support of the application. It is important to understand that it will not be possible to adduce further evidence at the oral stage; all the evidence must be included in the file.

The defendant has one month, after service on him of the application, to lodge a defence. This time limit can be extended by the President on a reasoned request. The defence must state

- the name and address of the defendant
- the arguments of fact and law relied on
- the form of order sought by the defendant
- the nature of any evidence offered by him

Other requirements with regard to the defence correspond with those for the application. In the defence it is customary to distinguish between defences on the merits and issues which go to the admissibility of the action. Lawyers in private practice will not usually be called upon to draft defences, since all direct actions are brought against institutions of the Community.

Thereafter there is usually a reply and a rejoinder. The time limits for service of these are set by the President. In a reply or rejoinder a party may offer further evidence but must give reasons for not doing so earlier. Article 42 of the Rules provides that no new plea in law may be raised in the course of proceedings, unless it is based on matters of law or of fact which come to light in the course of the written procedure.

Drafting the *requête* requires some degree of care. It defines the issues and contains all the Court will know about the plaintiff's case. There is no rule allowing amendments although in Case 92/78 *Simmenthal* v. *Commission* [1979] ECR 777, [1980] 1 CMLR 25, an amendment was allowed, apparently without comment.

Although a distinction is drawn between raising a new plea in law, which is not allowed, and raising new arguments, which is permitted, there is no rule with regard to departure from the original pleading. Therefore one can plead in reply arguments which, in an English action, might only be dealt with by an amendment of the particulars of claim. Be warned, however, that nothing can be added at the hearing.

Because an application must include the law, the facts, and the evidence, in an annexed bundle, it will be much longer than an English pleading: but, there is no merit in drafting very lengthy pleadings. It is best to be short and to the point. A practical point to note is that, although the pleading will be translated for the benefit of the Court, the annexes will not be. It is best to note those annexes which it is essential for the Court to have translated.

6.5.2   The preparatory inquiry

It is the Court which prescribes the measures of inquiry which it considers appropriate. If a party believes that certain facts might be proved by witnesses, or by reference to documents which are not annexed, he should ask for a preliminary enquiry in his pleadings. The *juge rapporteur* prepares a preliminary report upon which the Court will base its order. The Court can order the personal appearance of witnesses, request information and the production of documents, take oral testimony, order experts' reports, and inspect the place or thing in question. Note that the examination of witnesses takes place at the preparatory stage, not during the oral proceedings. In fact it is very rare for there to be any examination of witnesses; the Court prefers to put questions in writing.

6.5.3   The oral procedure

After the preparatory stage is completed the *juge rapporteur* will prepare a report for the hearing. This is delivered to the parties' lawyers before the hearing, so that there is an opportunity to correct any inaccuracies. It contains a summary of the facts, and the submissions, of the parties, together with recommendations as to whether a preparatory hearing or any other preparatory step should be taken. By the time of the hearing, the Court will have read this report, so there is no necessity for the plaintiff to open the case at the hearing. Later on, the report finds its way into the formal judgment in the part headed 'Facts and Issues'.

Advocates appear robed. The judges and the Advocate General are addressed as 'My Lord'. The President of the Court may be addressed as 'Mr President' which will happily translate as *Monsieur le Président*.

Unless the case is very complicated it is unlikely that more than 20 minutes will be allowed for advocacy. It is necessary to speak slowly because everything has to be translated into several languages. The best approach is for the advocate to begin by dealing with any points which were raised in his opponent's last pleading, because there will have been no opportunity to deal with them in any other way. The object of the hearing is to enable the advocate to comment on matters which he was unable to treat in the written pleadings or observations. One or two main points in the case can be emphasised, but there will be little time for flights of rhetoric; often it will be quite acceptable to state simply that the submissions are clearly set out in the pleadings, and that there is nothing more to add. The Court will want to ask questions, and dealing with them is the most important task. The plaintiff speaks first and there is an opportunity to reply. The Registrar of the Court has prepared Notes for the Guidance of Counsel for the Parties at Hearings before the European Court of Justice which are made available to all advocates.

Before the case is called on it is customary for counsel to be invited to meet the members of the Court in chambers. This is an opportunity to discuss procedural points, and for the Court to indicate the questions which may be asked.

At the end of the oral hearing the Advocate General may sometimes give his opinion but, usually, the case is adjourned for several weeks to allow time for him to prepare it. Counsel are not expected to attend when his opinion is delivered. A copy is delivered to them but they cannot comment on the opinion. The judgment of the Court is always reserved; counsel need not attend when this is delivered.

6.5.4 Interlocutory applications

The Court has power to prescribe interim measures under article 243 [186] of the Treaty. Article 242 [185] states that an application to the Court has no suspensory effect but the Court of Justice can, if it considers that circumstances so require, order that application of the contested act be suspended. Article 83 of the Rules of Procedure provides for these applications to be made by a separate document, which takes the same form as the main application but must state the subject matter of the proceedings, the circumstances giving rise to urgency and the pleas of fact and law establishing a *prima facie* case for the interim measures applied for.

Sometimes a party will wish the Court to make a decision on a preliminary objection, or on some other procedural issue. Article 91 of the Rules provides for such applications to be made by a separate document, setting out the form of the order sought and the grounds of fact and law relied on. Supporting documents must be annexed to it.

An action will be inadmissible if it is procedurally wrong, out of time, or if there is no *locus standi*. If the defendant considers that an action is inadmissible it will file a short defence raising the preliminary objection. The plaintiff may then file an answer. There is a preliminary hearing. If the defendant is successful then that is the end of the matter. If not, the defendant will file a defence in the ordinary way.

6.5.5 Referrals

Under article 234 [177] of the EC Treaty any court or tribunal in a Member State may refer a question to the European Court in order to obtain a ruling. Preliminary rulings under article 234 [177] are, by their very nature, dealt with in a slightly different way to direct actions. Referrals go straight to the Court of Justice; they are never dealt with in the Court of First Instance.

The procedure resembles an appeal by way of case stated. A copy of the reference is sent by the Court of Justice to the parties, to the

Member States, and to the Commission. They may all submit written observations within two months. The Commission will usually appear at the oral stage and Member States may attend if they are concerned about the outcome.

When a point of Community law is raised before the English High Court the procedure is governed by RSC Order 114 in Schedule 1 of the Civil Procedure Rules. An order may be made by the High Court on application, or of its own motion at any stage of the proceedings. The order has to set out the request for the preliminary ruling in a schedule which must follow a practice form, PF No.109. The proceedings in which the order is made are stayed, unless the High Court otherwise orders.

Whilst the content of the schedule is ultimately a matter for the court, it is common for the court to ask counsel to draft it. The court may amend the draft as it thinks fit. The rules specify the form of the schedule, and provide that it should set out a clear and succinct statement of the case, in order to enable the Court of Justice to consider and understand the issues of Community law raised, and to enable Member States and other interested parties to submit their observations. There is a consolidated practice direction which applies to proceedings in the Court of Appeal Civil Division (see Supreme Court Practice PD-001, and [1999] 2 CMLR 799). The schedule should

- identify the parties and summarise the nature and history of the proceedings
- summarise the salient facts, indicating whether these are proved or admitted or assumed
- make reference to the rules of national law (substantive and procedural) relevant to the dispute
- summarise the contentions of the parties so far as relevant
- explain why a ruling of the European Court is sought, identifying the EC provisions whose effect is in issue
- formulate, without avoidable complexity, the question(s) to which an answer is requested.

There are different procedural rules for other courts. A reference by the Crown Court must be sent to the Senior Master of the High Court who waits until the period for lodging an appeal has expired, and then forwards the reference to the European Court (Crown Court Rules SI 1982/1109 r.29). The rules applying in the Court of Appeal Criminal Division are the Criminal Appeal (References to European Court) Rules 1972 (SI 1972/1786). The County Court

Rules Order 19 r.15 now appear in Schedule 2 of the Civil Procedure Rules. No specific rules have been made for the Magistrates Courts.

There are particular procedural problems in the case of jury trials. Once the jury has been empanelled it is not practicable to refer a question to the European Court. But a point can be taken on a motion to quash the indictment. Also, under section 9 of the Criminal Justice Act 1987 the judge has power, in a serious fraud case, to hear a question of law at a preliminary hearing, and under section 40 of the Criminal Procedure and Investigations Act 1996 the Crown Court can make preliminary rulings.

6.6   Costs and legal aid

In the case of a referral the costs are a matter for the national court. In direct actions the Court gives a decision as to costs in its final judgment, or in the order which closes the proceedings, provided that the successful party has asked for them in his pleadings; the loser usually pays all the costs.

The European Court has its own power to grant legal aid (see article 76 of the Rules of Procedure (OJ C65 6.3.99 p1)). This power is quite separate from the ordinary national arrangements with regard to legal aid. An applicant must attach to his application 'a document from the competent authority certifying his lack of means' – what is meant by 'competent authority' is not defined. The Court makes the order without giving reasons, and there is no appeal. After the hearing, in its decision on costs, the Court can order the assisted party to repay some or all of the legal aid back to the Court.

6.7   Rights of audience

In the case of referrals the Court takes account of the national rules, so that a lawyer entitled to appear before the referring court will also be able to appear before the Court of Justice. In the case of direct actions private parties must be represented 'by a lawyer entitled to practise before a court of a Member State'; this includes solicitors. Member States and institutions of the Community have to be represented by an agent who may be assisted by an adviser, or by a lawyer entitled to practise before a court of a Member State. University teachers who are nationals of Member States whose law accords them a right of audience have the same rights as are accorded to lawyers entitled to practise before a court of a Member State. These provisions are to be found in article 17 of the Statute of the Court of Justice.

6.8   The Court of First Instance

Until August 1993 the jurisdiction of the Court of First Instance was limited to staff cases, and competition cases. By Council Decision (Euratom ECSC EEC) 93/350 (OJ L144 16.6.93 p21) its jurisdiction has been extended to actions brought by natural or legal persons under articles 230 [173], 232 [175], 235 [178], and 238 [181] of the EC Treaty, and under corresponding articles of the Euratom and ECSC Treaties. Under article 225 [168a] of the EC Treaty, as amended by Maastricht, the jurisdiction of the Court of First Instance can be extended to such further classes of cases as the Council may determine after a request by the Court of Justice. Some procedural provisions for the Court are set out in the decision that established the Court of First Instance, Council Decision (ECSC,EEC,Euratom) 88/591 (OJ L319 25.11.88, corrected by OJ L241 17.8.89 p1, and codified by OJ C215 21.8.89 p1). The decision has inserted a new Title IV into the Statute of the Court of Justice. Article 47 of the amended Statute states that where an application, or other procedural document, addressed to the Court of First Instance is lodged by mistake with the Court of Justice it must be transmitted to the other Court and vice versa. Where the Court of First Instance, or the Court of Justice, finds that it does not have jurisdiction it has to refer the matter to the other Court. The Court of First Instance can stay an action where the same issue is being litigated in both Courts at the same time.

The procedure before the Court of First Instance is governed by the Statute of the Court of Justice and the Rules of Procedure of the Court of First Instance (OJ L136 30.5.91 p1). (Note that the rules have since been amended and corrected many times.) *Mutatis mutandis* the rules will mirror those of the Court of Justice, but, unless the case is unusually difficult or important, there is no Advocate General. An amendment to the Rules of Procedure permits a single judge to adjudicate on appeals in the Court of First Instance (OJ L135 29.5.99 p92).

The Court of First Instance is more apt to deal with factual issues. For detailed guidance on the procedure the reader must refer to the Court's three Practice Notes: [2000] All ER (EC) 1, [1999] All ER (EC) 641, and [1999] All ER (EC) 545.

6.8.1 Appeals from the Court of First Instance

Appeals from the Court of First Instance to the Court of Justice must be made within two months of notification of the decision appealed against. Appeals are limited to points of law or grounds of lack of competence, breach of procedure before it which adversely affects the interests of the appellant, and infringement of Community law by the Court of First Instance. No appeal lies regarding only the amount of costs. The rules of the Court of Justice require that appeals should be brought by lodging an application at the registry of the Court of Justice or of the Court of First Instance. The application must contain

- the name and address of the appellant
- the names of the other parties to the proceedings before the Court of First Instance
- the pleas in law and legal arguments relied on
- the form of order sought by the appellant.

An appeal must seek to set aside, in whole or in part, the decision of the Court of First Instance. The appeal must ask for the same form of order, in whole or in part, as was sought at first instance and may not seek a different form of order. The subject matter of the proceedings at first instance may not be changed on appeal. A respondent has two months in which to lodge a response which must contain

- the name and address of the party lodging it
- the date on which notice of the appeal was served on him
- the pleas in law and legal arguments relied on
- the form of order sought by the respondent.

The response must seek to dismiss, in whole or in part, the appeal or to set aside, in whole or in part, the decision of the Court of First Instance. It must ask for the same form of order, in whole or in part, as that sought at first instance, and must not seek a different form of order. The subject matter of the proceedings may not be changed in the response.

CHAPTER 7
EFFECTIVE USE OF EC LAW

7.1 Introduction

In 26/62 *Van Gend en Loos* v. *Netherlands* [1963] ECR 1 it was said that the European Community constitutes a new legal order which gives rights to individuals as well as imposing obligations on Member States. In C46/93 & C48/93 *Brasserie du Pêcheur SA* v. *Germany* and *R* v. *Secretary of State* ex parte *Factortame* [1996] ECR I-1029, [1996] 1 CMLR 889, it was said the obligation to make good damage caused to individuals by breach of Community law cannot depend on domestic rules as to division of powers between constitutional bodies nor can the protection of rights under EC law vary according to whether a national or a Community authority is responsible.

Injunctions, declarations and interim relief are available in order to protect these rights, even to the extent of disapplying national legislation. Remedies must be made available on terms comparable to those in the case of analogous national laws. Damages for breach of the requirements of EU law are available in a public law context, and in a private law context if the EU law is directly effective; if the EU law has not been implemented, an action lies against the State. Implementing legislation must be read sympathetically in conformity with the requirements of EU law. But, if reliance is placed on a provision of EU law it must be intended to confer rights. In C178/94 *Dillenkofer* v. *Federal Republic of Germany* [1996] ECR I-4845 the European Court said that a failure by the state to take any measure to transpose a Directive constituted a serious breach of Community law and consequently gave rise to a right to reparation for individuals suffering injury if the results prescribed by the Directive entail the grant of individual rights whose content is identifiable and a causal link exists between the breach of the state's obligation and the loss and damage suffered.

In this chapter we will outline the principles of effective protection of rights in European Law as summarised above.

7.2 *Obtaining a reference*

If the case depends on interpreting EU law it is for the European Court to do the interpreting, but often the court will think that the law is so obvious that it needs no interpreting. Lower courts can avoid the issue by refusing a reference and leaving the parties to appeal if they wish: it is only where a question is raised before a court against whose decision there is no judicial remedy that the court must refer the matter to the Court of Justice.

Acte claire is a principle derived from the French courts. It was considered by the European Court, for the first time, in Cases 28–30/62 *Da Costa* [1963] ECR 31, [1963] CMLR 224. It amounts to this, that when the law is so clear as to admit of no reasonable doubt the courts of a Member State are entitled to judge the matter for themselves. Such a doctrine is attractive to the English court, where the natural reaction of the judge is to decide the matter before him without further ado.

In such a case it may be useful to point out that, although Community law may seem obvious, the court cannot know how this law is interpreted in other Member States. Each version of the Treaty is equally authoritative, and each version of the regulations and Directives. The law of the Community includes general principles from all the Member States. The principle of proportionality, the rule of reason, legal certainty, and legitimate expectation are concepts unknown to the English Court; it is in no way equipped to apply such principles for itself.

In Case 283/81 *CILFIT* v. *Ministry of Health* [1982] ECR 3415, [1983] 1 CMLR 472, a dispute arose between some wool importers and the Italian Ministry of Health. The dispute concerned the payment of an inspection levy in respect of wool imports from outside the Community. The firms concerned relied on a regulation which prohibited charges having an equivalent effect to a customs duty on 'animal products'. According to the Ministry the scope of the regulation was quite unequivocal and therefore precluded any need to make a reference to the Court for a preliminary ruling.

In the course of the judgment the European Court drew attention to several features of Community law which made it desirable to refer questions to the European Court, even in those cases where the answer might appear to be obvious. The obligation to refer a matter to the Court is based on cooperation, established with a view to ensuring the proper application and uniform interpretation of Community law in all the Member States. It seeks to prevent a

85

divergence of judicial opinion within the Community on questions of Community law.

It is possible that the correct application of Community law may be so obvious as to leave no scope for any reasonable doubt as to the manner in which questions raised are to be resolved; but, before it comes to such a conclusion, the national court must be convinced that the matter is equally obvious to the courts of the other Member States, and to the Court of Justice of the Community. The possibility must be assessed on the basis of the characteristic features of Community law, and the particular difficulties to which its interpretation gives rise. One of the difficulties is that Community law is drafted in several languages and each language is equally authentic. Another difficulty is that Community law uses its own terminology and legal concepts do not necessarily have the same meaning in Community law as in the law of the various Member States.

In *Bulmer* v. *Bollinger* [1974] Ch 401, [1974] 3 WLR 202, the Court of Appeal endeavoured to lay down guidelines as to those cases which might appropriately be referred to the Court of Justice. The suggestion by Lord Denning that the English court should decide the matter for itself when, in the light of all the circumstances, the delay, expense, and the difficulty of the point involved, it was just to do so may not be right when one considers that such a principle would lead to Community law developing along different lines in different jurisdictions. Lord Denning's views seem old fashioned in the current European climate.

If cost is an obstacle it should be pointed out that apart from drawing up the question, which has probably been done already, and any written observations which the parties may care to file, nothing needs to be done, and as to delay, a day trip to Luxembourg is all that will be needed.

7.3   Sympathetic interpretation

If the EU law is sufficiently clear no reference to the European Court will be necessary; the quarrel shifts to whether national legislation implements it. In Case 106/77 *Simmenthal* [1978] ECR 629, [1978] 3 CMLR 263, the European Court said that a national court which is called on, within the limits of its jurisdiction, to apply provisions of Community law is bound to give full effect to those provisions, if necessary refusing to apply conflicting provisions of national legislation, even if adopted subsequently. The case establishes the principle of priority of Community law. It was followed by Case 14/83 *Von Colson* [1984] ECR 1891, [1986] 2 CMLR 430. In the grounds of the judgment in the latter case the Court stated that in applying the national law, in particular the provisions of a national law specifically introduced in order to implement a Directive, national courts are required to interpret their national law in the light of the wording and purpose of the Directive. In the formal order of the Court the wording is slightly different:

> 'It is for the national court to interpret the legislation adopted for the implementation of a directive in conformity with the requirements of Community law, in so far as it is given discretion to so so under national law'.

That left a problem over what was to happen if the national law in question antedated the European measure. But in C-106/89 *Marleasing SA* v. *La Comercial* [1992] 1 CMLR 305 (the facts are related in Chapter 3 of this book) the Court said that in applying national law, whether the provisions in question were adopted before or after the Directive, the national court called upon to interpret it is required to do so, as far as possible, in the light of the wording and purpose of the Directive, in order to achieve the result pursued by the Directive, and thereby comply with article 249 [189] of the Treaty.

But there is a limit when it comes to crime. In C-688/95 *Arcaro* [1996] ECR I-4705, [1997] 1 CMLR 179, [1997] All ER(EC) 82, the Italian proprietor of a factory was prosecuted for discharging cadmium into a river. Had it not been for the failure of Italy to implement fully a directive on discharges into the aquatic environment he would have been convicted. The prosecutor appealed and the question was whether he could rely on the Directive. It was held that a Directive cannot itself, independently of national law, have the effect of determining or aggravating the criminal liability of a person.

The line of English authorities on the interpretatioin of implementing legislation begins with *McCarthy's Ltd* v. *Smith* [1979] 3 CMLR 44 & 381, [1979] 3 All ER 325. In this case Lord Denning, in a dissenting judgment, said that

> 'In construing our statutes we are entitled to look to the Treaty as an aid to construction; but not only as an aid but as an overriding force. If on close examination it should appear that our legislation is deficient or is inconsistent with Community law by some

oversight of our draftsmen then it is our bounden duty to give priority to Community law.'

In *Garland* v. *British Rail Engineering Ltd* [1983] 2 AC 751, [1982] 2 CMLR 174, Lord Diplock had to construe the words of the Sex Discrimination Act 1975 in the light of the obligation under article 141 [119] of the Treaty. He said that the words of a statute passed after the Treaty are to be construed, if they are reasonably capable of bearing such a meaning, as intended to carry out the obligation which is imposed by the Treaty, and not to be inconsistent with it.

In *Duke* v. *GEC Reliance Ltd* [1988] AC 618, [1988] 2 WLR 359, the plaintiff tried to rely on the words of Lord Diplock, in *Garland*, in construing the Equal Pay Act in the light of a Directive. The equal treatment Directive, Council Directive (EEC) 76/207 (OJ L39 14.2.76 p40), imposes a duty on the UK to implement the principle of equal treatment for men and women in employment. Mrs Duke tried to sue her employer for damages because she was required to retire at 60 instead of 65; but, in this she was unsuccessful, because the House of Lords held that the Directive was not of direct effect, and the Equal Pay Act 1970 was not passed in order to give effect to it.

In *Pickstone* v. *Freeman's Publishing* [1989] AC 66, [1988] 3 WLR 265, the House of Lords had again to construe the Equal Pay Act 1970. This time the problem was to construe a section which had been inserted in the Act in order to give effect to the equal pay Directive, Council Directive (EEC) 75/117 (OJ L45 19.2.75 p19). The method chosen to avoid any difficulty was to adopt a teleological interpretation of the English statute. Lord Keith said:

'It is sufficient to say that the words must be construed purposively in order to give effect to the manifest broad intention of the maker of the regulations and Parliament'.

The importance of those words cannot be underestimated. For the first time an English statute was interpreted in a European way. The change went unnoticed at the time and to this day its consequences have not been realised. If this is the method of interpreting such legislation one wonders why British draftsmen should go through the labour of turning perfectly good Community Directives into British style statutes. Would it not be simpler to enact them as they stand?

The *Pickstone* case was confirmed in *Litster* v. *Forth Dry Dock Co Ltd* [1989] 2 WLR 634, [1989] 1 All ER 1134, but in none of the above cases did the House of Lords confront the constitutional issues involved in a direct clash between Community law and a UK statute.

7.4   Disapplying national legislation

In *R* v. *Secretary of State for Transport* ex parte *Factortame Ltd* [1990] 2 AC 85, [1989] 3 CMLR 1, the House of Lords had to decide what was to be done when there was so direct a conflict between European and English legislation that it was not possible to solve it by sympathetic interpretation. The appellants were a number of Spanish owners of British trawlers. The Merchant Shipping Act 1988 introduced very strict rules concerning fishing in United Kingdom waters by Community nationals. These rules had the effect of preventing the appellants from using British waters. They asked for a judicial review, claiming that the law was discriminatory, and consequently contrary to the Treaty of Rome. Lord Bridge said that by virtue of section 2(4) of the European Communities Act 1972 the Merchant Shipping Act 1988 was to be read subject to directly enforceable Community rights. It was the same as if there was a section in the 1988 Act which said that it was to take effect without prejudice to the directly enforceable Community rights of nationals of any Member State of the Community. It was quite clear that there was a doubt whether the Merchant Shipping Act was compatible with Community law, and that a question should be referred to the European Court.

A problem then arose as to what was to be done in the meantime. It would take two years for the matter to come before the European Court, by which time the appellants would be ruined. As we shall see later in this chapter, it is not entirely certain that there will always be a remedy in damages against a Member State for a breach of Community law, and the European Court of Justice has no power to order interim measures in a case referred to it under article 234 [177] of the Treaty. The appellants therefore asked the English court for interim relief in the form of an order, pending final judgment, disapplying the Merchant Shipping Act and restraining the Secretary of State from enforcing it against the appellants. The House of Lords refused such interim relief because, said Lord Bridge, it was not possible to obtain an injunction against the Crown in judicial review proceedings, and there was a presumption that English law accorded with Community law until it was declared otherwise.

The European Court of Justice disagreed. In Case C-213/89 *Factortame* v. *Secretary of State* [1990] ECR I-2433, [1990] 3 CMLR 375, (*Factortame I*) it said that it is for national courts to ensure the legal protection which persons derive from the direct effect of the provisions of Community law. If the only obstacle which precluded the English court from granting interim relief was a rule of national law, it had to set aside that rule. The House of Lords was therefore obliged to grant an interim injunction, suspending the operation of an act of Parliament. The reader must bear the suspense; we shall return to the history of this case in a moment.

7.5 Remedies

Before EU law can be used it must be shown that the EU law is intended to confer rights. In *Bowden* v. *Secretary of State for Environment* (17 December 1997 QBD unreported) an action by some fishermen who claimed for damage to shellfish beds caused by a failure of the UK to comply with the Bathing Water Directive and the Shellfish Waters Directive was struck out because nothing in the Directives entailed the grant of rights.

In competition law, in particular, the Treaty or regulations made under it will be designed to grant substantive rights. In such cases an injunction can be obtained in a private context in an English court for breach of European law; an example is the case of *Holleran* v. *Daniel Thwaites plc* [1989] 2 CMLR 917, in which the tenants of some tied public houses refused to sign the new tenancy agreement that the brewers had offered them. They claimed that it was contrary to a regulation on beer supply agreements, and they were granted an injunction preventing the brewers from exercising their contractual right to claim possession.

It is now clear that damages may be obtained in private law in an English court for breach of directly enforceable Community law. In such cases it is usually said that there is a breach of statutory duty, the statute being the European Communities Act 1972. In *Garden Cottage Foods Limited* v. *Milk Marketing Board* [1984] 1 AC 130, [1983] 3 WLR 143, it appears to have been accepted that damages would be available against a statutory authority. The Milk Marketing Board was subject not only to British legislation, but also to various Council Directives relating to the common organisation of the market in milk and milk products. In 1982 the Milk Marketing Board told the appellants that it would no longer be willing to supply bulk butter to them. Garden Cottage Foods Limited brought an action in which it claimed that there had been a breach of article 82 [86] of the EC Treaty. Article 82 [86] forbids the abuse of a dominant position in the market.

Garden Cottage asked for an interim injunction. In this they were unsuccessful, although it was not doubted that in an appropriate case an injunction might be granted. Lord Diplock said that since article 82[86] was intended not only to promote the general prosperity of the common market, but also to benefit private individuals, to whom loss or damage is caused, it was capable of giving rise to a civil action for damages. Lord Wilberforce seemed reluctant to support this conclusion, but nowadays the case is regarded as supporting the proposition that damages are available, for contravention of directly effective provisions, in at a private law context.

In a public law context, the first case to consider is *Bourgoin SA* v. *Ministry of Agriculture* [1986] QB 716, [1986] 1 CMLR 267. Some French turkey breeders sued the Minister of Agriculture for damages for refusing to allow the import of their poultry. The minister's action was a breach of article 28 [30] of the Treaty, which deals with free movement of goods. There is a history to this case which is set out in Chapter 9 of this book. The Court of Appeal held that there could be no action against a minister of the Crown for innocently exercising his legislative powers. The case was settled and therefore the European Court never had a chance to consider these doubtful reasons; subsequent cases have shown that the defendant was right to compromise.

In the joined cases C-6/90 and C-9/90 *Frankovich* v. *Republic of Italy* and *Bonifaci* v. *Republic of Italy* [1993] 2 CMLR 66, the Court said that the Italian government was obliged to make good the damage suffered by individuals as a result of its failure to implement Council Directive 80/987 (EEC) (OJ L283 28.10.80 p23). Directive 80/987 is designed to ensure that employees will have some protection against the loss of their wages, in the form of a guarantee payment, in the event of the insolvency of their employer. Signor Francovich brought an action for his wages against his insolvent employers, but they had nothing left with which to pay him. He therefore asked the Italian Republic to pay him his guarantee; but the government refused to pay him because it had not implemented the Directive. That being so, he sued the Italian state claiming either that he was entitled to rely upon the Directive, and on that basis must be paid his guarantee, or, alternatively, that he was entitled to damages for the failure to implement the Directive.

His first claim was unsuccessful; the European Court held that he could not rely upon the words of the Directive because it was not sufficiently precise and unconditional to be directly effective. But his alternative claim, for damages for failure to implement the Directive, succeeded. The Court said that in order to obtain damages against the state, for failure to implement a Directive, the following conditions must apply. First, the Directive must be calculated to confer rights on individuals. Second, the subject matter of those rights must be identified by reference to the provisions of the Directive. Third, the existence of a causal link between the infringement of the obligation incumbent upon the Member State and the damage suffered must be shown.

The Court also stated that, although it was for the legal system of each Member State to lay down the procedures to safeguard the rights of individuals under Community law, the conditions concerning compensation for damage could not be less favourable than those applicable to similar claims of an internal nature, and could not be so arranged as to make it virtually impossible or excessively difficult to obtain compensation.

In C-221/89 *R* v. *Secretary of State for Transport* ex parte *Factortame* [1991] 1 ECR 3905, [1991] 3 CMLR 589 (*Factortame* II), the European Court of Justice held that it was contrary to Community law, and in particular article 43 [52] of the Treaty for a Member State to impose conditions as to nationality, residence and domicile of the owners of fishing vessels such as those laid down by the registration system in the UK. In the light of *Francovich* one wonders why the British government was spending public money on arguing that it was right in *Factortame*, but every litigant wants to put off the evil day and consequently the matter came back to the European Court in joined cases C-46/93,C-48/93 *Brasserie du Pêcheur SA* v. *Germany* and *R* v. *Secretary of State* ex parte *Factortame* [1996] ECR I-1029, [1996] 1 CMLR 889 (*Factortame III*), and the Court then had to consider whether Member States are obliged to make good damage caused to individuals by breaches of Community law when the national legislature was responsible for the infringement. The European Court simply repeated what it had said in *Francovich*, namely that it is a principle of European Community law that Member States are obliged to make good loss and damage caused to individuals by breaches of community law. The Court went on to say that the conditions for liability cannot differ from those governing the Community; in like circumstances the Community would be liable under article 288 [215] of the Treaty. The protection of rights which individuals derive from Community law cannot vary depending on whether a national or a Community authority is responsible for the damage.

7.6 Limits

Member States may apply their own rules as to liability, but not so as to make the remedy for breach of EC law excessively difficult to obtain. For example, in 199/92 *Amministrazione delle Finanze dello Stato* v. *SpA San Georgio* [1983] ECR 3595 the San Giorgio Dairy was entitled to the repayment of some export charges that had been levied in contravention of article 28 [30] of the Treaty. But in order to get its money back the dairy had to provide documentary proof that the charges had not been passed on to someone else, which was practically impossible. The European Court held that any require-ment of proof which had the effect of making it virtually impossible or excessively difficult to secure repayment was contrary to Com-munity law.

The breach must, however, be sufficiently serious before damages will be awarded for failure to implement EU law. In C-392/93 *R* v. *HM Treasury* ex parte *British Telecom plc* [1996] I ECR 1631; [1996] 2 CMLR 217, the UK failed to implement an obscure provision in one of the Purchasing Directives. These Directives set out a tedious, complicated and largely incomprehensible procurement procedure to be followed by entities funded or regulated by the state. According to the European Court an error in implementing the Directive did not form the basis for a claim in damages because the UK could be forgiven for misunderstanding the Directive.

By contrast, in C178/94 *Dillenkofer* v. *Federal Republic of Germany* [1996] ECR I-4845, [1996] 3 CMLR 469, Germany failed to imple-ment Council Directive 90/314/EEC (OJ L158 23.6.90) at all. This is a Directive that guarantees to customers the reimbursement of money paid to a package holiday company if it becomes insolvent. The European Court ruled that a failure to take any measure to fulfil the Directive constituted a serious breach of Community law and consequently gave rise to a right to reparation. A right to reparation for individuals suffering injury as a result of a failure to implement European law arises if the results prescribed by the Directive entail the grant to individuals of rights whose content is identifiable, and a causal link exists between the breach of the state's obligation and the loss and damage suffered.

In *R* v. *Secretary of State* ex parte *Factortame* (No 5) [1999] 4 All ER 907 the House of Lords had the opportunity to consider how these principles are to be applied after the European Court in *Factortame III* had ruled that the UK had to pay damages to the Spanish fishermen who had been prevented from fishing in British waters, if the breach could be shown to be sufficiently serious. The House of Lords identified four factors that made the breach serious, namely

- discrimination on the ground of nationality
- the fact that the Secretary of State knew that the fishermen would suffer damage
- the fact that the UK adopted primary legislation so that interim relief could not be obtained save by intervention of the European Court
- the hostile attitude of the Commission.

As to the measure of damages the House of Lords considered that the criteria that the Community law required to be satisfied were that there should be full reparation, that the reparation should be effective as a means of enforcing Community law, and that there should be no discrimination in the way the Court treated breaches of national law and breaches of Community law. The fishermen argued that penal damages ought to be awarded, but the Court treated the breach like a breach of statutory duty, and English law is that unless the statute expressly provided that penal damages may be awarded only compensatory damage should be awarded.

7.7   *Declarations*

A declaration may be obtained that national legislation does not comply with EC law. In *Equal Opportunities Commission* v. *Secretary of State for Employment* [1995] 1 AC 1, [1994] 2 WLR 409, [1994] 1 All ER 910, the Equal Opportunities Commission sought judicial review against the Secretary of State for a declaration that the Employment Protection (Consolidation) Act 1978 was incompatible with EU law. The incompatibility arose because of a provision, since repealed, that part-time workers had to be employed for five years before they were entitled to make claims for unfair dismissal, whereas full time workers needed only to be employed for two years. This indirectly discriminated against women, who formed a high proportion of the part-time work force. The House of Lords made the declaration that there was an incompatibility with European law. But the Court refused to make a further declaration that the Secretary of State was in breach of the provisions of the Equal Treatment Directive, 76/207 (OJ L39 14.2.76 p40), that required Member States to introduce measures to abolish laws that were contrary to the principle of equal treatment. The Equal Opportunities Commission had asked for this declaration so that employees of private employers would be able to pursue actions for damages against the state under the *Francovich* principle. The Court refused because in any claim under the *Francovich* principle different considerations would apply and the Attorney General would be the defendant.

The last point resulted in the failure of the applicant to obtain a declaration in *R* v. *Secretary of State for Employment* ex parte *Seymour Smith* [1997] 1 WLR 473. The applicant had been unable to pursue her claim for unfair dismissal against her employer on account of the operation of the Unfair Dismissal (Variation of Qualifying Period) Order 1985, which she said was incompatible with the Equal Treatment Directive. The House of Lords refused to grant her a declaration, saying that it would serve no useful purpose. She would not be able to pursue her employer as a result of a declaration because the Directive had no direct effect. The House of Lords was not prepared to allow her to circumvent the rules on direct effect by granting a declaration. The question whether the award of compensation for the right not to be dismissed amounted to 'pay' within article 141 [119] of the Treaty was, however, referred to the European Court; in C167/97 *R* v. *Secretary of State for Employment* ex parte *Seymour Smith* [1999] 2 AC 554, [1999] All ER (EC) 97 the European Court decided that it was pay.

Judicial review is available where a minister acts in contravention of EU law. For example in *R* v. *Ministry of Agriculture* ex parte *Bell Lines* [1984] 2 CMLR 502 the question was whether imports of dairy products from Ireland could be restricted to certain ports and the importers obtained an order requiring the Minister to designate certain other ports.

7.8 Proportionality

If the question of the applicability of Community law is in question the European Court may be minded to apply its principles of proportionality. In *Francovich* and *Factortame* it was said that any breach must be *sufficiently* serious and the European Court appreciates the practical difficulties in implementing Community law in the circumstances which may apply in different Member States. In the period up to the repeal of the Shops Act 1950 an attempt was made by several traders to show that Sunday trading rules in the UK were contrary to the right to free movement enshrined in article 28 [30] of the Treaty (as to which see Chapter 9). The argument was that if there was no Sunday trading there would be less trade between the UK and the rest of the European Union. Had they been successful it would have presaged actions against the state for failure to implement free movement provisons. But, in C267/91 *Keck and Mithouard* [1992] ECR I-6097, [1995] 1 CMLR 101, the European Court said that the application to products from other Member States of national provisions restricting or prohibiting certain selling arrangements is not such as to hinder directly or indirectly, actually or potentially, trade between Member States within the meaning of the rule in *Dassonville* so long as those provisions apply to all relevant traders operating within the national territory, and so long as they affect in the same manner, in law and in fact, the marketing of domestic products and of those from other Member States. Effectively the European Court entertained an argument based on proportionality.

7.9 Unlawful Community measures

In the case of unlawful Community acts, it used to be thought that so long as the Community measure was not declared void by the European Court it had to be complied with, but since C143/88 & 92/89 *Zuckerfabrik Suderdithmarschen AG* v. *Hauptzollamt Itzehoe* [1991] ECR I-415, [1993] 3 CMLR 1, it appears that a domestic court may grant interlocutory relief on the same basis as the European Court. Damages must be determined by national law and procedure, they do not come within article 288 [215] of the Treaty. If a court of a Member State suspects that a Community measure may be void it must stay the proceedings and refer a question to the European Court.

CHAPTER 8
PLEADINGS

8.1 Introduction

The European Court has been at pains to prevent undue formalism in its proceedings. There are, however, certain minimum requirements which have to be met and in this chapter we shall consider how to go about drafting an article 234 [177] reference, observations by the parties in such a reference, and an application or *requête* in a direct action.

8.2 Article 234 [177] references

The point to keep in mind is that content is more important than form. In this chapter the first example given is of an order made in the High Court for an article 234 [177] reference. This is primarily a matter for the court, but it is customary to call upon counsel to agree the form of the order. *R* v. *Immigration Appeal Tribunal* ex parte *Antonissen* [1989] 2 CMLR 957 may be referred to as a practical example of the points to bear in mind when requesting the Court to make a reference; the exchange between counsel and the Court is there reported in full.

The information contained in a reference must be sufficient to enable the European Court to consider, and understand the issues of Community law raised, and to enable governments of Member States, and other interested parties, to make observations. The Commission will usually make observations, even if nobody else does. The European Court has issued advice on the contents of references and this advice has now been incorporated into RSC Order 114 in Schedule 1 of the Civil Procedure Rules and related practice directions.

An order may be made by the High Court on application, or of its own motion at any stage of the proceedings. The order has to set out the request for the preliminary ruling in a schedule which must follow a practice form, PF No.109. The proceedings in which the order is made are stayed, unless the High Court otherwise orders. Guidance is given in a consolidated practice direction which applies to proceedings in the Court of Appeal Civil Division (Supreme Court Practice PD-031 and [1999] 2 CMLR 799). Reference may also be made to Case 141–143/81 *Holdijk* [1982] ECR 1299, [1983] 2 CMLR 635, where the European Court discussed the content of a reference. Whilst the schedule is ultimately a matter for the court, it is common for the court to ask counsel to draft it. The court may amend the draft as it thinks fit.

The example that follows is based on Case 138–139/86 *Direct Cosmetics Limited* v. *Commissioners of Customs and Excise* [1988] ECR 3937, [1988] 3 CMLR 333. The case was chosen because it is a practical example of how EC law impinges on practice in the United Kingdom. The issues, much developed in the case, had to do with the circumstances in which the United Kingdom may derogate from the 6th Directive on value added tax. In order to be entitled to make such a derogation the United Kingdom must notify the Commission who may then make the appropriate decision. Those interested in the problem may like to look at *Fine Art Developments plc* v. *Commissioners of Customs and Excise* [1996] 2 CMLR 710, in which an unsuccessful attempt was made to circumvent the *Direct Cosmetics* case.

A practical point to note is that the European Court Reports are the only official reports for the European Court. In pleadings references should be given to these reports rather than any others.

When a case is filed at the European Court it is given a reference number. Cases are given numbers in chronological order followed by the year, for example '146/77'. When the Court of First Instance was established in 1988 the court registry began to place a letter before the number: 'C', for the European Court of Justice (e.g. C-999/90), and 'T', standing for *Tribunal*, for the Court of First Instance (e.g. T-999/90).

DRAFT ARTICLE 234 [177] REFERENCE

IN THE HIGH COURT OF JUSTICE   No . . . . .
QUEEN'S BENCH DIVISION

B E T W E E N:

    VERY FRILLY TRADERS PLC   Appellant

    and

    COMMISSIONERS OF CUSTOMS AND EXCISE

    Respondents

It is ordered that the questions set out in the Schedule hereto concerning the interpretation of Sixth Council Directive (EEC) 77/388 of 17 May 1977 on the harmonisation of the laws of Member States relating to turnover taxes – Common system of value added tax: uniform basis of assessment and on the validity of Council Decision (EEC) 85/369 of 13 June 1985, be referred to the Court of Justice of the European Communities for a preliminary ruling in accordance with article 234 EC, formerly article 177 of the Treaty Establishing the European Community.

And it is ordered that all further proceedings in the above mentioned cause be stayed until the said Court of Justice has given its ruling on the said questions or until further order.

SCHEDULE

(1)   The appellant company is a dealer in frilly items and the respondents are the Commissioners for Customs and Excise, being the body responsible in the United Kingdom for the collection and administration of value added tax.

(2)   The appellant specialises in direct sales of very frilly items sold through agents in offices, factories and clubs.

(3)   The scheme operates in the following way. The products are delivered to agents who sell them at the company's catalogue price; if an agent sells a frilly item within 14 days she may retain 20% of the price, but otherwise she must account to the appellant for the full price . . . *etc.*

(4)   The agents are not liable to value added tax because their turnover is below the relevant limit laid down by UK legislation in accordance with article 24 of Directive (EEC) 77/388.

(5) As a result of the above trade scheme the final taxable base for the purposes of value added tax is not the final value of sale to the consumer. Consequently no tax is paid on the difference between the final price and the price previously charged ... *etc*

(6) In the United Kingdom the Sixth Directive is implemented by the Finance Act 1977.

(7) On the ... day of ... 19... the United Kingdom notified the Commission that a measure derogating from Article 11.A.1(a) of the 6th Directive had been made by paragraph 3 schedule 4 of the Finance Act 1977.

(8) Paragraph 3 of schedule 4 of the Finance Act 1977 reads as follows: 'The Commissioners may by notice in writing ... direct that the value of any such supply shall be ... taken to be its open market value ... *etc*.'

(9) Paragraph 3 of schedule 4 is authorised by Council Decision (EEC) 85/369 of 13 June 1985 which was adopted pursuant to article 27 of the 6th Directive.

(10) On ... day of ... 19... the Commissioners served a notice in the following form directing that the value of goods supplied by Very Frilly Traders PLC under the above trade scheme should be taken to be the open market value for sale by retail and ... *etc*.

(11) The appellants appealed against that notice to the Value Added Tax Tribunal. On the ... day of ... the Tribunal found in favour of the Commissioners. The appellants appealed to the High Court under section 40 of the Value Added Tax Act 1983.

(12) The following are agreed facts:

(a) That the trading scheme described above was lawful and was not entered into with a view to avoiding the payment of value added tax.

(b) ... *etc*.

(13) The appellants contend that:

(a) Article 27 of the Directive must be interpreted as not permitting a derogating measure where the taxpayer carries on business in a certain manner without any intention to obtain a tax advantage, and that therefore the Commission decision was invalid.

(b) The notice sent to the Commission in accordance with Article 27 of the Directive on the ... day of ... 19... does not mention tax avoidance and that therefore the Decision made by the Commission on ... is invalid.

(14) The respondents contend that:

(a) Upon its proper interpretation article 27 authorises an exemption because ... *etc.*

(b) Although the notice sent to the Commission referred only to tax evasion the cases mentioned in the notice concerned only tax avoidance and that accordingly the Commission was entitled to make a decision permitting a derogation ... *etc.*

(15) The proceedings having been stayed by order of Mr Justice ... on the ... day of ..., the Court of Justice, pursuant to the provisions of article 234 EC, formerly article 177, of the Treaty Establishing the European Community, is requested to give a preliminary ruling on the following questions:

(1) Whether, upon the true construction of article 27 of the Sixth Council Directive (EEC) 77/388 of 17 May 1977, the Commission may adopt a measure derogating from the rule set out in article 11.A.1(a) of that Directive, where the taxable person carries on a business in a particular manner without any intention of obtaining a tax advantage but for commercial reasons.

(2) Whether a measure that falls outside the terms of the request for authorisation made to the Commission under article 27 of the Directive is invalid.

DRAFT WRITTEN OBSERVATIONS ON AN ARTICLE 234 [177] REFERENCE FOR A PRELIMINARY RULING

IN THE COURT OF JUSTICE   Case C-999/94
OF THE EUROPEAN COMMUNITIES

In the matter of a reference to the Court under article 234 EC, formerly article 177 of the EC Treaty, by the High Court of Justice, Queen's Bench Division, for a preliminary ruling in the matter pending before the Court between:

VERY FRILLY TRADERS PLC

and

COMMISSIONERS OF CUSTOMS AND EXCISE

OBSERVATIONS OF THE COMMISSIONERS FOR CUSTOMS AND EXCISE

On the facts:

(1) The facts set out in the reference require explanation. It should be noted that undertakings which have recourse to the methods of trading mentioned therein are not all of the same size and are not equally significant from the point of the functioning of the system of value added tax ... *etc.*

(2) Failure to apply the derogating measures would lead to distortion of competition ... *etc.*

Submissions

(3) The Commissioners of Customs and Excise have nothing further to add concerning their contentions on the second question set out in the reference.

(4) As to the first question, it was said in Case 138-139/86 *Direct Cosmetics Limited* v. *Commissioners for Customs and Excise* [1988] ECR 3937 that ... *etc.*

IN CONCLUSION the Commissioners of Customs and Excise submit that the questions referred to the Court should be answered as follows:

(1) Article 27(1) of the 6th Directive permits the adoption of a measure derogating from the basic rule set out in article 11,A.1(a) of that Directive, even where the taxable person carries on business without any intention of obtaining a commercial advantage and for commercial reasons.

(2) There are no factors affecting the validity of Council Decision 85/369 of 13 June 1985 authorising a derogating measure requested by the United Kingdom.

(Signature of Counsel)

Dated ...

Instructed by Solicitors

(Address for service)

8.3   *Pleadings in direct actions*

The most frequent example of a direct application is a competition case. Such actions are heard in the Court of First Instance. The rules of procedure with regard to the form and contents of an application are set out in article 44 of the rules of the Court of First Instance (OJ L136 30.5.91 p1), and do not differ materially from the equivalent rule in the Court of Justice, namely article 38 of the Rules of Procedure of the Court of Justice (OJ L176 4.7.91 p7). The requirements are that the application must state the name and address of the applicant, the designation of the party against whom the application is made, the subject matter of the proceedings and a summary of the pleas in law on which the application is based, the form of order sought by the applicant, and, where appropriate, the nature of any evidence offered in support.

The following draft for an application in a direct action is based upon Case 155/79 *A M & S Europe Ltd* v. *EC Commission* [1982] ECR 1575, [1982] 2 CMLR 264, which concerns the question of whether in-house lawyers should be able to claim privilege in competition matters. It is a topic that needs to be revisited. Such a case would now commence in the Court of First Instance, because it is brought under article 230 [173] of the Treaty by a natural or legal person: see article 3 of Council Decision (ECSC,EEC,Euratom) 88/591 (OJ L319 25.11.88 p1, corrected version OJ C215 21.8.89 p1) establishing the Court of First Instance, as amended by Council Decision (Euratom ECSC EEC) 93/350 (OJ L144 16.6.93 p21). Although no particular form is specified applications will usually be headed by the names of the applicant and defendant, followed by a short title such as 'Application made under articles 230 EC and 231 EC, formerly articles 173 and 174, of the Treaty Establishing the European Community for a declaration that Council Regulation ... is void'. Purists would then begin the body of the pleadings with the words 'May it please the Court to declare that...' followed by the proposed order in imitation of the French draftsmen. Submissions are then followed by the 'conclusions' or form of the order required.

A defence will take the same form as the application, answering each point in turn and containing the conclusion that the application should be dismissed and that the plaintiff should pay the costs. Lawyers in private practice will not be likely to be called upon to draft a defence since the Commission will usually be the defendant.

Since an application has, in itself, no suspensory effect it may be necessary to make a separate application under article 242 [185] and

243 [186] of the Treaty in order to suspend the application of a decision which has been taken. Under article 104 of the Rules of Procedure of the Court of First Instance such an interim application takes the same form as the main application but must state the subject matter of the proceedings, the circumstances giving rise to urgency, and the pleas of fact and law establishing a prima facie case for the interim measures applied for.

DRAFT APPLICATION IN A DIRECT ACTION

IN THE COURT OF FIRST INSTANCE OF THE EUROPEAN COMMUNITIES

Between:

Dreadful Plc of . . . . represented by N. Fees QC and CU. Later Solicitor of Messrs Payup, London with an address for service in Luxembourg at the Chambers of Messrs Paieplus of . . . .

Applicant

and

Commission of the European Communities, represented by A. Ferret, legal adviser, acting as agent, with an address for service in Luxembourg at the office of G. Fromage, a member of the Commission's Legal Department . . .

Defendant

Application under articles 230 EC and 231 EC, formerly articles 173 and 174, of the Treaty Establishing the European Community for a declaration that Commission Decision . . ./. . . of the . . . . is void

May it please the Court to:

(a) Declare the Commission Decision . . ./. . . of 4th July 19. . . void.

(b) Order the Defendant to pay the costs.

POINTS OF FACT

(1) Dreadful Plc is a company incorporated in England which manufactures widgets which are sold under the trade name 'Hobson's Choice'.

---

(2)   On the 1st day of January 19... the Member of the Commission responsible for competition policy directed investigation to be made of the applicant, pursuant to Article 14 of Regulation 17 of the Council.

(3)   On the 10th January 19... three officials of the Commission carried out an investigation at the applicant's premises in Bradford the purpose of which was to investigate '... the competitive conditions concerning the production and distribution of widgets in order to certify that there is no infringement of Article 81 EC and 82 EC'. During the course of the investigation ... *etc.*

(4)   At the conclusion of that investigation the officials left the premises taking with them copies of a certain number of documents and leaving with Mr Gradgrind the managing director a written request for further specified documents. The written request states ... *etc.*

(5)   By letter dated the 12th day of March 19... Dreadful Plc sent to the Commission photocopies of certain documents namely ... but at the same time refused to make available others which its legal advisers considered were covered by legal privilege.

(6)   By decision of 4th day of July 19..., taken under article 14(3) of Regulation 17, the Commission required Dreadful Plc to produce those specific documents for which legal privilege had been claimed as set out in a schedule ... *etc.*

(7)   The decision of the 4th day of July 19... requires the applicant to disclose to the Commission's inspector the entire contents of the documents.

(8)   The Applicant's solicitors gave the following explanation as to why the documents ought to be privileged supported by the documents in the annexed file and listed in the schedule hereto: ... *etc.*

(9)   Document ... in the annexed file proves that ... *etc.*

SUBMISSIONS

(10)   The Applicant submits that the documents referred to in the decision of the Commission consisted of letters between an independent lawyer and his client.

(11)   In Case 155/79 *AM & S Ltd* v. *EC Commission* [1982] ECR 1575 the Advocate General said that ... the reasoning was followed in ... *etc.*

(12)   The decision was an abuse of power because ... *etc.*

(13) The applicant submits that the decision was void on the grounds that it was an abuse of power and also contrary to a fundamental principle of Community law, in that it required the production of documents which had been exchanged after the commencement of proceedings, and which were made between a client and an independent lawyer.

CONCLUSION

May it please the Court to:

(a) Declare the Commission Decision ... of 4th July 19... void.

(b) Order the Commission to pay the costs.

Dated .... (Signature of legal representative)

8.4   Further reading

Precedents may be found in both the following

Atkin's Court Forms. Butterworths, London.
European Courts Procedure. Sweet and Maxwell, London.

CHAPTER 9
FREE MOVEMENT OF GOODS

9.1 Introduction

Four freedoms are established by the European Union: free movement of goods, of persons, of services and of capital; but the greatest of these is free movement of goods. The general policy of the Community on free movement of goods is set out in article 3 [3] of the EC Treaty; the prohibition, as between Member States, of customs duties and quantitative restrictions on the import and export of goods, and all other measures having equivalent effect. 'Quantitative restrictions' in this context means quotas. The detailed provisions of the Treaty are set out in articles 23 [9] to 31 [37].

Article 23(1) [9(1)] states that the Community is based upon a common customs union. In relation to third countries a common customs tariff (CCT) is adopted and the duties under this tariff are fixed by the Council acting by a qualified majority. Products coming from third countries are considered in free circulation in Member States once they have crossed the tariff wall.

A full customs union was achieved by July 1968 and therefore cases on direct barriers to trade are now rare, but in C-16/94 *Edouard Dubois Fils SA* v. *Garanor Exploitation SA* [1995] 1 ALL ER (EC) 821 such an issue did arise. A privately administered international road station was levying a transit charge. This was held to be illegal because it was for the state to bear the costs of any frontier controls.

It is now the concealed and indirect barriers to trade which most exercise the Commission. Article 28 [30] prohibits quantitative restrictions on imports and all measures having an equivalent effect. Article 29 does the same for exports. Article 30 [36], in a way typical for Community law, provides for derogations from the general principles set out in article 28 [30]. The exceptions provided for by article 30 [36] (the full terms are set out later in this chapter) include justifications on the grounds of public morality, public policy, and public health.

9.2   Definition of terms

Terms encountered in this area of Community law include

- equivalent effect
- the rule of reason
- parallel imports
- proportionality.

An attempt will be made to explain and illustrate some of these expressions. Proportionality is discussed at sections 4.7.4 and 7.8.

9.2.1   Equivalent effect

There is a distinction between the term equivalent effect as it is used, on the one hand, in relation to customs duties and, on the other hand, in connection with quantitative restrictions; although they are clearly connected. First, we shall look at customs duties.

Gingerbread men are a vital element in the economy of Belgium and Luxembourg. This accounts for the Royal and Grand Ducal decrees of February 1960 that increased the special duty levied on the imports of that anthropomorphous confection. The defendants endeavoured to justify the charge by arguing that it was simply the counterpart of internal charges affecting similar domestic products. The Court, in Cases 2 & 3/62 *EC Commission* v. *Luxembourg and Belgium* [1962] ECR 425, [1963] CMLR 199, held that what was important was that the charge jeopardised the objectives of the Treaty and was the result not of a Community procedure, but of a unilateral decision. Any duty imposed unilaterally that applied to a product imported by a Member State, but not to a similar national product, and which, by altering the price, had the same effect on free movement of goods as a customs duty, was unlawful. In Case 158/82 *EC Commission* v. *Denmark* [1983] ECR 3573, [1984] 2 CMLR 658, the charge appeared in the guise of a charge made for the health inspection of peanuts. A charge having equivalent effect to a customs duty was there defined in the following way:

> 'The Court has consistently held that any pecuniary charge, whatever its designation or mode of application, which is imposed unilaterally on goods by reason of the fact that they cross a frontier, and which is not a customs duty in the strict sense, constitutes a charge having an effect equivalent to a customs duty ... even if it is not imposed on behalf of the state.'

The case arose because of a Danish law which required importers to pay laboratory charges for health checks on their peanuts. For domestic products such charges were paid for from domestic taxes.

Charges for health checks are allowed, if they are part of a general system of internal dues, applied systematically, in accordance with the same criteria, to both national products and imported or exported goods. Denmark was unable to show that this was the case. But, charges can be justified on the alternative ground that they represent payment for a service rendered to the importer; provided that the sum charged is in proportion to the service. The idea that justifications will avail only in proportion to their purposes, which is called 'proportionality', is a general one in Community law.

For quantitative restrictions the definition of the meaning of 'equivalent effect' is commonly known as the Rule in *Dassonville*. Monsieur Dassonville had imported some Scotch whisky from France into Belgium. He was prosecuted because he did not have the certificate of origin which was required by Belgian law. French law did not require him to have a certificate, so it is not surprising that he did not have one. The case was referred to the European Court. In Case 8/74 *Procureur du Roi* v. *Dassonville* [1974] ECR 837, [1974] 2 CMLR 436, the European Court formulated the rule as follows:

> 'All trading rules enacted by member states which are capable of hindering directly or indirectly, actually or potentially, intra-Community trade are to be considered as measures having effect equivalent to quantitative restrictions.'

9.2.2   The rule of reason

A requirement that a product should have 'Made in England', or some such legend, stamped upon it is a venerable way of discouraging imports. Such practices fall within article 28 [30]; though not in all circumstances. In Case 120/78 *Rewe-Zentral AG* v. *Bundesmonopolverwaltung für Branntwein* [1979] ECR 649, [1979] 3 CMLR 494, otherwise known as the *Cassis de Dijon* case, the problem was that French liqueurs could not be imported into Germany because of German requirements as to their alcohol content. The Court of Justice held that the fixing of minimum alcohol content for alcoholic beverages fell within article 28 [30], but observed that it would be possible to protect the consumer by requiring an indication of origin, and of the alcohol content, in the packaging of products; but that requirement would have to be subject to the principle of proportionality.

Cassis de Dijon thus deals with the problems which arise when obstacles to movement within the Community result from disparities between national laws relating to marketing of products. In the absence of common rules, on the marketing of alcohol for example, such anomalies are bound to arise, and will be defended by the Member State concerned on laudable grounds such as protection of the consumer. The rule which the Court has developed to deal with such problems is known as the *rule of reason*.

The rule of reason is a principle which the Court has developed. It is a justification for conduct which might fall within article 30 [36], but it does not derive from article 30 [36]. It is an example of the European Court filling in gaps. In the *Cassis de Dijon* case the Court expressed the rule as follows:

> 'Obstacles to movement within the Community resulting from disparities between the national laws relating to the marketing of the products in question must be accepted in so far as those provisions may be recognised as being necessary in order to satisfy mandatory requirements relating in particular to the effectiveness of fiscal supervision, the protection of public health, the fairness of commercial transactions and the defence of the consumer.'

This rule is now subject to a gloss added by C-267/91 *Keck & Mithouard* [1993] ECR I-6097, [1995] 1 CMLR 101, which is described later in the next section.

9.2.2.1 Sunday trading

For those who worship Mammon, the Shops Act 1950 was a constant source of irritation. What this had to do with article 28 [30] of the Treaty may become clearer to those who have time to consider the arguments in Case 145/88 *Torfaen BC* v. *B & Q plc* ([1989] ECR 3851; [1990] 1 CMLR 337). The Borough Council of Torfaen, where tea with the minister after morning Chapel is regarded as an indulgence, prosecuted the defendant company for opening a do-it-yourself store on Sunday. The defence relied on the rule in Dassonville, because the ban on Sunday trading was, so they said, capable of hindering, directly or indirectly, actually or potentially, intra-Community trade. The ban had restricted sales in their shops and had thereby restricted the value of imports from other Member States.

The prosecution relied on the *Cassis de Dijon* case, arguing that the Sunday trading rules were mandatory requirements to do with working conditions, the health and welfare of workers, and typical Welsh Sundays.

A question was therefore referred to the European Court of Justice as to whether the ban on Sunday trading was a measure equivalent to a quantitative restriction on imports. The Court replied that article 28 [30] must be interpreted as meaning that the prohibition which it lays down does not apply to national rules prohibiting retailers from opening their premises on Sunday where the restrictive effects on Community trade which may result therefrom do not exceed the effects intrinsic to rules of that kind.

Both sides emerged triumphant and promptly fell out over who had won. Another reference to the European Court was necessary to clarify the real issues. The litigants had suffered from two characteristics of the European Court: that upon an article 234 [177] reference it cannot make any findings of fact, and that it will only answer the question put; it hardly troubles itself over whether its answer is helpful. It is therefore incumbent upon the national court to take care about how it phrases its questions.

In Case C-169/91 *Stoke on Trent City Council* v. *B & Q plc* [1993] 1 CMLR 426, however, it was pointed out that the national court was left in a quandary if it was asked to make up its mind whether the restrictive effects on Community trade of the Sunday trading rules were disproportionate. The Advocate General said that it was a joint task for the European and the national court to decide whether a national measure was compatible with EC law. But, the Court decided to give a simple answer to the question. It ruled that article 28 [30] is to be interpreted as meaning that the prohibition which it lays down does not apply to national legislation prohibiting retailers from opening their premises on Sundays.

The question to ask oneself is why anyone would ever have imagined a Welsh Sunday would have any effect upon trade within the EC. The rule of reason is perhaps better translated as a rule of common sense. Ultimately the argument was to sink into oblivion with the repeal of the Shops Act. The legacy of all this dispute is C-267-268/91 *Keck & Mithouard* [1992] ECR I-6097, [1995] 1 CMLR 101, a case which put a further gloss on *Dassonville*. Mr Keck and Mr Mithouard were prosecuted by the French Directorate for Competition and Prevention of Fraud for selling beer at a loss in two supermarkets near the German border. This was an offence under French law, but they objected that it was contrary to article 28 [30] in that the Germans could sell beer at whatever loss they pleased. The European Court remarked that it was tired of the increasing tendency of traders to invoke article 28 [30] as a means of challenging any rules that limited their trade even where the rules were not aimed at products from other Member States.

Accordingly the Court revisited the *Cassis de Dijon* case and said that by contrast with what had previously been decided, the application to products from other Member States of national provisions restricting or prohibiting certain selling arrangements was not such as to hinder directly or indirectly, actually or potentially, trade between Member States within the meaning of *Dassonville* so long as those provisions applied to all relevant trades operating within the national territory and so long as they affect in the same manner, in law and fact, the marketing of domestic products and those from other Member States.

9.2.3 Parallel imports

Article 28 [30] applies to the measures of a Member State, but it also affects private arrangements. The cases where this happens are, usually, those involving parallel imports. The situation can happen where, for example, the owner of a patent tries to compartmentalise the market by selling his goods at a higher price in one country than in another. The enterprising trader who slips across the border in order to import goods which have been marketed elsewhere at a lower price is known as a parallel importer.

The parallel importer benefits from article 28 [30]. Case 15/74 *Centrafarm BV* v. *Stirling Drug Inc* [1974] ECR 1147, [1974] 2 CMLR 480, was a case which arose because Stirling Drug was the holder of patents relating to drugs for urinary infections in several Community countries. Centrafarm imported the drugs from England and Germany into the Netherlands. The drugs had been put on the market in England by subsidiaries of Stirling Drug. In the Netherlands they could be sold at half the price charged by the owner of the patent. It was held that a patentee could not prevent the import of drugs into a third country where they had already been marketed with his consent. Article 30 [36] could not be relied on in a case where the patent owner had thus volunteered to put his drugs on the unified market.

Parallel trading and the EU competition rules combine to create problems when a manufacturer endeavours to protect his trademark in, for example, designer clothing. Council Directive (EEC) 89/104 (OJ L40 11.2.89 p1) is designed to harmonise the laws of Member States with regard to trade marks. There is a principle known as 'exhaustion of rights' illustrated by the following case.

In C355/96 *Silhouette International Schmied Gmbh & Co KG* v. *Hartlauer Handelgesellschaft mbH* [1998] ECR I-4799, [1998] 2 CMLR 953, [1998] All ER (EC) 769), what happened was that Silhouette, a manufacturer of sophisticated spectacles, refused to supply Hartlauer with any of its goods for distribution in Austria. The reason was that Hautlauer sold cheap spectacles and Silhouette did not want to spoil its image. But Hartlauer managed to buy some Silhouette frames from a Bulgarian buyer in Sofia, and these it proceeded to sell in Austria. Hautlauer applied for an injunction to protect its trademark but the action was dismissed by the Austrian court. The question for the European Court was whether a proprietor of a trademark was entitled to rely on Directive 89/104 to protect his interest. The European Court replied that the Directive was designed so as to provide a uniform code in the European Economic Area with regard to the exhaustion of trademark rights. The position was that if a trader put his goods on sale within the EEA there was nothing to stop a parallel importer from buying them in one country and selling them in others. But there was no principle of international exhaustion of rights, so if a trader sold his goods outside the EEA, a parallel importer was not entitled to acquire them there and resell them in the EEA in breach of trademark laws.

As it happened Austria had not implemented the Directive as it should, and this accounted for why it was not possible to obtain an injunction in the Austrian courts, but the European Court reminded the Austrian court of its duty to interpret its laws so far as possible to accord with the Directive.

By contrast in C189/96 *Parfums Christian Dior SA* v. *Evora BV* [1998] RPC 166 the plaintiff was not able to prevent the sale of products obtained by parallel import after the plaintiff had placed them on the market within the EEA.

It used to be thought that article 28 [30] might apply to the conduct of private individuals, such as a policy of stocking only British goods or a campaign to boycott French apples (proposed by certain politicians as revenge in the beef war) but in Case 311/85 *Vereeniging van Vlaamse Reisbureaus* v. *Social Dienst van de Plaatselijke*

en Gewestelijke Overheidsdiensten [1987] ECR 3801, [1989] 4 CMLR
213, the Court said that articles 28 [30] and 29 [34] of the Treaty
concern only public measures, not the conduct of undertakings.

9.3   Excuses

Since the selfish interests of Member States are met by restrictions of
imports, they will try to justify their recalcitrance by reference to
article 30 [36]. The test set out in article 30 [36] is as follows:

> *Article 30 [36].* The provisions of Articles 28 [30] and 29 [34] shall
> not preclude prohibitions or restrictions on imports, exports or
> goods in transit justified on grounds of public morality, public
> policy or public security; the protection of health and life of
> humans, animals or plants; the protection of national treasures
> possession artistic, historic or archaeological value; or the pro-
> tection of industrial and commercial property. Such prohibitions
> or restrictions shall not, however, constitute a means of arbitrary
> discrimination or a disguised restriction on trade between
> Member States.

The cases on article 30 [36] involve *inter alia* French turkeys, German
beer and Dutch wives.

9.3.1   French turkeys

Case 40/82 *EC Commission* v. *United Kingdom* [1982] ECR 2793,
[1982] 3 CMLR 497, is an object lesson in what can go wrong in
putting too much trust in exceptions. As a general rule the European Court will construe exceptions narrowly. The background to
the case is that the French government was heavily subsidising
French turkey breeders, to the annoyance of English farmers. In
1981 the Minister of Agriculture decided to impose a ban on French
poultry imports. The reason was supposed to be an outbreak of
Newcastle disease, a dreadful infection of that festive fowl and
others. It was not long before Christmas. The European Court was
later to observe that 'certain established facts suggest that the real
aim of the 1981 measures was to block, for commercial and economic reasons, imports of poultry products from other member
states, in particular from France'.

The Commission brought proceedings against the United Kingdom alleging a breach of article 28 [30]. The United Kingdom lost. As usually happens in this kind of case, the United Kingdom relied on article 30 [36], contending that the ban was justified by reason of protecting the health of British birds. The Court, however, held that such a prohibition must not constitute a means of arbitrary discrimination or a disguised restriction on trade.

That was not the end of the matter. The producers, having established their rights in the European Court, looked around for a remedy; they decided to sue for damages, relying on the direct effect of article 28 [30]. In *Bourgoin SA* v. *Ministry of Agriculture Fisheries and Food* [1986] QB 716, [1986] 1 CMLR 267, the Minister of Agriculture found himself being sued for a very large sum of money indeed. It is interesting to see three judges of the Court of Appeal grappling with the argument that article 28 [30] is of direct effect, and that therefore the English courts have a duty to protect that right to the same extent as a domestic right of a similar nature. Only Oliver LJ grasped the nettle that logically this must mean damages. Parker LJ and Nourse LJ said that there was no remedy in damages against a minister innocently exercising his legislative powers. It would have been even more interesting to see what the House of Lords and the European Court would have said about it. The plaintiff obtained leave to appeal, but the action was settled for £3.5 million. Nowadays that figure would be much larger because, since the decision in Cases C-6/90 and C-9/90 *Frankovich* v. *Republic of Italy* [1993] 2 CMLR 66 (see section 7.5 for the facts) an action for damages will lie against a Member State for its failure to implement EC law. The likely considerations in assessing the quantum of such a claim were considered in *R* v. *Secretary of State* ex parte *Factortame (No 5)* [1999] 4 All ER 907.

At the time of writing the Commission was about to commence an action against France over its ban on importation of British beef. It is against the background of decisions like those in the *Bourgouin* case that the Court will develop its jurisprudence.

9.3.2 German beer

In Case 178/84 *Re Purity Requirements for Beer: EC Commission* v. *Germany* [1987] ECR 1227, [1988] 1 CMLR 780, a complaint was made that German laws stipulated such stringent requirements for the ingredients of beer that foreign brewers could not compete in the German market. It was not that they were prevented from importing their chemical concoctions; it was simply that if they did then, under German law, they were not allowed to call their products beer.

The defence naturally relied on article 30 [36], pointing out the many dangers to healthy German drinkers. The German laws were said to be necessary in order to protect the German consumer from confusion as to what he was drinking, and it was said that the health of the nation might be at risk if German beer drinkers were to drink beers produced, and widely consumed, in other Member States.

Alas, such noble sentiments were to no avail. It was pointed out that the additives forbidden in German beer were generously allowed in soft drinks. German teetotalers did not benefit from solicitude for their health, so, evidently, health was by no means the reason for the beer purity laws. The moral is that when a Member State prohibits the addition of additives to imported beer, but allows them in soft drinks, the prohibition cannot be said to be justified on the grounds of public health within the terms of article 30 [36].

9.3.3   Dutch dolls

National predelictions can sometimes be discerned in those cases which are considered by the European Court. In Case 121/85 *Conegate Limited* v. *HM Customs and Excise* [1986] 3 ECR 1007, [1986] 1 CMLR 739, the Court had to consider the question which arose when customs officials seized some Dutch dolls, variously described as 'Miss World Specials' and 'Rubber Ladies', which were being imported into Britain. Conegate Limited complained that the ban on importation of those articles was contrary to article 28 [30] of the Treaty. The United Kingdom contended that the restriction was justified on the grounds of public morality.

The Court found that the ban on imports was not justified. Although public morality was a matter for each Member State to lay down for itself, it was observed that only the importation of the articles was forbidden; their manufacture was perfectly permissible in the United Kingdom. It followed that, even though the customs legislation was not adopted with the intention of discriminating against goods from Member States, there was, in fact, arbitrary discrimination within the meaning of article 30 [36]. A ban on the imports of particular products cannot be justified on the grounds of public morality, within the meaning of article 30 [36] of the EC

Treaty, unless comparable restrictions on the domestic sale and manufacture of such products exist and are applied.

9.4   *The public procurement régime*

The right to free movement of goods cannot be viewed in isolation, but must be seen in the light of the rights to freedom of establishment and freedom to provide services which the Treaty guarantees. The relationship is demonstrated by the Community Directives on public procurement.

The public procurement Directives are intended to make it practicable for businesses throughout the Community to compete for large contracts that are awarded by governments and public authorities. These contracts account for some 15% of the gross domestic product of the Community. Governments and public authorities, if left to their own devices, buy nationally; suppliers from other Member States cannot compete if technical specifications are national in character, or if they are not made aware of the proposed contracts.

In order to understand the public procurement regime the reader must refer to six main Directives. Four of these set out the detailed procedures which must be followed when entities award public contracts, namely:

- Council Directive 93/37/EEC of 14 June 1993 concerning the coordination of procedures for the award of public works contracts (OJ L199 9.8.93 p54)
- Council Directive 93/36/EEC coordinating procedures for the award of public supply contracts (OJ No L199 9.8.93 p1)
- Council Directive 92/50 relating to the coordination of procedures for the award of public service contracts (OJ L209 24.7.92 p1)
- Council Directive 93/38/EEC of 14 June 1993 coordinating the procurement procedures of entities operating in the water, energy, transport and telecommunications sectors (OJ L199 9.8.93 p84).

The above Directives are known respectively as the Works, Supplies, Services, and Utilities Directives. They are all, save for the Services Directive, consolidating Directives, with a long history of amendments. They have all been amended to take account of WTO and GPA requirements by European Parliament and Council

Directive 97/52 (OJ L328 28.11.91 p1). The Directives set out procedures which must be followed by purchasing entities in order to ensure that contracts are awarded openly. The Directives affect contracts worth more than certain threshold values. In order to accommodate changes made to the international arrangements for trade and embodied in the WTO (formerly GATT) Government Purchasing Agreement (the GPA), the Directives were amended.

There are two Directives, namely the Compliance Directive and the Utilities Remedies Directive, which require Member States to make adequate arrangements for aggrieved suppliers, service providers and contractors to seek redress if they are unfairly treated, or if the procedures set out in the Purchasing Directives are not followed. The full titles of these two Directives are as follows:

- Council Directive 89/665 of 21 December 1989 on coordination of the laws, regulations and administrative provisions relating to the application of review procedures to the award of public supply and public works contracts (OJ L395 30.12.89 p33)
- Council Directive 92/13/EEC of 25 February 1992 coordinating the laws, regulations and administrative provisions relating to the application of Community rules on the procurement procedures of entities operating in the water, energy, transport and telecommunications sectors (OJ L76 23.3.92 p14).

9.4.1 Thresholds

The Directives apply only to contracts worth more than certain threshold values and the thresholds are reviewed annually. To take account of the requirements of the WTO and GPA some of the thresholds are given in Special Drawing Rights (SDR). For the period 1 January 2000 to 31 December 2000 the main thresholds were fixed as follows. For works contracts the limit is £3 611 395 (SDR 5 000 000, €5 358 153), whether it be in the private sector or the public sector. For purchasing by public authorities subject to the WTO Government Purchasing Agreement (Central Government Purchases) the limits are, for supplies and services, £93 896 (SDR 130 000 €139 312). For other public sector purchasing authorities (sub-central government) supplies and services: £144 456 (SDR 200 000, €214 326). Some service contracts have a lower threshold; principal exceptions concern telecommunications, research and development and subsidised services. For these kinds of contracts the threshold is £134 800.

For purchases by the utilities, in the water, electricity, urban transport, airports and ports sectors the limit is £288 912 (SDR 400 000 €428 653) for supplies and services, and for works contracts £3 611 395 (SDR 5 000 000 €5 358 153). In the case of the oil, gas, coal and railways sectors the limit is: £269 600 (€400 000) for supplies and services, and £3 370 000 (€5 000 000) for works. In the telecommunications sector the limit is £404 400 (€600 000) for supplies and services, and £3 370 000 (€5 000 000) for works.

Threshold values at the time of writing (mid-2000) were set out in the Official Journal at OJ 1999 C379 p2. Up to date values are available from the website of HM Treasury, together with a wealth of other material on public procurement, at: http://www.hm-treasury.gov.uk. The reader should look for the link called Guidance which leads to a page called Procurement Guidance.

9.4.2 Procedures

If the purchasing Directives apply then certain fixed procedures, called 'open', 'restricted' and 'negotiated', must be applied to the process of awarding a contract. As a general rule a contract must be advertised by means of a notice in the *Official Journal* – in practice this means the Tenders Electronic Daily database, now available on a website. Tenders may be requested on the basis of lowest price or most economic advantage. Specifications must be expressed in European standards. There are strict time limits for the delivery of bids. If unfair procedures are used the supplier can bring an action for damages or an injunction in the High Court, but there is a three month time limit for this. The implementing Regulations at the time of writing were as follows:

- The Public Supply Contracts Regulations (SI 1995 No 201)
- The Public Services Contracts Regulations (SI 1993 No 3228)
- The Public Works Contracts Regulations (SI 1991 No 2680)
- The Utilities Contracts Regulations (SI 1996 No 2911).

The system has become far too complicated and it is doubtful whether it achieves its purpose. At the time of writing the Commission was proposing that entities which operate under real conditions of competition, in particular the telecommunications sector, should not come within the purview of the Utilities Directive and that there should be a consolidation of the Directives for the public sector (see COM 2000 275 and 2000 276). The package of measures adopted by the Commission has the objective of simplifying and clarifying the existing rules and adapting them to modern administration. For complex contracts the new system will permit a dialogue between awarding authorities and tenderers.

CHAPTER 10
FREE MOVEMENT OF PERSONS

10.1   Introduction

The internal market comprises an area without internal frontiers in which the free movement of goods, persons, services and capital is ensured in accordance with the provisions of the Treaty (see article 14 [7a]). The right to freedom of movement for workers in the Union is ensured by articles 39 [48] to 42 [51] of the Treaty, and the related rights of establishment and freedom to provide services are to be found in articles 49 [59] to 55 [66]. These rights are part of an overall scheme set out in article 2 [B] to maintain and develop the Union as

> 'an area of freedom, security and justice, in which the free movement of persons is assured in conjunction with appropriate measures with respect to external borders controls, immigration, asylum and the prevention and combating of crime'.

The Amsterdam Treaty added a new title, consisting of articles 61 [73i] to 69 [73q], which is headed 'Visas, Asylum, Immigration and Other Policies related to Free Movement of Persons'.

It was the Maastricht Treaty that introduced the concept of citizenship of the Union, but article 17 [8] of the Union Treaty states that this citizenship complements and does not replace national citizenship. Every person holding the nationality of a Member State is a citizen of the Union and under article 18 [8a] citizens of the Union enjoy the right to move freely within territory of the Member States, subject to the limitations and conditions laid down in the Treaty. Section 7 of the Immigration Act 1988 recognises this right by stating that persons exercising enforceable Community rights do not require leave to enter the United Kingdom. Whether article 18 [8a] confers directly effective rights of residence, not provided elsewhere in the Treaty or by other legislation, is still an open question although the Advocate General in C-85/96 *Martinez Sala* v.

Freistaat Bayern [1998] ECR I-2691 said that the limitation in article 18 concerns only the exercise of the right, not its existence.

10.2 Nationality

The right to free movement applies to nationals of Member States. Each Member State has made a declaration stating what persons it regards as its nationals. The United Kingdom declaration (OJ C 23 28.1.83 p1) defines its nationals, for Community purposes, as including British citizens; persons who are British subjects by virtue of Part IV of the British Nationality Act 1981 and who have the right of abode in the UK and are therefore exempt from UK immigration control; and British Dependent Territories citizens who acquired their citizenship from connection with Gibraltar. The question of the legal effectiveness of this declaration has not been fully examined by the European Court.

The right of a citizen of the Union to free movement is not absolute but subject to to the limitations and conditions laid down in the Treaty. The right generally depends upon whether he is a worker, is establishing himself in another Member State, or is a provider or recipient of services. Restrictions can be placed on the right to free movement on grounds of public policy, public security, or public health: see article 46 [56] of the Treaty. Problems arise over the meaning and scope of the terms 'worker', 'public policy', and 'services'.

10.3 Workers

Article 39 [48] of the Treaty establishes the right to freedom of movement for workers in the Community. This freedom entails the abolition of any discrimination based on nationality, as regards employment, remuneration, and conditions of work. It also entails the right, subject to limitations on grounds of public policy, public security, or public health, to accept offers of employment actually made, to move freely within Member States for this purpose, to stay in a Member State for the purposes of employment, in accordance with the provisions governing the employment of nationals of the state, and to remain there after having been employed. But article 39 [48] does not apply to employment in the public service, although this exception is supposed to be interpreted narrowly. In Case C-

473/93 *Commission* v. *Luxembourg* [1996] ECR I-3207, [1996] 3 CMLR 981, it was held that Luxembourg was in breach of article 39 [48] by applying a nationality requirement to positions in public research, education, health, inland transport, telecommunications, water, gas and electricity.

Article 39 [48] is not restricted to actions by Member States, as is shown by Case C-415/93 *Union Royale Belge des Sociétés de Football Association ASBL* v. *Jean-Marc Bosman* [1995] ECR I-4921, [1996] 1 CMLR 645, [1996] All ER (EC) 97, which shows that it extends more widely. Mr Bosman was a footballer who played for RC Liège. In 1990, finding that at the end of the season he was not offered a suitable contract, he decided to accept an offer from a French second division club, US Dunkerque. Unfortunately under the rules of UEFA he could not be employed by the French club unless they paid a transfer fee. Mr Bosman was also prejudiced by a rule that football clubs could only field a limited number of foreign players. The European Court held that both the transfer fee and the rule on foreign players were contrary to article 39 [48].

In Case 66/85 *Lawrie-Blum* v. *Land Baden Württemberg* ([1986] ECR 2121; [1987] 3 CMLR 389) a worker was defined as a person who for a period of time performs services for, or under, the direction of another person, and receives remuneration in return. Part-time work will do, even if the income derived from the occupation is less than that which the Member State concerned regards as sufficient for subsistence, provided that he is pursuing an activity which is effective and genuine (see C-53/81 *DM Levin* v. *Staatssecretaris Van Justitie* [1982] ECR 1035). Case 118/75 *Watson* v. *Belmann* [1976] ECR 1185, [1982] 2 CMLR 552, seems to imply that it is possible to recognise as workers those who have not previously received an offer of employment in another state.

A similar sentiment was expressed in Case 48/75 *Royer* [1976] ECR 497, [1976] 2 CMLR 619, but the extent to which Community law protects those who look for work but find none is not clear. Under the provisions of the present Immigration Rules, which have been made under the Immigration Act 1971, a national of a Member State loses his right to remain if he does not acquire employment within six months. In Case 292/89 *R* v. *Immigration Appeal Tribunal* ex parte *Antonissen* [1991] 2 CMLR 373 ECJ, the European Court had to consider whether this restriction was contrary to Community law. It ruled that a national of a Member State who has not found work after six months may be required to leave, unless he provides evidence that he is continuing to seek employment and has a genuine chance of being engaged.

It is proposed to make legislation clarifying the rights of those who are looking for work, and also that of wives who are left stranded after a divorce to remain in the country where their husbands have taken them – see the Council proposal for amendments to Regulation 1612/68 and 68/360 at OJ C344 12.11.98 pp 9 and 12.

10.4 Family members

A series of regulations and directives augment the rights set out in the Treaty. Council Directive 73/148/EEC abolishes restrictions with regard to establishment and provision of services. Council Regulation (EEC) 1612/68 (OJ L257 19.10.68 p2; Sp edn 1968 (II) p475) gives effect to the free movement provisions in the Treaty with regard to employment. It states that any national of a Member State has the right to take up an activity as an employed person within the territory of another Member State. Workers who are not nationals of a Member State do not have this right, but the regulation provides that, irrespective of their nationality, members of a worker's family are entitled to instal themselves with a worker who is a national of one Member State and who is employed in another. Council proposals for amendments to Regulation 1612/68 are contained in OJ C344 12.11.98 p9.

The family, for these purposes, extends to a spouse and dependants under the age of 21, and dependent relatives in the ascending line. A spouse has an autonomous right to remain after three years under Regulation 1612/68. The Immigration Act 1971, by contrast, does not give an automatic right of entry to a spouse or other dependent relatives. The Home Office rules made under the Act no longer contain the notorious primary purpose rule (under which the spouse had to prove that the primary purpose of a marriage was not to obtain the right to enter the UK) but there is still a requirement to show that each spouse intends to live permanently with the other and that they will have adequate accommodation without recourse to public funds (see the Statement of Changes in Immigration Rules HC 395, as amended by HC 26 with effect from 5 June 1997).

Indefinite leave to remain is not granted in the first instance. A spouse has to apply for indefinite leave after a year and must show at that stage that he or she still intends to live permanently together with the other individual. Home Office rules require parents and grandparents dependent on persons settled in the UK to show that they have no close relatives to turn to in their own country. The Home Office rules on children are equally complicated. Where both parents are settled in the UK their children will be granted leave to enter. Where only one parent is settled in the UK a child may be granted leave only if that parent has had sole responsibility for the upbringing of the child or if there are serious or compelling considerations which make exclusion undesirable.

The conflict between the Home Office rules and the relevant European Regulations has bizarre consequences. For example a man who is not a Community national, who marries a woman who is a British citizen, will not be able to join her as of right in the United Kingdom, but he will be able to join her in another Member State, if she exercises her right of free movement to go there.

The question was decided in C-370/90 *R* v. *Immigration Appeal Tribunal and Surinder Singh* ex parte *Secretary of State for the Home Department* [1992] ECR I-4265, [1992] 3 All ER 798, in which the husband Mr Surinder Singh, an Indian national, married a British wife and they went to live in Germany. They returned to the United Kingdom in order to open a business. But the marriage failed and a decree *nisi* was granted. His limited leave to remain was cut short and he was ordered to be deported. The Court of Justice held, on a reference from the Divisional Court, that article 43 [52] of the Treaty and Council Directive (EEC) 73/148 (OJ L172 28.6.73 p14)) require a Member State to grant leave to enter and reside in its territory to the spouse, of whatever nationality, of a national of that state who has gone, with that spouse, to another Member State in order to work there as an employed person, as envisaged by article 39 [48] of the Treaty, and returns to establish herself or himself as envisaged by article 43 [52] of the Treaty in the state of which he or she is a national. A spouse must enjoy at least the same rights as would be granted to him or her under Community law if his or her spouse entered and resided in another Member State.

But Cases 35 and 36/82 *Re Morson and Jhanjan* [1982] ECR 3723, [1983] 2 CMLR 221, show that the Treaty provisions on free movement of persons cannot be applied unless there is a factor which links them to the situations which are governed by Community law. So Mr Tombofa, a Nigerian national against whom the Home Secretary made a decision to deport after he was convicted of an attempted robbery, was unable to take advantage of the EC rules when he married a United Kingdom citizen. His counsel's hopeful submission that his wife was a recipient of services because she listened to Radio Luxembourg, so bringing into play the Directive which implements the right to free movement in relation to establishment and services, Council Directive (EEC) 64/221 (OJ L56 4.4.64 p850, Sp edn 1963–64 p1150), was rejected: *R* v. *Secretary of State for Home Affairs* ex parte *Tombofa* [1988] 2 CMLR 609 CA.

The right of retired and incapacitated workers, and their families, to remain in the territory of a Member State, after having been employed there, is dealt with in Council Regulation (EEC) 1251/70 (OJ L142 30.6.70 p24, Sp edn 1970 (II) p402). But in *R* v. *Secretary of State for the Home Department* ex parte *Botta (Jacqueline)* [1987] Imm AR 80, [1987] 2 CMLR 189, the Court of Appeal said that where a wife from a country which is not a Member State had come to the United Kingdom with a German national she could not remain here after her husband was deported. In 267/83 *Aissatou Diatta* v. *Land Berlin* [1985] ECR 567, [1986] 2 CMLR 164, however, Mrs Diatta, a Sengalese national, married a Frenchman who lived in Berlin. Soon after the marriage they separated, but the husband remained in Germany. The European Court held that she was entitled to remain in Germany because under Regulation 1612/68 she was only required to live in the same country, not necessarily under the same roof as her husband.

In Germany difficulties sometimes arise because certain occupations are open only to German nationals or nationals of Member States. Thus in 131/85 *Gul* v. *Regierungspräsident Düsseldorf* [1986] ECR 1573, [1987] 1 CMLR 501, a Turkish doctor married a British wife while she was working in Germany. This meant, of course, that he was entitled to live in Germany under the terms of Regulation 1612/68. He was, however, refused a permanent licence to practise medicine. On his appeal to the European Court it was said that this was wrong. A spouse was entitled to be treated in the same way as a national of the host state with regard to access to his profession. By contrast in C64–65/96 *Land Nordrheim-Westfalen* v. *Ueker* [1997] 3 CMLR 963, [1997] ECR 1-3171, the foreign wife of a German national was forbidden to obtain a permanent state job as a language teacher. The Court held that EU law was not breached because her spouse had never exercised free movement rights.

Council Directive (EEC) 68/360 (OJ L257 19.10.68 p13, Sp edn 1968 (II) p485) makes provisions for documentation. Article 3 of this Directive provides that Member States shall allow workers, and their families, to enter their territories simply on production of a valid identity card or passport. No entry visa or equivalent may be demanded, save from members of the family who are not nationals of Member States. Member States are obliged to accord to such person every facility for obtaining any necessary visas. As proof of the right of residence a document has to be issued which must include a statement that it is issued pursuant to Regulation (EEC) No 1612/68. It is proposed to amend this Directive so as to make the formalities simpler, and instead of a permit there will be a Residence Permit for a Citizen of the European Union (see OJ C344 12.11.98 p12).

For the purposes of recognition of the right of residence a residence permit can only have a declaratory and probative force. In C48/75 *Royer* [1976] ECR 497 a French national was detected in Belgium and expelled because he did not have a residence permit. He had gone there to join his wife who ran a café and dance hall in Liège. The European Court held that a mere failure to comply with the formalities regarding entry of aliens was not so threatening to public policy as to justify his expulsion.

10.4.1   The *Baumbast* case

Baumbast v. *Secretary of State* (26 April 1999 – Immigration Appeal Tribunal TH/2769/96) raises a number of issues that await decision by the ECJ and illustrates the problems which arise for the the expatriate worker. Mr Baumbast married a Colombian national, and then worked in the UK for a while. His wife and children obtained EC residence documents. He then found that he could not earn enough in the UK and was obliged to work in China for various German companies, but the family maintained a house in England and their children went to school there. Mrs Baumbast applied for the whole family to have indefinite leave, but this was refused on the ground that Mr Baumbast was not exercising any EU rights – he no longer had any rights as a worker. The European Court was asked to rule on whether Mr Baumbast nevertheless enjoyed a directly effective right of residence under article 18 [8a] of the Treaty. As to the children, they had been entitled to begin their education in the UK as members of a worker's family under Regulation (EEC) 1612/68, but the question was asked whether they were entitled to continue that education after their father ceased to be a worker and whether their mother was entitled to remain in the UK to care for them.

10.5   *Public policy*

The meaning of public policy is expanded by Council Directive (EEC) 64/221 (OJ 56 4.4.64 p850, Sp edn 1963–64 p1150) which applies to the employed, self-employed, and recipients of services. The Directive relates to all measures concerning entry, issue or renewal of residence permits, or expulsion taken by Member States on grounds of public security, or public health. Such grounds must not be invoked to serve economic ends. They must be based exclusively on personal conduct. Previous criminal convictions do not in themselves constitute grounds for the taking of such measures. Expiry of an identity card or passport does not justify expulsion.

The concept of public policy was discussed in one of the first United Kingdom cases to be referred to the European Court: Case 41/74 *Van Duyn* v. *Home Office* [1974] ECR 1337, [1975] 1 CMLR 1. At that time it was not obvious that all the above legislation is of direct effect. Miss Van Duyn, a Dutch national, claimed that she was entitled to enter the United Kingdom and remain there in order to take up employment at the Hubbard College of Scientology. She asked for a declaration in the Chancery Division, and a number of questions were then referred to the Court of Justice. The European Court held that the provisions of article 39 [48] of the Treaty and Directive 64/221 were directly effective; but the United Kingdom had acted lawfully because membership of the Church of Scientology constituted 'conduct' of a kind which would justify a refusal of leave to enter within article 3 of the latter Directive.

The concept of public policy in Community law was also examined in Case 36/75 *Rutili* v. *Minister for the Interior* [1975] ECR 1219; [1976] 1 CMLR 140. That was a case where the French Minister for the Interior had imposed on an Italian national restrictions that prohibited him from living in certain French *départements*. It transpired that the reason for this was his trade union activities, which were regarded as 'likely to disturb public policy'.

On a reference to the Court of Justice it was said that the concept of public policy must be interpreted strictly, so that its scope cannot be determined unilaterally by each Member State without being subject to control by the institutions of the Community. Article 33 [39] of the Treaty prohibits discrimination on the grounds of nationality, and it followed that measures restricting rights of residence may not be imposed, except in cases where such measures are equally applied to the nationals of a Member State.

Case 30/77 *Regina* v. *Bouchereau* [1977] ECR 1999, [1977] 2 CMLR 800, was a reference from the Marlborough Street magistrates court. Monsieur Bouchereau was a French national who had been convicted of possession of a small quantity of drugs. He was fined £35 but the magistrate was minded to recommend his deportation. The Court of Justice ruled that the mere fact that a crime had been committed, or that there were previous convictions, was not enough to constitute grounds for deportation; there had also to be 'a genuine and sufficiently serious threat affecting one of the fundamental interests of society'.

In Cases 115 & 116/81 *Adoui and Cornaille* v. *Belgium* [1982] ECR 1665, [1982] 3 CMLR 631, two French waitresses were refused a permit to live in Belgium. It was alleged that the ladies worked in a bar where it was suspected that immoral things went on. The Belgian court, in a reference to the European Court, asked for a definition of public policy.

The Advocate General seemed somewhat piqued at this question. He said that the first point to emphasise was that Community law does not define or purport to give an independent definition of public policy. In the Community Treaties there are numerous expressions derived from the laws of the Member States whose interpretation involves reference to principles, rules, and concepts peculiar to those States. The expression 'public policy' fell within that category. Within national legal systems there were areas of uncertainty. It was therefore pointless to ask the Court for a definition of public policy. The Court ruled, however, that a Member State could not refuse access to its territory by reason of conduct which was not subject to repressive measures in respect of its own nationals, and this was sufficient to decide the case.

The European Court reaffirmed its views in C384/96 *Criminal Proceedings against Donatella Calfa* [1999] All ER (EC) 850, 1999 1 NLR 333. The fashionable Ms Calfa, an Italian, had spent her holiday in Crete, where she was charged with possession of some drugs, found guilty and sentenced to three months imprisonment. She was also expelled for life from Greek territory and appealed to the Arios Pagos about this part of her sentence. She claimed that articles 17 [8], 18 [8a] and 49 [59] of the Treaty and Directive 64/221 did not allow her to be expelled for life unless a comparable measure could be taken against a Greek national.

Following *Van Duyn* and *Adoui*, and also C111/95 *R* v. *Secretary of State for Home Department* ex parte *Radiom* [1997] ECR I-3342, the European Court held that Ms Calfa could not be excluded from

Greece for life. Greek law did not comply with European law, at any rate in so far as she was automatically excluded for life, without any account taken of her personal conduct or the danger she represented to society.

10.5.1 Recommendations for deportation

The above provisions, in particular Council Directive (EEC) 64/221, have practical effects in proceedings before UK courts. Article 9 of this Directive stipulates that, where there is no right of appeal to a court of law, or where such appeal may only be in respect of the legal validity of the decision, a decision ordering the expulsion of the holder of a residence permit from a territory shall not be taken, until an opinion has been obtained from a competent authority of the host country before which the person concerned enjoys such rights of defence as the domestic law of the country provides. The United Kingdom has not enacted any legislation to take account of this requirement. The position under English law is that a court before whom a person is convicted of an offence has the power to recommend deportation. This has the effect of depriving the defendant of any appeal to the Immigration Appeal Tribunal against a decision to make a deportation order. The guidelines on sentencing set out in *R* v. *Nazari* (1980) 71 Cr App Rep 87, [1980] 1 WLR 1366, apply both to those who are nationals of Member States and those who are not.

In Case 131/79 *Santillo* [1980] ECR 1585, [1980] 2 CMLR 308, the Court of Justice ruled that a recommendation by the court is an 'opinion' within article 9 of Directive 64/221. The opinion must, however, be sufficiently proximate in time to the decision ordering expulsion to provide an assurance that there are no new factors to be taken into consideration; and, the lapse of several years, as may happen in the case of a person sentenced to imprisonment, is liable to deprive the recommendation of its function as an opinion.

In C175/94 *R* v. *Secretary of State for Home Department* ex parte *John Gallagher* [1995] ECR 1-4253, [1996] 1 CMLR 557 the European Court was asked whether Article 9 of the Directive precluded the competent authority from being appointed by the same administrative authority that took the decision on expulsion. Mr Gallagher was an Irishman who had been sentenced in Ireland for possession of two rifles. In 1991 he came to England where he was arrested and served with an exclusion order. Under the Prevention of Terrorism

(Temporary Provisions) Act 1989 his rights were severely limited. He was entitled to make written representations, and if he did so the Secretary of State was obliged to refer the matter to a person nominated by the Secretary of State. In practice this amounted to a short interview with a man who refused to give his name. The European Court held that provided he was independent and followed a procedure which enabled Mr Gallagher to present his case it did not matter that the competent authority was nameless and appointed by the Secretary of State.

In *R* v. *Secretary of State for the Home Department* ex parte *Santillo* (1981) 73 Cr App Rep 71, Lord Donaldson said that no court should make an order recommending deportation without full enquiry into the circumstances and should give reasons for its decisions if a recommendation is to be made. In *R* v. *Secretary of State for the Home Department* ex parte *Dannenberg* [1984] QB 766, [1984] 2 WLR 855, the Court of Appeal quashed a deportation order because no reasons were given by the justices, or the Secretary of State, and the failure to give reasons was a breach of Council Directive 64/221.

In *R* v. *Escauriaza* [1989] 3 CMLR 281, 87 Cr App Rep 344, the Court of Appeal said that the public policy requirements of Community law are simply mirrored by the law and practice of England. The requirement that there should be a threat to one of the fundamental interests of society was said simply to mean that the presence of the appellant was to the detriment of the United Kingdom. Whether the European Court would agree that mere detriment is a sufficient definition of the requirements of public policy is questionable.

10.6   Non-workers

Three directives on the right of residence for students, retired persons and other members of the non-working population came into effect on 1 July 1992 as part of the programme to establish the single market. Member States are required, under Council Directive 90/364 (EEC) (OJ L180 13.7.90 p26), to grant a right of residence to nationals of Member States who do not enjoy this right under other provisions of Community law. Under Council Directive (EEC) 93/96 (OJ L317 18.12.93 p59) a student can stay for the duration of his course, and, under Council Directive 90/365 (EEC) (OJ L180 13.11.90 p28), a person who has retired and is in receipt of a pension can stay in any Member State. These rights are all made subject to a condition not to become a burden on the social security system of the host state. Spouses and dependent relatives, irrespective of nationality, are entitled to instal themselves with the holder of the right of residence.

Council Directive 90/365, unlike Council Regulation 1251/70 (above) that allows a worker to remain in a Member State after he has retired, does not require a retired worker to have exercised a Community right of free movement before his retirement.

10.7 Tourists and priests

It appears from Cases 286/82 & 26/83 *Luisi and Carbone* v. *Ministero del Tesoro* [1984] ECR 377, [1985] 3 CMLR 52, and C384/96 *Criminal Proceedings against Donatella Calfa* [1999] All ER (EC) 850, 1999 1 NLR 333, that tourists come within the category of recipients of services and thus would be protected by Council Directive 64/221 (above). The Court said that the freedom to provide services includes the freedom for the recipients of services to go to another Member State in order to receive a service there, and that tourists, persons receiving medical treatment, and persons travelling for the purpose of education or business are to be regarded as recipients of services.

An interesting problem is whether a member of a religious order can be said to be a provider or recipient of services. In Case 196/87 *Steymann* v. *Staatssecretaris van Justitie* [1989] 1 CMLR 449, [1988] ECR 6159 the Advocate General relied upon the *Luisi and Carbone* case in his opinion. The Court decided that participation in a community based on religion is within the Community law on free movement, but only to the extent that it can be regarded as economic activity. Hermits and contemplatives might do better to rely on Council Directive (EEC) 90/364 (above).

10.8 Visas, asylum, immigration and other policies

The Amsterdam Treaty added a new title, Title IV [Title III A], consisting of articles 61 [73i] to 69 [73q], which is headed 'Visas, Asylum, Immigration and Other Policies related to Free Movement of Persons'. Whereas articles 39 [48] to 55 [66] relate to free movement of persons, services and capital within the Community, the new title is concerned with establishing an area of freedom, security and justice within which citizens of the Union will be able to exercise their rights and from which others are to be excluded. Measures under this title are to be taken in the period of five years from the entry into force of the Treaty of Amsterdam on 1 May 1999. Thus, under article 61 [73i] the Council is to adopt

> 'measures with respect to external border controls, asylum and immigration' and under Article 62[73j] 'standards and procedures to be followed by Member States in carrying out checks on persons at such borders'.

Other parts of the Title include provision for the taking of measures on judicial cooperation in civil matters (see article 65 [73m]).

Council Regulation (EC) 574/99 (OJ L72 18.3.99 p2) has been made under this part of the Treaty. This regulation is concerned with determining the third countries whose nationals must be in possession of visas when crossing the external borders of the Member States. Nationals of third countries on the common list in the Annex are required to be in possession of visas when crossing the external borders of the Member States (this is a corollary of Schengen). In 2001 the Commission must draw up a progress report on the harmonisation of visa policies.

10.8.1   The Dublin Convention

At Maastricht the Member States set their hands to a declaration that they would consider their asylum policies with the aim of harmonising aspects of them by the beginning of 1993. The process of harmonisation had really begun before this declaration with the signing of the Convention Determining the State Responsible for Examining Applications for Asylum Lodged in One of the Member States of the European Communities, commonly known as the Dublin Convention, on 15 June 1990.

The Convention has now been ratified by all the Member States and came into force on 1 September 1997. Its object is to avoid the unseemly spectacle of orbiting refugees. It requires applications for asylum to be examined by one Member State. The pecking order begins with the state where the applicant's family is legally resident, and is followed, respectively, by the state where he has a valid residence permit or visa; when it can be proved that he has irregularly crossed a border from outside the EC, the state so entered; the state responsible for controlling his entry into the territory of the

Member States; and finally, the first Member State with whom the application is lodged.

The United Kingdom gets off lightly because refugees have to swim or use parachutes. In *R* v. *Secretary of State* ex parte *Mehmet Colak* (*The Times* 6 July 93), a Turkish Kurd asked for political asylum in the United Kingdom, having travelled via Paris, where he spent four hours in a transit lounge. The Home Office said that, in accordance with the Dublin Convention, he should have his claim considered in Paris, which was the first country he went to after leaving Turkey. On an application for judicial review, Mehmet Colak contended that, as a result of the single market without frontiers established by article 14 [7a] of the EC Treaty, there was no power to return him from one Member State to another. But the court held that the article 14 [7a] did not bar the Secretary of State from returning him to France; so much for Europe without frontiers.

10.9   Third country agreements

The Union has made a variety of agreements with third countries containing provisions on free movement and establishment. It is important to refer not only to the agreements but also to their protocols, and related decisions or regulations. The agreements vary depending on how anxious the parties are to join the Union. The longest standing and most advanced of the agreements is the Association Agreement with Turkey (OJ L217 19.12.64) which was signed at Ankara in 1963.

The agreements with Central and Eastern European Countries are known as Europe Agreements; these have been concluded with Poland, Hungary, the Czech Republic, Slovakia, Romania, Bulgaria, Slovenia, Lithuania, Estonia and Latvia.

The agreements with independent states of the former Soviet Union are known as Partnership Agreements; these have been concluded with the Ukraine, the Russian Federation, Kazakhstan, Kirgizstan, Moldova, Belarus (not ratified at the time of writing, mid-2000), Georgia, Armenia, Azerbaijan, and Uzbekistan.

The agreements with certain North African states are known as Cooperation Agreements, and have been concluded with Morocco, Tunisia, Algeria, and San Marino (again not ratified at the time of writing).

In 12/86 *Demirel* v. *Stadt Schwabisch Gmund* [1987] ECR 3719; [1989] 1 CMLR 421, the European Court said that a provision in an agreement with a non-Member State is directly applicable when, regard being had to its wording and the purpose and nature of the agreement, it contains a clear and precise obligation which is not subject in its implementation or effects to the adoption of any subsequent measure. For example, the Poland Agreement (OJ L348 31.12.93 p2) grants establishment rights to Polish companies and natural persons which must fall within this category. Article 44(3) of that agreement reads as follows:

> Each member state shall grant, from entry into force of this Agreement a treatment no less favourable than that accorded to its own companies and nationals for the establishment of Polish companies and nationals as defined in article 48 and shall grant in the operation of Polish companies and nationals established in its territory a treatment no less favourable than that accorded to its own companies and nationals.

C-386/95 *Suleyman Eker* v. *Land Baden-Württemberg* [1997] ECR I-2697 concerns a question arising on the interpretation of article 6 of the EEC–Turkey Association Council Decision (1/80) of 19 September 1980 on the development of the Association. The Turkey Agreement protects Turkish workers once they have obtained work permits within the Union. Article 6 of the Decision states that a Turkish worker is entitled to renewal of his work permit after one year's residence, and after three years he can respond to another offer of employment with an employer of his choice. Mr Suleyman Ecker married a German national and obtained employment for three months, but then moved to another employer. He separated from his wife and she commenced divorce proceedings. The question the European Court of Justice was asked to decide was whether article 6 of the EEC–Turkey Association Council Decision required him to be continuously employed for one year with the same employer, or whether employment with more than one employer was enough if he had applied for his permit to be renewed with a view to employment with his current employer. The Court held that only continuous employment with the one employer would do.

10.10 Extradition

Police and judicial cooperation in criminal matters is the subject of Title VI of the Union Treaty. This Title, which is outside the EC Treaty, does not confer any legislative powers on the Council, but instead requires cooperation at government level. The law on extradition between Member States is governed by the European Convention on Extradition. This was opened for signature by the Members of the Council of Europe on 13 December 1957, but it was not until 1990 that it was finally ratified as a consequence of the provision for greater cooperation on criminal matters contained in the Union Treaty. The Convention is not limited to the European Union – Turkey and Norway, for example, are parties.

The Extradition Convention is implemented in the United Kingdom by the Extradition Act 1989 and the European Convention on Extradition Order 1990, SI 1990/1507. The procedure under Part III of the Act applies to Convention extraditions. What distinguishes such committals is the much simplified procedure. It is not necessary for the court of committal to satisfy itself that there is evidence sufficient to warrant a trial; it is assumed that the requesting state is sufficiently civilised to provide proper safeguards for the accused. All that is necessary is the production of the original warrant of arrest together with details of the offences and the relevant enactments under which the charges are brought. Extradition can, however, be refused on the grounds that the offence is of a political nature, and purely military offences are excluded altogether from the Convention.

Section 1 of the Extradition Act provides that a person who is accused of an extradition crime may be arrested and returned to a foreign state in accordance with the procedures set out in the Act. An 'extradition crime' means conduct in a foreign state which, if it occurred in the UK, would constitute an offence punishable with 12 months imprisonment or more and which, however described in the law of the foreign state, is so punishable under that law. A person cannot be dealt with except in pursuance of an authority to proceed issued by the Secretary of State in pursuance of an extradition request. The extradition request must be accompanied by particulars of the person whose return is requested, particulars of the offence (including information sufficient to justify the issue of a warrant for his arrest under the Act), and a copy of the warrant. Copies must be served on the person whose return is requested. Where the European Convention on Extradition Order 1990 applies it is sufficient merely to furnish information sufficient to justify the issue of a warrant; it is not necessary to provide evidence of a prima facie case.

A person who has been arrested must be brought before a magistrate. The magistrate has powers like, as nearly as may be, those he would have on a summary trial. Where an authority to proceed has been issued and the court is satisfied that the offence to which the authority relates is an extradition crime the magistrate must commit the person to custody or on bail to await the Secretary of State's decision as to his return.

Under the Extraditon Convention there is a general restriction on return if the offence is political, or military, if the purpose is to prosecute the person for his race, religion, nationality or political opinions, or if he might be prejudiced or punished by reasons of his race, religion, nationality or political opinions.

Application can be made for habeas corpus. Where a person is committed the court must inform him in ordinary language of his right to make an application for habeas corpus and must give notice of the committal to the Secretary of State. A person committed must not be returned until the expiration of 15 days or as long as habeas corpus proceedings are pending.

The Divisional Court can order the applicant's discharge if by reason of the trivial nature of the offence, by reason of the passage of time, or because the accusation against him is not made in good faith in the interests of justice it would, having regard to all the circumstances, be unjust or oppressive to return him.

Where a person is committed and is not discharged the Secretary of State may order him to be returned but, without prejudice to his general discretion, the Secretary of State may not make an order if by reason of the trivial nature thereof the offence, by reason of the passage of time, or because the accusation against the applicant is not made in good faith, in the interests of justice it would, having regard to all the circumstances, be unjust or oppressive to return him.

The Secretary of State must give notice of an intention to make an order and the person has 15 days commencing with the date that notice is given to make representations. He may not be returned until seven days after the warrant is issued. He may seek judicial review in this period and may not be removed so long as judicial review is pending.

Under article 14 of the Convention a person who has been extradited may not be proceeded against for any offence prior to his surrender other than the one for which he was extradited.

10.11 Schengen

The *Schengen Acquis* consists of the Schengen Agreement of 14 June 1985, originally made between Germany, France, Luxembourg and the Netherlands, and the Convention of 19 June 1990 applying the Schengen Agreement. The object of the Schengen Agreement is to reduce common frontier controls between the contracting parties and abolish internal controls. The Convention establishes common entry conditions for nationals from outside the Union who wish to cross the external borders of the Schengen states. Under article 2 internal borders may be crossed without any checks. Crossings of external borders are subject to checks and airports count as external borders. Entry may be granted for up to three months. A visa for longer visits must be issued by a Member State in accordance with its own legislation. All Member States are signatories to Schengen save for Denmark, Ireland and the UK.

The machinery for adopting EU measures on the crossing of external borders, asylum and other related subjects is contained in Title IV [IIIa] of the Treaty. The application of this Title is subject to two protocols on the position of the United Kingdom and Ireland, and Denmark; the protocols except them from the effect of Schengen. Under Article 1 of its Protocol the UK can continue to exercise border controls for the purpose of verifying the right to enter the UK of citizens of the EEA and their dependants and determining whether or not to grant other persons permission to enter the UK.

CHAPTER 11
FREEDOM OF ESTABLISHMENT AND PROVISION OF SERVICES

11.1 Introduction

Article 43 [52] of the EC Treaty confers on the self-employed the right to establish themselves in other Member States. This freedom of establishment includes the right not only to take up and pursue activities as self-employed persons, but also to set up and manage undertakings, companies, and firms. Article 47 [57] is an important corollary to this, in that it provides for the issue of Directives for the mutual recognition of formal qualifications. Article 48 [58] states that companies or firms formed in accordance with the law of a Member State, and having their registered office, central administration, or principal place of business within the Community, shall, for the purposes of the provisions on freedom of establishment, be treated in the same way as natural persons who are nationals of Member States. Freedom to provide services is dealt with separately in articles 49 [59] to 55 [66]. Article 45 [55] derogates from the provisions on freedom of establishment in respect of activities which are connected with the exercise of official authority in the host state. Transport services are governed by the separate title in the Treaty which deals with that activity.

11.2 The qualification Directives

There is no point in having a right of establishment if there is no system for the mutual recognition of qualifications. This has prompted the Commission to introduce a general Directive on the recognition of qualifications, Council Directive 89/48 (OJ L19 24.1.89 p46), implemented in the UK by the European Communities (Recognition of Professional Qualifications) Regulations SI 1991/ 824. The Directive is described, in its full title, as a general system for the recognition of higher education diplomas awarded on completion of professional education and training of at least three years' duration. A series of Directives which apply to the medical profession make specific provision for the mutual recognition of qualifications throughout the Community, but in the case of most other professions there are no particular Directives and the general Directive applies.

The Directive applies to a national of a Member State who wishes to pursue his profession in another Member State. If he holds a diploma from a Member State, he is entitled to pursue his profession anywhere in the Community on the same terms as those which apply to nationals of the host state. The problem which arises when the laws of one Member State insist upon a diploma, but the laws of another do not, is dealt with by a requirement that the applicant should have pursued his profession, full time, for two years, and possess evidence of one or more formal qualifications. Member States can require applicants to undergo an adaptation period, or take an aptitude test; generally it is for the applicant to decide which.

A second general system for the recognition of professional education and training complements the first. Council Directive 92/51 (OJ L209 24.7.92 p25) covers levels of education and training not covered by the earlier Directive, such as those for artificial limb makers and probation officers. Where the taking up of a profession regulated by Council Directive 92/51 is subject to the possession of a diploma, the host state cannot refuse to allow a national of a Member State to take up his occupation on the same conditions as those that apply to its own nationals.

European Parliament and Council Directive (EC) 99/42 (OJ L201 31.7.99 p77) is designed to consolidate and simplify legislation relating to a wide range of occupations. It repeals earlier measures that had been made on a piecemeal basis, such as the redundant Council Directive (EEC) 82/489 (OJ L218 27.7.82 p24) on hairdressers, and substitutes a general system for recognition of qualifications. Included in a long list of affected occupations in the appendix to the Directive are manufacturers of textiles, itinerant tradesmen, hawkers and pedlars.

11.3 Lawyers and the Community

Three Directives affect lawyers,

- Council Directive (EEC) 89/48 (OJ L19 24.1.89 p46), the general Directive on the provision of services and recognition of qualifications
- Council Directive (EEC) 77/249 (OJ No L78 26.3.77 p17), a Directive on establishment
- European Parliament and Council Directive (EC) 98/5 (OJ L 77 14.3.98 p36) on permanent establishment.

There are three directives because there are three ways in which a lawyer may wish to provide his services: he may want to become a member of the profession in the host state, he may wish to provide services in the host state but still operate from his home state using his professional title there, or he may wish to establish himself in the host state but use his home qualifications. The Member States have different policies as regards foreign lawyers. In France, for example, all lawyers are expected to be members of the French legal profession, whatever law they may profess, but in the UK there has never been any objection to a foreign lawyer providing legal services provided that he does not profess to be a barrister or solicitor.

A lawyer may ask to have his diploma recognised with a view to establishing himself as a member of the profession in another state in accordance with Council Directive 89/48 (OJ L19 24.1.89 p46), but the host state may stipulate either an adaptation period, or an aptitude test. In the UK the Bar Council and the Law Society have devised aptitude tests including examinations on English law and procedure.

Under Council Directive (EEC) 77/249 (OJ No L78 26.3.77 p17) a lawyer can provide legal services in another Member State, but there is nothing in this Directive which relates to the establishment of an office in another Member State. It stipulates that a lawyer providing services in another Member State shall adopt the professional title used in the Member State from which he comes. Activities relating to the representation of a client in legal proceedings have to be pursued under the conditions laid down for lawyers established in the host state, with the exception of any conditions requiring residence, or registration with a professional organisation in that state.

With regard to representation of a client in litigation, Member States may require lawyers to work in conjunction with a lawyer who practises before the national court. The European Communities (Services of Lawyers) Order SI 1978/1910, amended by SI 1980/1964, implements the Directive in the UK and states that a lawyer from another Member State can provide any service, including appearing before a court, provided that he is instructed along with a United Kingdom advocate, barrister or solicitor. A lawyer from outside the United Kingdom has to decide which role he wishes to play, be it barrister, advocate, or solicitor, for the purposes of the proceedings. If he is instructed with a solicitor he cannot provide the services of a barrister, and vice versa. Likewise, a salaried lawyer, acting with a barrister or advocate in proceedings, can provide services only to the extent that a barrister or advocate in employment may do so.

A lawyer from another Member State cannot engage in conveyancing or probate work, but there are no other restrictions on non-contentious work. A competent authority (the Law Society or the Bar Council) can request him to verify his status as a Community lawyer. Article 4 of Directive 77/249 requires that a Community lawyer should observe the rules of professional conduct of the host state. This is without prejudice to his duty to observe the rules of conduct prevailing in his own Member State. It puts him in double jeopardy. Those contemplating forays onto the continent had best remember this.

The rule for non-contentious work is modified because article 4(4) speaks only of 'respect for the rules ... which govern the profession in the host Member State'; but the rules on professional secrecy, conflict of interest, publicity, and privilege may be entirely different in another Member State. A common lawyer will often write 'without prejudice' at the head of a letter but he should note that these words may not mean anything in another Member State. The Common Code of Conduct (see section 11.3.1 below) seeks to resolve the problems caused by such inconsistent professional rules.

In the United Kingdom complaints concerning the conduct of Community lawyers can be made to the Law Society, Bar Council, or equivalent bodies in Scotland and Northern Ireland. The Community lawyer has rights in disciplinary proceedings equivalent to those of a United Kingdom lawyer; the disciplinary authority concerned, if it upholds the complaint, must report its finding to the Community lawyer's own professional authority, and may limit his right to provide services in the United Kingdom.

European Parliament and Council Directive (EC) 98/5 is designed to facilitate the practice of the profession of lawyer on a permanent basis in a Member State other than that in which the qualification was obtained. It had to be implemented by 14 March

2000. It states that any lawyer shall be entitled to pursue certain professional activities including giving advice on the law of his home state, on Community law, on international law, and on the law of the host State in any other Member State on a permanent basis, and under his home country professional title. As in the case of Directive 77/249, however, the foreign lawyer may have to act in conjunction with a local lawyer in legal proceedings, and may not be entitled to administer estates or engage in conveyancing. He must register with the competent authority in the host state. And, irrespective of the rules of professional conduct to which he is subject in his home State, a lawyer practising under his home-country professional title is subject to the same rules of professional conduct as lawyers practising under the relevant professional title of the host Member State. In the event of failure by a lawyer practising under his home-country professional title to fulfil the obligations in force in the host Member State, the rules of procedure, penalties and remedies provided for in the host State apply, but before initiating proceedings the competent authority must inform the like authority in the home State, and must cooperate with that authority.

A lawyer who has practised with his home title under Directive 98/5 for at least three years will gain exemption from the requirements (to complete an adaptation period or take an aptitude test) set out in article 4(1)(b) of the general Directive on the recognition of diplomas, Directive 89/48/EEC (OJ L19 24.1.89 p16).

11.3.1 The Common Code of Conduct

The Comité Consultatif des Barreaux Européens (CCBE) is the liaison body in the European Community for the legal professions in the Member States. To this body was delegated the task of formulating the Directive relating to establishment.

In 1977 the Committee formulated the Declaration of Perugia on the principles of professional conduct of the professional legal regulatory bodies of the European Community. This does not amount to a code of professional conduct, but it is a statement of common principles. It also contains a little practical advice:

'In some Community countries, all communications between lawyers are regarded as being confidential. This principle is recognised in Belgium, France, Italy, Luxembourg and the Netherlands. The law of the other countries does not accept this as a general principle... In order to avoid any possibility of misunderstanding which might arise from the disclosure of something said in confidence, the Consultative Committee considers it prudent that a lawyer who wishes to communicate something in confidence to a colleague ... should ask beforehand whether and to what extent his colleague is able to treat it as such.'

In 1988 a Common Code of Conduct was adopted at Strasbourg. A revised version was adopted in 1998. The purpose of the Code is to minimise the problems which may arise from double deontology; that is to say, the application of more than one set of national professional rules of conduct to a particular situation. Article 5 of the Code attempts to deal with the problem concerning communications between lawyers of different Member States. It states that, if a lawyer sending a communication to another lawyer in another Member State wishes it to remain confidential or without prejudice, he should clearly express this intention when communicating the document. If the recipient is unable to ensure its status as confidential, he should return it to the sender without examining its contents. The explanatory memorandum which is appended to the Code contains a useful summary of the different national rules on confidentiality as they apply in each of the Member States. The European Court recognised the principle of confidentiality in Case 155/79 *A M & S Ltd* v. *E C Commission* [1982] ECR 1575, [1983] QB 878, and the principle is now enshrined in article 2 of the Code.

The Code applies to cross-border activities only. Its provisions include articles relating to the independence of the profession, confidentiality, client funds, insurance, fee sharing and contingency fees. The Code reflects the position in all Member States that unregulated agreements for contingency fees are regarded as contrary to the proper administration of justice.

11.3.2 Professional rules

The Common Code of Conduct was incorporated into the Code of Conduct of the Bar of England and Wales in 31 March 1990 and, since 1 September 1990, it has formed part of both the Solicitors Practice Rules 1990 (Rule 16) and the Solicitors' Overseas Practice Rules 1990 (Rule 4).

The Solicitors Overseas Practice Rules 1990 (which must now be read in the light of the Establishment Directive) allow solicitors to be in partnership outside England and Wales with lawyers of other jurisdictions, but such a partnership may only practise in England and Wales, or hold itself out as so practising, if all the non-solicitor partners are on the register of foreign lawyers that the Law Society now has to maintain under section 89 of the Courts and Legal Services Act 1990. The way was made open for multinational practices by section 66 of that act, and such arrangements are now permitted by amendments to the Solicitors Practice Rules made by the Multi-National Legal Practice Rules 1991. When such a partnership practises in England, the foreign lawyer is required to register with the Law Society so that clients will receive the same kind of protection that they would receive if a purely English firm was instructed; detailed rules are set out in Schedule 14 of the Act.

On 25 March 2000 the Bar Council adopted a new Code of Conduct for practice at the Bar of England and Wales. The code applies to international work whether a barrister is practising in England and Wales or abroad. A registered European lawyer must comply with the Code of Conduct in the manner provided for by the Registered European Lawyers Rules. The Rules are set out in Annex B of the Code, and require a registerred European lawyer to pay a subscription to the Bar Council, and to be insured. Where the professional activities of the European Lawyer in question may, but for the European Communities (Services of Lawyers) Order 1978, SI 1978/1910, be lawfully provided only by a solicitor or barrister, he must act in conjunction with a solicitor or barrister who is entitled to practise before the court, tribunal, or public authority concerned and who could lawfully provide those professional activities. The Order does not entitle a European Lawyer to carry out conveyancing.

A practising barrister can accept instructions from a 'professional client', which includes a solicitor, an employed barrister or registered European lawyer, any practising barrister or registered European lawyer acting on his own behalf, and any foreign lawyer in any matter that does not involve the barrister in supplying advocacy services.

The Foreign Lawyers (Chambers) Rules are part of the Bar Code of Conduct, and they enable foreign lawyers to practise from the chambers of an English barrister. A foreign lawyer must give a written undertaking to comply with the Bar Code of Conduct. He must be insured and must obtain the written consent of the Bar Council to his so practising. Copies of his undertaking and a certificate of insurance must be provided to the Bar Council.

The EC Directives do not apply as between the constituent parts of the United Kingdom, so that bizarrely Scottish lawyers are worse off than European lawyers with regard to practice in England. Under section 60 of the Courts and Legal Services Act 1990, and section 30 of the Law Reform (Miscellaneous Provisions) (Scotland) Act 1990, the Lord Chancellor has the power to make regulations to cure this anomaly. So far he has not done so, although he is a Scotsman.

Council Directive (EC) 98/5 (OJ L77 14.3.98 p36) is implemented by the European Communities (Lawyers Practice) Regulations 2000, SI 2000/1119, which apply to both branches of the profession. The Regulations are designed to facilitate the practice of European lawyers on a permanent basis in the UK and provides for the system of registration.

11.4 Jurisprudence

Prior to the enactment of the Establishment Directive the European Court had to adjudicate in several cases where the professional rules of Member States restricted the right of lawyers to provide their services. In the absence of an establishment Directive the litigants had resort to the direct effects of the Treaty. 427/85 *Commission* v. *Germany* [1988] ECR 1123 is the leading case. It concerned an action brought by the Commission accusing Germany of a failure to fulfil its obligations under articles 49 [59] and 50 [60] of the EC Treaty and Council Directive 77/249. The Commission criticised a German law which required the foreign lawyer to be dogged at every stage. He had to act in conjunction with a German lawyer even in cases where there was no requirement for representation by a lawyer. It required the German lawyer to be the authorised representative in the proceedings. It prevented the foreign lawyer from appearing in court unless accompanied by the German lawyer. The foreign lawyer could not even visit his client in prison unless accompanied by the German lawyer. The co-involvement of the foreign lawyer had to be proved at each stage. The European Court held that these restrictions were contrary both to the Directive and to the Treaty. The Establishment Directive has to be read in the light of this case.

CHAPTER 12
COMPETITION

12.1   Introduction

The European Union contains a market economy. Competition is supposed to lie at the heart of this economy and to be crucial to the protection of consumers' interests and the efficient allocation of resources. Undertakings try to gain an advantage over their rivals by offering more attractive terms to customers or by developing better products or more effective ways of meeting their requirements. In theory competition encourages and enhances economic growth. In practice however, even though his pies are the best on the High Street, the baker cannot sell any if the supermarket gives its pies away.

Article 3(g) [3(g)] of the EC Treaty states that the activities of the Community include a system for ensuring that competition in the internal market is not distorted. The fundamental rules on competition are contained in articles 81 [85] and 82 [86] of the Treaty. These rules apply to any enterprise trading directly or indirectly in the Community, no matter where it is established; Japanese or US companies are, therefore, as much affected as any Community enterprise. Article 81(1) [85(1)] of the Treaty prohibits agreements which may affect trade between Member States, and article 81(2) [85(2)] declares contracts containing such restrictions void (although if the restrictive terms are severable, only the severable parts are void).

Article 81(3) [85(3)] of the Treaty gives the Commission the power to exempt practices which have certain redeeming beneficial effects. As well as making application to the Commission for exemption, companies may sometimes need to check with the Commission in order to reassure themselves that their agreements do not offend against the competition rules; the latter procedure is known as an application for 'negative clearance'. EC Council Regulation No 17 (OJ 13 21.2.62 p204, Sp edn 1959-62 p87) sets out the procedure by which applications are made to the Commission both for negative clearance and exemption under article 81 [85].

12.2   *The Treaty provisions*

The Treaty rules are so important that they are best set out in full.

Rules Applying to Undertakings

Article 81 [85]. 1.   The following shall be prohibited as incompatible with the common market: all agreements between undertakings, decisions by associations of undertakings and concerted practices which may affect trade between Member States and which have as their object or effect the prevention restriction or distortion of competition within the common market, and in particular those which:

(a)   directly or indirectly fix purchase or selling prices or any other trading conditions;

(b)   limit or control production, markets, technical development, or investment;

(c)   share markets or sources of supply;

(d)   apply dissimilar conditions to equivalent transactions with other trading parties, thereby placing them at a competitive disadvantage;

(e)   make the conclusion of contracts subject to acceptance by other parties of supplementary obligations which, by their nature or according to commercial usage, have no connection with the subject matter of such contracts.

2.   Any agreements or decisions prohibited pursuant to this Article shall be automatically void.

3.   The provisions of Paragraph 1 may, however, be declared inapplicable in the case of:

–   any agreement or category of agreement between undertakings;

–   any decisions or category of decisions by associations of undertakings;

–   any concerted practice or category of concerted practices;

which contributes to improving the production or distribution of goods or to promoting technical or economic progress, while allowing consumers a fair share of the resulting benefit, and which does not:

(a) impose on the undertakings concerned restrictions which are not indispensable to the attainment of these objectives;
(b) afford such undertakings the possiblity of eliminating competition in respect of a substantial part of the products in question.

Article 82 [86]. Any abuse by one or more undertakings of a dominant position within the common market or in a substantial part of it shall be prohibited as incompatible with the common market in so far as it may affect trade between the Member States.

Such abuse may, in particular, consist in:

(a) directly or indirectly imposing unfair purchase or selling prices or other unfair trading conditions;
(b) limiting production, markets or technical development to the prejudice of consumers;
(c) applying dissimilar conditions to equivalent transactions with other trading parties, thereby placing them at a competitive disadvantage;
(d) making the conclusion of contracts subject to the acceptance by the other parties of supplementary obligations which, by their nature or according to commercial usage, have no connection with the subject of such contracts.

12.2.1 Application of article 81 [85]

Agreements falling within article 81(1) [85(1)] are automatically void. The scope of such a prohibition is wide. It can extend to 'horizontal' agreements such as cartels, market sharing, and price fixing between supplier and supplier. It also extends, with rather less justification, to 'vertical' agreements such as distribution, licensing, and exclusive purchasing agreements between different levels in the trade; the Commission usually grants exemption for many arrangements of this kind. The European Court is also prepared to accept that sometimes a degree of market protection is necessary before a distributor can be expected to take the risk of entering the market at all.

In Case 258/78 *Nungesser* v. *Commission* [1982] ECR 2105, [1983] 1 CMLR 278 (the *Maize Seeds* case), there was a licensing agreement for the exploitation of some plant breeders' rights which the Commission contended was contrary to article 81(1) [85(1)]. The Court held that the agreement was permissible, since otherwise there would be no incentive for anyone to risk introducing novel crop varieties onto the market. When the Court adopts such reasoning it is sometimes said to apply a 'rule of reason', and the test it applies is whether the terms in question are really necessary to secure access to the market. The Court went so far as to allow a clause which conferred on the plaintiffs an exclusive territory, and protected them from competition from the owners of the plant breeders' rights. However, the judgment made clear that an exclusive licence, with absolute territorial protection, which would eliminate competition from third parties and cut out parallel imports, would go far beyond what was necessary for the improvement of production or distribution or the promotion of technical progress.

Only those parts of the agreement which are incompatible with article 81 [85] are affected. The consequence of this nullity for other parts of the agreement is no concern of Community law. The way in which the English courts will apply this blue pencil test is not quite clear. In *Chemidus Wavin Ltd* v. *Société pour la Transformation et l'Exploitation des Résines Industrielles SA* [1978] 3 CMLR 514, the Court of Appeal doubted whether it was really a question of severance in the way the English courts use that term in considering whether covenants are void as being in restraint of trade, and, if they are to any extent void, whether those covenants can be severed so as to save part of the covenant, although another part may be bad. Buckley LJ said that one may have to consider whether, after the excisions required by article 81 [85], the contract could be said to fail for lack of consideration, or might have so changed its character as not to be the sort of contract that the parties intended to enter into at all.

The prohibition under article 81 may even be transient. In *Passmore* v. *Morland plc* [1999] 1 CMLR 1129, [1999] 3 All ER 1005, the Court of Appeal said that a beer supply agreement which was void when the claimant entered into a lease on a public house could become enforceable when the size of the defendant's business shrank so that the beer ties no longer had a material effect on trade.

An agreement or practice must be one which may affect trade between Member States before it is subject to article 81 [85]. In Case 56/65 *Société Technique Minière* v. *Maschinenbau Ulm GmbH* [1966] ECR 235, [1966] CMLR 418, it was said that this means that it must be possible to foresee, with a sufficient degree of probability, on the basis of a set of objective factors of law or fact, that the agreement in question may have an influence on the pattern of trade between Member States. The influence may be direct or indirect, actual or potential.

An agreement extending over the whole of the territory of a Member State, by its very nature, has the effect of reinforcing the compartmentalisation of the market on a national basis. Case 8/72 *Cementhandelaren* v. *Commission* [1972] ECR 977, [1973] CMLR 7, arose out of a number of decisions made by the Netherlands Cement Dealers Association. The trade in cement in the Netherlands was regulated, not by agreement but by the decisions of this association. The Association introduced a purely national cartel whereby the price of cement was fixed, for sales of less than 100 tonnes, and, for larger sales, a target price applied. The Court said that this arrangement would hold up the economic interpenetration which the Treaty was designed to bring about, and thus offended article 81 [85].

The kinds of agreements affected by article 81 are not confined to contracts in the legal sense. In Case 41/69 *ACF Chemiefarma NV* v. *EC Commission* [1970] ECR 661 several companies entered into an agreement fixing prices and quotas for the export of quinine. A gentlemen's agreement extended its provisions to all sales within the Common Market. It was held that such an agreement, if it contains clauses restricting competition in the Common Market, may fall under the prohibition contained in article 81(1).

Article 81 [85] extends to concerted practices. A concerted practice, sometimes called 'concertation', does not have all the elements of a contract, but may arise out of coordination which becomes apparent from the behaviour of the participants. Of course, the companies concerned will excuse themselves by saying that there is no collusion; everyone just happens to be charging the same price. In the *Dyestuffs* case, Case 48/69 *Imperial Chemical Industries Limited* v. *EC Commission* [1972] ECR 619, [1972] CMLR 557, the meaning of 'concerted practices' was discussed. It was said that article 81 distinguishes the concept of concerted practices from that of agreements between enterprises in order to bring under the prohibition of article 81 a form of coordination between undertakings which, without going so far as to amount to an agreement properly so called, knowingly substitutes a practical cooperation between them for the risks of competition. Although parallel behaviour may not, by itself, amount to a concerted practice, it may be strong evidence of such a practice, if it leads to conditions of competition which do not correspond to normal conditions.

The facts of the *Dyestuffs* case were quite striking. From January 1964 to October 1967 three general and uniform increases in the prices of dyestuffs took place in the Community. ICI argued that this extraordinary coincidence was the result of 'price leadership' by one undertaking. It was said that such a situation would arise where there was an oligopoly, that is to say a market which consists of a small number of large firms. In its grounds of judgment the Court said that, if parallel conduct is such as to enable those concerned to attempt to stabilise prices at a level different from that to which competition would have led, and to consolidate established positions, to the detriment of effective freedom of movement of products in the Common Market, it was particularly strong evidence of a concerted practice.

At the time this case arose the United Kingdom was not a member of the Community, so the case is also interesting from the point of view of the attitude of the Court to the position of subsidiaries established within the Community. It was said that by making use of its subsidiaries in the Community ICI was able to ensure that its decisions were implemented on the market. The fact that a subsidiary has separate legal personality is not sufficient to exclude the possiblity of imputing its conduct to the parent company. Such may be the case particularly where the subsidiary, although having separate legal personality, does not decide independently upon its own conduct on the market but carries out, in all material respects, the instructions given to it by the parent company.

Where a subsidiary does not enjoy real autonomy in determining its course of action in the market, the prohibitions set out in article 81(1) [85(1)] may be considered inapplicable in the relationship between it and the parent company, with which it forms one economic unit. In view of the unity of the group thus formed, the actions of the subsidiaries may in certain circumstances be attributed to the parent company.

The *Dyestuffs* case contains the first mention of a principle, now established, that an undertaking is an entity which may include a parent company and its subsidiaries: for a more recent application of the principle see C-73/95 *Viho* v. *Commission* [1996] ECR I-5457 discussed below.

ICI contended that, because it was a company from outside the Community, there was no jurisdiction. The Court rejected that argument; an agreement does not have to be made within the Community, or even between Community companies, for its effects to be felt within the Community. The European Court justifies its jurisdiction in such cases by means of this reasoning, known as the 'effects doctrine'.

The *Dyestuffs* case can be contrasted with the *Wood Pulp* case, Case 89/85 *A Ahlström Osakeyhtio and others* v. *Commission* [1993] ECR I-1307, in which the Commission asserted that certain producers of wood pulp had concerted on their prices by means of a system of quarterly price announcements. The European Court held that that conduct could not in itself amount to concertation. There was communication between producers because of periodic price announcements, but these announcements did not lessen each undetaking's uncertainty about what others would do; therefore concertation was not the only plausible explanation for their parallel conduct. 'Concertation' was a new fangled word for concerted practices, and the Court used the classic definition, namely a form of coordination between undertakings which, without having been taken to the stage where an agreement so called has been concluded, knowingly substitutes for the risks of competition practical cooperation between them.

Case 15/74 *Centrafarm BV* v. *Sterling Drug Inc* [1974] ECR 1147, [1974] 2 CMLR 480, is a case where there was an arrangement between the proprietor of parallel patents in various Member States and his licensees. It clarifies the principle that article 81[85] has no place in collusion between a parent and its subsidiary company, if they both form one economic unit, where the subsidiary has no freedom and the collusive conduct has to do with the internal allocation of tasks between the undertakings. In C-73/95 *Viho* v. *Commission* [1996] ECR I-5457, what happened was that Viho lodged a complaint against the Parker Pen Company about a system whereby it restricted its subsidiaries to distributing its products in their allocated territories. The European Court agreed with the Commission that the subsidiaries were wholly dependent on Parker Pen UK and enjoyed no real autonomy.

Article 81 [85] contains no definition of 'undertaking'. The term seems to be left deliberately vague: it appears to include undertakings in the economic or commercial sense. Defined in this way even an individual may be an undertaking. Commission Decision (EEC) 76/743 *Re Reuter/BASF AG* [1976] 2 CMLR D44 (OJ L254 17.9.76 p10) arose because of a complaint by Dr Reuter, a research chemist, who held shares in a group of companies. He complained about a non-competition clause which had been imposed on him. It was part of a contract made when a group of companies controlled by him had been sold. The Commission regarded Dr Reuter as an undertaking because he engaged in economic activity through the group of firms which remained under his control and by exploiting the results of his own research.

The reference, in article 81 [85], to decisions by associations of undertakings is designed to include decisions by trade associations, as happened in the *Cementhandelaren* case. In the United Kingdom a series of agreements and decisions by the Publishers Association and its members had the effect of restricting the market in books, and controlling their retail prices. This arrangement was known as the Net Book Agreement; it was notified to the Commission soon after the United Kingdom joined the Community, but remained valid until the Commission had time to consider it because it was an 'old agreement', that is to say one which was in existence before article 81 [85] was brought into effect. It was not until 1986 that the Commission decided to prohibit it, by Commission Decision (EEC) 89/44 (OJ L22 26.1.89 p12). The publishers made an application for exemption under the provisions of article 81(3) [85(3)] of the Treaty; it was refused and pending the outcome of annulment proceedings the European Court was persuaded to suspend the operation of the decision. The lesson the Commission learned from the subsequent litigation is that it should make a thorough examination of the economic consequences of trade agreements before commencing proceedings.

Before the Court of First Instance it was argued that the issues had already been decided by the Restrictive Practices Court in the United Kingdom in 1962. But the Court said that a Commission decision cannot be vitiated on the ground that it does not specifically rebut the previous findings of a national court. It was found that the Commission had considered the 1962 judgment, and that national judicial practices cannot prevail in the application of the EC competition rules (Case T-66/89 *Publishers Association* v. *EC Commission* [1992] ECR II-1995, [1992] 5 CMLR 120).

The appeal to the European Court of Justice (C360/92P [1995] ECR I-23, [1995] 5 CMLR 33) was not heard until 1995; this is not untypical of the delays in this kind of case. By the time the case was considered in the higher court a more critical approach to competition law had developed. The judgment showed that the Commission had failed to take account of the benefits derived from the Net Book Agreement, in particular for the English language area of the Union, and it should not have ignored findings by national courts. It was also important that the agreement did not require the publisher to fix a price for a book unless he chose to market it as a net book.

Agreements which have as their object or effect the distortion of competition fall within the terms of article 81 [85]. Several examples of such agreements are given in subparagraphs (a) to (e) of article 81(1). The list is not exhaustive, but it does indicate the sorts of agreements which require careful consideration. One should be careful when drafting or construing, *inter alia*, the following:

- price fixing agreements
- market sharing arrangements
- distribution agreements
- patent licences
- know-how licences
- agreements fixing discounts or other trading conditions and differentiating them according to the particular distributor or customer
- agreements preventing parallel imports
- export bans.

The requirements that an agreement should have as its object or effect the prevention, restriction or distortion of competition are to be read disjunctively. In Case 56/65 *Société Technique Minière* v. *Maschinenbau Ulm GmbH* [1966] ECR 235, [1966] CMLR 357, the Court explained that those requirements are not cumulative but alternative. It found that it was necessary to consider the precise purpose of the agreement, in the economic context in which it is applied. But if that analysis failed to reveal a sufficiently deleterious effect on competition, the consequences of the agreement should also be considered.

Cases 56 and 58/64 *Consten SARL and Grundig Verkaufs* v. *EEC Commission* [1966] ECR 299, [1966] CMLR 418, arose out of an agreement whereby Consten were granted sole distribution rights in France for the products of Grundig. It was said that, for the purposes of the application of article 85(1), there was no need to take account of the concrete effects of the agreement when it has as its object the prevention, restriction or distortion of competition. The *Consten* case is, by the way, a leading case in the competition law generally, and is useful not only with regard to the substantive law in this area, but also its procedural aspects.

12.3 Special sectors

The basic principle is that the competition rules apply to all sectors of the economy, but agriculture is treated as a special case, and transport has its own detailed rules. Coal and steel are not covered by the competition rules of the EC Treaty because of article 305 [232] which states that provisions of the ECSC Treaty are not affected; the ECSC has competition rules of its own.

Article 36 [42] of the EEC Treaty states that the Treaty articles relating to competition apply to the production and trade in agricultural products only to the extent determined by the Council. Council Regulation (EEC) 26/62 (OJ 30 20.4.62 p993, Sp edn 1959-62 p129) has applied the competition rules to production and trade in agricultural products, but not where the agreement forms part of a national market organisation. Nearly all agricultural products are subject to such a market organisation. The question whether the rules of a market organisation fell within the exemption in Regulation 26/62 was the subject of C319/93 *Dijkstra* v. *Friesland (Frico Domo) Cooperatie BA* [1995] ECR I-4471, [1996] 5 CMLR 178. The case turned on the interpretation of Article 2 of the Regulation 26/62. Some dairy farmers, who had withdrawn from a cooperative which was part of the market organisation, found that they were still subject to fees levied on their milk revenue. Advocate General Tesauro pointed out that these conditions could not be regarded as conforming with the objects of the common agricultural policy. The Court sympathised and said that if there was any doubt whether the criteria for exception in article 2 of Regulation 26/62 applied a national court should allow the parties to seek a decision from the Commission, as provided for in article 2.

Transport was originally included within the purview of Regulation 17. For a while it was exempted by Council Regulation 141/62 (OJ 124 28.11.62 p2751, Sp edn 1959–62 p291) but in 1968 it was brought back into the fold by Council Regulation 1017/68 (OJ L175 23.7.68 p1, Sp edn 1968 (I) p302). This applied the rules of competition to transport by rail, road, and inland transport. Maritime transport was made subject to detailed rules by Council Regulation (EEC) 4056/86 (OJ L378 31.12.86 p4). Air transport between Member States has been made subject to detailed rules by Council Regulation (EEC) 3975/87 (OJ L374 31.12.87 p1); this regulation applies, as amended by Council Regulation (EEC) 2410/92 (OJ L240 24.8.92 p18) to air transport, whether national or international, between Community airports.

Where there are no detailed rules on competition, article 81 [85] of the Treaty is not directly applicable. This is because, until the entry into force of implementing Directives, the transitional rules of articles 84 [88] and 85 [89] of the Treaty apply. Under these transitional rules it is for Member States to rule on the application of the competition rules, and for the Commission to record, under a procedure set out in article 85 [89], any infringements that have not been brought to an end. Agreements do not become automatically void under article 82 [85] until the transitional procedure has taken place. The position was discussed in Case 66/86 *Ahmeed Saeed Flugreisen and Silver Line Reisebüro* v. *Zentralezur Bekämpfung Unlauteren Wettbewerbs eV* [1989] ECR 803, [1990] 4 CMLR 102, and Cases 209 to 213/84 *Ministère Public* v. *Asjes* [1986] ECR 1425, [1986] 3 CMLR 173. Air transport between the Community and third countries is governed by a network of bilateral agreements. There is a proposal to apply competition rules to certain categories of such agreements: see (OJ C165 31.5.97 p14).

12.4   Minor agreements

The Court of Justice has applied a *de minimis* principle: trade must be affected to an appreciable extent before article 81 [85] will apply. In Case 19/77 *Miller International Schallplatten GmbH* v. *Commission* [1978] ECR 131, [1978] 2 CMLR 334, Advocate General Warner said that, in order for this plea to be accepted, the breach 'must indeed be negligible'. It appears, therefore, that the principle is of limited effect. It may well be that the offending party has a small share of the market in general, but if the market is sufficiently defined the share will be greater. Miller International was a producer of records and cassettes. It was true that it had a small share of the market in those goods, but half its repertoire consisted of recordings for children. In the children's market it had a leading position and could not escape the effects of article 81 [85].

The Commission has issued a Notice on Minor Agreements (OJ C372 9.12.97 p13). This states that in its view agreements do not fall under the prohibition in article 81(1) if the aggregate market shares held by all of the participating undertakings do not exceed on any of the relevant markets the following thresholds, namely 5% where the agreement is made between undertakings operating at the same level of production or of marketing (horizontal agreements), and 10% where the agreement is made between undertakings operating at different economic levels (vertical agreements). In the case of mixed horizontal/vertical agreements, or where the agreement is difficult to classify, the 5% threshold will apply.

The Notice does not rule out the applicability of article 81(1) [85(1)] in the following cases:

- horizontal agreements which have as their object to fix prices, limit production or sales, or to share markets or sources of supply
- vertical agreements which have as their object to fix resale prices or to confer territorial protection on the participating undertakings or on third undertakings.

12.5   *The* **Tipp-Ex** *case*

Commission Decision 87/407, *Tipp-Ex* (OJ 1987 L222 10.8.87 p1) is by no means a remarkable case, but it serves as a useful example of how Community competition law works in practice, and is a salutary example of what can go wrong. Tipp-Ex Vertrieb GmbH & Co KG was described as a company with a strong position in the market for correction paper and fluids, but by no means occupying a dominant position. At that time awareness of the competition rules was less acute, and the wordprocessor had yet to oust the typist's little white bottle. The proceedings concerned agreements and concerted practices between Tipp-Ex and its exclusive distributors in several Member States.

One of the distributors of Tipp-Ex was a French company, ISA, which bought Tipp-Ex products and then resold them on the German market. In other words, it engaged in parallel importing, thus undercutting other exclusive distributors. Tipp-Ex then brought pressure to bear in order to cut off the parallel market. ISA complained to the Commission.

During the Commission investigation a variety of evidence was unearthed. There was a telex to another distributor which ended with the sentence: 'We hope that you are able to help us to cut out the parallel market'. Another telex addressed to various distributors asked whether it made sense for an exclusive distributor to place his distributorship in jeopardy, and stated that action would be taken. Another telex to a company which had delivered supplies to ISA said: 'Although it is impossible on legal grounds to stop supplies, special prices should no longer apply'.

The system used by Tipp-Ex depended mainly on oral agreements, but, at a later stage, written standard form contracts were drawn up. These contained clauses restricting sales outside the contract territory: 'With regard to EEC Member States not included in the contract territory the Authorised Dealer undertakes not to engage in active sales.' There were also clauses protecting the contract territory: 'The Supplier shall not supply the contract goods to distributors who to his knowledge intend to resell them in the contract territory.'

It was easy for the Commission to make out a case from the above evidence. Tipp-Ex decided to rely on what amounts to a plea in mitigation. Its first submission was that prior to 1982 it had no knowledge of article 81 [85] of the Treaty. This did not impress the Commission. Its most heartrending plea was that it had 'instructed a lawyer to draw up a standard form contract with a view to placing its relations on a legally sound basis', and 'relied on the opinion of a lawyer who spent a considerable amount of time dealing with the legal questions involved and charged commensurately high fees'.

Altogether it was a sad case. The Commission found, using a typical phrase, that the conduct of Tipp-Ex and its dealers amounted at least to a concerted practice. It was moved to compassion, however, by the expressed readiness of Tipp-Ex to put its house in order. A fine of 400,000 ECU, which is very modest by current standards, was imposed.

12.6   Exemptions

The Commission has the power to exempt agreements from the effect of article 81(1) [85(1)] of the Treaty. It can declare article 81(1) inapplicable, if the agreement contributes to improving the production or distribution of goods or to promoting technical or economic progress while allowing consumers a fair share of the resulting benefit. Regulation 17 (OJ 13 21.2.62 p204, Sp edn 1959–60 p87) creates a system whereby undertakings can apply to the Commission for exemption.

The purpose of the exemption procedure is to allow undertakings to enter into arrangements that, taken as a whole, offer economic benefits, although they would otherwise be forbidden. A manufacturer might argue, for example, that his distributor should have an exclusive territory in which to promote a new product, as an incentive to sales and a means of increasing competition between different brands. Two manufacturers might wish to come to an agreement which would enable each to specialise in a particular product, instead of both manufacturing the entire range.

If an application for exemption is successful the Commission will make a decision declaring article 81(1) [85(1)] to be inapplicable. Under article 8 of Regulation 17 the exemption is issued for a specified period. In practice this period is unlikely to be longer than about five years. The Commission may revoke or amend its decision or prohibit specific acts by the parties.

It is sometimes difficult to know whether to notify an agreement. If in doubt it is usually best to notify. The Commission can impose fines of up to 10% of turnover on undertakings which intentionally or negligently infringe articles 81[85] or 82[86]. Under article 15 of Regulation 17, however, fines cannot be imposed in respect of acts that take place in the period after notification and before a decision is taken under article 81(3) [85(3)] of the Treaty. Under Commission Regulation 1216/1999 (OJ L148 15.6.99 p5), in the case of vertical agreements, an exception dates back to the date when the agreement was made; this is a recent and welcome reform.

12.6.1   Block exemptions

In order to obviate the need for the Commission to examine, on an individual basis, many agreements which have the same basic objectives there is a system of 'block exemptions'. Block exemptions are set out in several regulations, each of which exempts a category of agreements from the provisions of article 81(1) [85(1)] of the Treaty.

Technology transfer agreements are covered by Commission Regulation 240/96 (OJ L131 9.2.96 p2), motor vehicle distribution and servicing is covered by Commission Regulation 1475/95 (OJ L145 25.6.95 p25), specialisation agreements by Commission Regulation 417/85 (OJ L54 22.2.85 p5), and research and development agreements by Commission Regulation 418/85 (OJ L53 22.2.85 p5). 'Specialisation agreements' are reciprocal arrangements where each party agrees with the other not to manufacture certain products so that they can each concentrate on fewer production lines.

Vertical agreements or concerted practices entered into between two or more undertakings, each of which operates, for the purposes of the agreement, at a different level of the production or distribution chain, and relating to the conditions under which the parties may purchase, sell or resell certain goods and services are covered by Commission Regulation (EC) 2790/1999 (OJ L336 29.12.99 p21). This regulation introduces a new and more liberal régime for vertical arrangements replacing Commission Regulation 1983/83 (OJ L173 30.6.83 p1) on exclusive distribution agreements, Commission Regulation 1984/83 (OJ L173 30.6.83 p5) on exclusive purchasing, and Commission Regulation 4087/88 (OJ L359 28.12.88 p46 on franchising agreements.

The block exemptions regulations contain lists of terms which are permissible, the so-called *white clauses*, and lists of forbidden terms, the so-called *black clauses*. Some of the regulations take effect automatically without the need for notification to the Commission. Other regulations contain provisions for an 'opposition procedure'. The opposition procedure is a process which requires that, in certain cases, the Commission must be notified before the exemption applies. For example under the Regulation 417/85 on specialisation agreements undertakings with an aggregate turnover in excess of a certain threshold must notify the agreement to the Commission which then has six months in which to oppose the exemption.

The substitution of a single regulation covering vertical agreements is part of a modernisation process concerning competition procedures, the outlines of which may be understood by reading the Commission White Paper on Modernising the Rules for Implementing Articles 85 and 86 [81 and 82] (OJ C132 12.5.99 p1).

12.7   *Negative clearance*

The negative clearance procedure allows undertakings to ascertain whether the Commission considers that their arrangements are prohibited under article 81 [85] or 82 [86] of the Treaty. If the application is successful the Commission will make a decision certifying that, on the basis of the facts in its possession, there are no grounds under articles [81] 85(1) or [82] 86 of the Treaty for action on its part in respect of the arrangements or behaviour. An application for negative clearance will normally be made at the same time, and, indeed, on the same form as an application for exemption.

If the agreement has been drawn in such a way that it clearly falls within one of the block exemptions there will be little point in notifying it to the Commission; unless the company wishes to draw attention to itself.

12.8   Abuse of a dominant position

Article 82 [86] of the Treaty differs from article 81 [85] in that it is concerned not with collusive activity but the dominance of under-takings whose position is powerful enough for them to bully others. The leading case in this area is Case 6/72 *Europemballage Corporation and Continental Can Company Inc* v. *EC Commission* [1979] ECR 215, [1973] CMLR 199. The Continental Can Company of New York set up a company called Europemballage which was registered in Delaware. Europemballage then took over a Netherlands company, Thomassen. The arrangement gave Continental Can a powerful position in the European packaging market. The Commission found that by purchasing 80% of the shares in Thomassen, Continental Can had infringed article 82, and required the company to put an end to the infringement. Continental Can appealed to the European Court.

The first problem in the Continental Can case was to determine whether article 82 [86] applied at all; because the article would appear to be concerned not with the acquisition of a dominant position, but its abuse. In its grounds of judgment the Court said that abuse may occur if an undertaking in a dominant position so strengthens its position that the degree of dominance reached substantially fetters competition, so that the only undertakings remaining in the market are those whose behaviour depends on the dominant one. The judgment was not, however, a satisfactory basis for the development of a jurisprudence on mergers.

The Court then turned to what became the real issue in the case, namely whether there had been an abuse of dominance in the relevant market. The definition of the relevant market is central to all cases under article 82. In the *Brass Band Instruments* decision (OJ L286 9.10.87 p36), the history of which has already been described (see Chapter 2), the relevant market was the market for brass band instruments. It was fairly easy to define: brass bands cannot easily switch to using pianos and harmonicas. Case 27/76 *United Brands Co* v. *EC Commission* [1978] ECR 207, [1987] 1 CMLR 429, involved the interesting question whether, in the case of an importer of bananas, the relevant market was soft fruit or bananas. The Com-mission submitted that there is a demand for bananas which is distinct from the demand for other fresh fruit, especially as the banana is such a very important part of the diet of certain sections of the community. The report of the case occupies some 144 pages, thus demonstrating how much can be said about bananas. It was held that the relevant market is the banana market.

Firms are subject to three main sources of competitive restraint: demand substitutability, supply substitutability, and potential competition. The market is determined by looking at 'demand substitutability', that is to say the extent to which other products are available on the market; 'supply substitutability', or whether other manufacturers can enter the market; the geographical market; and the temporal market. Demand substitutability is measured by 'cross-elasticity of demand' which is a function of the ease with which customers will switch to other products if there is a price rise. In the *Continental Can* case the Commission failed to show that customers could not conveniently switch from the tin cans provided by the plaintiffs to glass containers. The metal closures provided by the plaintiffs were not expensive to transport, so they could easily be shipped in from other manufacturers. Moreover, food canners could easily produce cans themselves if they wished.

The Commission has issued a Notice on Market Definition (OJ C372 9.12.97 p5; [1998] 4 CMLR 177) which explains how the Commission approaches the problem of defining the relevant market. The Notice defines a relevant product market as comprising all those products and/or services which are regarded as interchangeable or substitutable by the consumer by reason of the product's characteristics, price or intended use. The relevant geographical market comprises the area in which the undertakings concerned are involved in the supply of and demand for products or services in which the conditions of competition are sufficiently homogeneous and which can be distinguished from neighbouring areas because the conditions of competition are appreciably different in those areas.

12.8.1 Dominance

In the *United Brands* case (above) dominance was defined as a position of economic strength enjoyed by an undertaking which enables it to hinder the maintenance of effective competition on the relevant market by allowing it to behave to an appreciable extent independently of its competitors and customers, and ultimately of consumers.

Market share does not necessarily indicate that there is a position of dominance. The Commission, however, takes the view that a dominant position is reached where an undertaking has acquired a 40–45% market share.

12.8.2   Abuse

Abuse may be 'exclusionary', such as predatory pricing, loyalty rebates and refusal to supply; or 'exploitative' such as charging unfairly high prices, tying, or imposing unfairly low prices on suppliers. In the *Brass Band Instruments* case the abuse was a refusal to supply. Likewise, in the *United Brands* case the plaintiff had used its strong position in the market in order to refuse to supply bananas to a distributor. In its decision in *Eurofix/Hilti* (OJ L65 11.3.88 p19) the Commission found there was an abuse when there was a tying arrangement. Hilti sold nail guns. It pursued a policy of tying the sale of nails to patented cartridge strips so that independent nail manufacturers could not enter the market; it was impossible to get nails except from Hilti. The decision was upheld in C53/92P *Hilti AG v. Commission* [1994] ECR I-667, [1994] 4 CMLR 614. The *Continental Can* case shows that abuse may consist not merely of unfair trading, but also changing the very structure of the market. Mere dominance, however, does not amount to an abuse; therefore article 82 [86] is not a satisfactory basis for the control of mergers, and specific regulations have had to be made to deal with that.

12.9   Mergers

Because the *Continental Can* case did not provide a good basis for the development of law on mergers, two regulations were enacted. Council Regulation (EEC) 4064/89 (OJ L395 30.12.89 p1 as corrected amended and republished at OJ L257 21.9.90 p14), which were later amended again by Council Regulation (EC) 1310/97 (OJ L180 9.7.91 p1), contain the substantive law on mergers. The regulations apply to all mergers which have a Community dimension. For a merger to have a Community dimension it has to be very large and it is defined in article 1 of the Regulation as follows (note that reference to ECUs has now been superseded by euros):

1. Without prejudice to Article 22 this Regulation shall apply to all concentrations with a Community dimension as defined in paragraphs 2 and 3.

2. For the purposes of this Regulation, a concentration has a Community dimension where:

(a) the combined aggregate worldwide turnover of all the undertakings concerned is more than ECU 5,000 million; and
(b) the aggregate Community-wide turnover of each of at least two of the undertakings concerned is more than ECU 250 million,

unless each of undertakings concerned achieves more than two-thirds of its aggregate Community-wide turnover within one and the same Member State.

3. For the purposes of this Regulation, a concentration that does not meet the thresholds laid down in paragraph 2 has a Community dimension where:

(a) the combined aggregate worldwide turnover of all the undertakings concerned is more than ECU 2,500 million;
(b) in each of at least three Member States, the combined aggregate turnover of all the undertakings concerned is more than ECU 100 million;
(c) in each of at least three Member States included for the purpose of point (b), the aggregate turnover of each of at least two of the undertakings concerned is more than ECU 25 million; and
(d) the aggregate Community-wide turnover of each of at least two of the undertakings concerned is more than ECU 100 million,

unless each of the undertakings concerned achieves more than two-thirds of its aggregate Community-wide turnover within one and the same Member State.

The procedural rules on notifications, time limits, and hearings are set out in Commission Regulation (EC) 447/98 (OJ L61 2.3.98 p1). The regulation contains an annexed note explaining the procedure. Some 23 copies of a complicated form (Form CO) have to be provided. The form specifies the information that must be provided when an undertaking notifies the Commission of a concentration with a Community dimension. The required information includes details of ownership and control, personal and financial links, and conditions in the affected markets.

12.10   Regulation 17

Council Regulation 17 (OJ 13 21.2.62 p24, Sp edn 1959–62 p87) governs not only the procedure with regard to applications for exemption and negative clearance, but also the powers of the Commission to impose fines and conduct investigations into matters relating to competition.

12.10.1   Exemption and negative clearance

The procedure for applying for exemption and negative clearance is set out in Commission Regulation 3385/94 (OJ L377 31.12.94 p28), which replaced the Commission Regulation (EEC) 27/62 (OJ L35 11.5.62 p.118, Sp edn 1959–62 p132). The regulation prescribes a form, Form A/B, which must be used when notifying agreements. Many copies are required: one for the Commission and one for each Member State. Detailed explanatory notes are included in an appendix to the regulation.

An application for negative clearance does not automatically count as an application for exemption; though both applications will usually be made on the same form. The information given on the form is detailed and relates to the market for the goods or services, the structure of the companies involved, details of the proposed arrangements, and the reasons why an application is being made for negative clearance or exemption. Even if the application is only made as a precaution, in order to obtain an exemption the applicant must state how the proposed arrangements are said to improve production or distribution, or promote technical and economic progress.

12.10.2   Complaints

Complaints of infringement of articles 81 [85] or 82 [86] of the Treaty can be made under article 3 of Regulation 17. Regulation (EC) 2841/98 (OJ L354 30.12.98 p18) sets out the procedure. Those entitled to make an application are Member States and natural or legal persons who can claim a legitimate interest; but the Commission may also act on its own initiative, so those unable to show strictly that they have a legitimate interest can still complain, and hope that the Commission will take up the cudgels on their behalf.

In competition cases a complaint might be, for example, that there is an agreement or cartel which distorts competition in the Community, or that a company has abused a dominant position in the common market. The complaint does not have to take any particular form; a letter will do. As a general rule, however, the complaint will identify the parties, give details of the infringements of the Treaty, show that the complainant has a legitimate interest, contain any evidence and documents relied on, state what steps have been taken to bring the infringement to an end, and declare that the contents are correct.

The party against whom a complaint is made will receive a statement of objections from the Commission identifying the issues. At the same time the Commission fixes the time limit in which the company has an opportunity to reply. The time limit may not be less than two weeks, and may be extended. The Commission will usually inform the company of the contents of its file by means of an annex attached to the statement of objections, although certain documents may be withheld on the grounds of confidentiality. The Commission is obliged to have regard to the legitimate interests of undertakings in the protection of business secrets and other confidential information and it will set a date by which parties may indicate parts of the objections which contain such information.

In its reply the company may set out all the matters relevant to its defence, and attach any relevant documents in proof of the facts relied on. If it so requests, in its written comments, the company is entitled in appropriate cases to have an oral hearing before the Commission. The hearing is informal, before a hearing officer appointed for the purpose. The public are not admitted; the hearing is an administrative one, an opportunity for the company to be heard. Statements by each person heard must be recorded on tape. Persons appearing before the Commission may be assisted by lawyers. Third parties may be heard, if they have a sufficient interest. The outcome of this procedure will be a decision by the Commission. Appeals against such decisions lie to the Court of First Instance.

12.10.3 Comfort letters

In practice exemptions are rare. Negative clearance may be unnecessary where the parties have in fact drafted their agreement with the object of avoiding the effects of article 81 [85], and many problems are dealt with in an informal manner. There is scope for renegotiating the agreement, or sometimes the Commission may require amendments to be made. More often than not the Commission will send a 'comfort letter' saying that the Commission is closing its file and that there is no reason to take further action; sometimes the letter will say that the agreement merits exemption. The national courts are supposed to take such a letter into account when dealing with competition cases, as was said in Case 99/79 *Lancôme SA* v. *Etos BV* [1980] ECR 2511, [1981] 2 CMLR 164, but a comfort letter does not actually confer any exemption. In *Inntrepreneur Estates* v. *Mason* [1993] 2 CMLR 293, in the Queen's Bench Division, the judge considered the guidance issued by the Commission in its Notice on Cooperation between National Courts and the Commission in Applying Articles 81 [85] and 82 [86] (OJ C39 13.2.93 p6), namely that national courts should have regard to a comfort letter as factual element. But he was not at all satisfied that it resolved the issue of whether an individual exemption was likely to be granted.

12.11   Hearings

Article 19 of Regulation 17 provides that the Commission shall give parties an opportunity to be heard before it takes any decision on negative clearance, exemption or fines. The procedure is set out in Commission Regulation (EC) 2842/98 (OJ L354 30.12.98 p18) which replaces Commission Regulation (EEC) 99/63 (OJ 127 20.8.63 p2268, Sp edn 1963–64 p47).

A company, or it may be an undertaking or association, against whom, for example, a complaint has been made will receive a statement of objections from the Commission which identifies the issues. At the same time the Commission fixes the time limit, usually six or eight weeks, during which the company has an opportunity to reply. The time limit may not be less than two weeks and may be extended. The Commission will usually inform the company of the contents of its file by means of an annex attached to the statement of objections, although certain documents may be withheld on the grounds of confidentiality.

In its reply the company may set out all the matters relevant to its defence and attach any relevant documents in proof of the facts relied on. If it so requests, in its written comments, the company is entitled to have an oral hearing before the Commission. The hearing is informal, before an official called the Hearing Officer, and the public are not admitted but minutes are kept which are read and approved by each person heard. Persons appearing before the Commission may be assisted by lawyers. Third parties may be heard if they have a sufficient interest.

The Hearing Officer does not give a judgment; it is an administrative hearing only. Any decision will be drafted by DG IV (the department of the Commission which deals with competition matters). An appeal against a decision will lie to the Court of First Instance.

12.12 Powers of the Commission

In order to carry out its tasks, the first need of the Commission is to acquire information. Under article 11 of Regulation 17 it can request information from companies and other undertakings. If the request is refused, the Commission can proceed by way of a decision to demand information. Under article 15 there is power to impose fines of up to €5000 where, whether intentionally or negligently, either no information or incorrect information is supplied.

Under article 14(1) the Commission may authorise its officials to examine books and business records, take copies, ask for on the spot explanations, and enter premises; but there is no obligation to comply. If a request made under article 14(1) does not prove to be sufficient, it can proceed under article 14(3) by making a decision ordering an undertaking to submit to investigation; this time the undertaking is bound to comply. There is, however, no necessity for the Commission to go through the preliminary stage of the procedure under article 14(1). It can proceed directly to a decision under article 14(3) without warning the company, and arrive unannounced.

Compliance is enforced with assistance of the 'competent authority' in the Member State. In the United Kingdom the competent authority is the Director General of Fair Trading who can apply for appropriate injunctions to enforce the powers of the Commission. What happens in practice is that the Commission officials come armed with the decision ordering the company to submit to the investigation. If it refuses, an application is made without notice in the Commercial Court for an injunction restraining the company from destroying any documents and requiring it to admit the officials of the Commission to carry out their investigation.

It is difficult to know what advice to give to a client who is faced with a request for information from the Commission. The first point to note is that there is no right of silence. There may be a temptation to give inadequate information on the first request, but carelessness at this stage may be difficult to rectify later on, since the Commission may be disinclined to believe a later explanation. Any statement which departs significantly from reality will amount to incorrect information within article 15, and will incur liability to a fine. If the initial request for information under article 11(1) is widely drawn, as is often the case, it may be best to wait for the Commission to demand information under article 11(5), since it must then specify what information is required.

If the inspector arrives uninvited there will be an explanatory memorandum attached to his warrant, setting out his powers. Article 14 does not specifically say that he has the power to search, but there is a duty to assist him to the extent of actually producing the specific documents required (Commission Decision 80/334 *Fabbrica Pisana* (OJ L75 21.3.80 p30)). Tactically it is best to answer his questions fully, and favourable points should be emphasised rather than left for the hearing.

Legal professional privilege may be claimed, but only to a limited extent. Case 155/79 *AM & S Ltd* v. *EC Commission* [1982] ECR 1575, [1982] 2 CMLR 264, sets out the limits of legal privilege as it applies in Community law. Privilege may not be claimed in respect of communications to in-house lawyers. Communications to independent lawyers may be privileged if made after proceedings were commenced.

As has already been mentioned, a finding that an undertaking has infringed article 81(1) [85(1)] or article 82 [86] of the Treaty will result in a fine of up to 10% of turnover. If an agreement is notified to the Commission, however, no fine can be imposed for acts done after notification and before the Commission decision provided that they fall within the limits of the activity described in the notification. Fines are enforced by registration in the High Court which then enforces them as if they were an ordinary judgment (see RSC Order 71, CPR Schedule 1). There is a Commission notice on the calculation of fines (OJ C9 14.1.98 p3) which indicates that minor infractions attract fines of from €1000 to €1 million, and in serious matters the fines may range up to €20 million. But sometimes these guidelines are exceeded. For an account of a Commission decision in which British Sugar was fined €39.6 million and Tate and Lyle €7 million in respect of price fixing agreements, see *The Times*, 15 October 1998.

Since the *Camera Care* case, Case 792/79R *Camera Care Ltd* v. *EC Commission* [1980] ECR 131, [1980] 1 CMLR 334, it has been recognised that the Commission also has the power to make interim orders. An example of this is provided by the Commission Decision in *Brass Band Instruments* (OJ L286 9.10.87 p36). This case has already been mentioned as a general illustration of the powers of the Commission in Chapter 2. Boosey and Hawkes the brass band instrument makers had managed to obtain a dominant position in the market for brass band instruments. They refused to supply parts to their competitor, Brass Band Instruments. The Commission, on a complaint, by way of an interim decision, ordered Boosey and Hawkes to supply the parts on pain of a penalty of 1000 ECU per day.

12.13   Cooperation with national courts

In *Garden Cottage Foods* v. *Milk Marketing Board* [1984] 1 AC 130, [1983] 3 CMLR 43, it was said that an abuse of a dominant position would give rise to an action in damages; articles 81 [85] and 82 [86] of the Treaty are directly applicable law. One can see, therefore, that in the *Brass Band Instruments* case it would have been possible to apply for an interim injunction and damages rather than proceeding by way of a complaint to the Commission. The enforcement of EC competition law is thus a task that can be undertaken by either the Commission or the courts in Member States, but the Commission, because of its limited resources, prefers people to use their national courts.

In Case T-24/90 *Automec Srl* v. *EC Commission* [1992] 5 CMLR 431 the applicant was an Italian car dealer who complained that BMW had violated article 81 [85] by refusing to continue his dealership. He asked the Commission to grant him an injunction to compel BMW to resume supplies. The Commission rejected his complaint because the Italian courts were already seized of the matter. He appealed to the Court of First Instance, who said that under article 81(1) [85(1)] the Commission was not empowered to grant an injunction ordering BMW to supply him. The Commission had a discretionary power to conduct an investigation, were entitled to prioritise matters in that regard, and were entitled to refer him to the Italian courts.

It was the *Automec* case that prompted the Commission to issue a Notice on Cooperation between National Courts and the Commission in Applying Articles 81 [85] and 82 [86] (OJ C39 13.2.93 p6). The problem was how to avoid conflicts and divide responsibility for the application of competition law between national courts and the Commission; the purpose of the notice was to achieve effective cooperation between them. In the notice the Commission pointed out the advantages of using national courts, namely that the Commission cannot award damages, that national courts can adopt interim measures more rapidly, that national courts can combine EU and national law claims, and that the Commission cannot award costs. Since the *Automec* case the Commission has devoted itself to proceedings which have particular political, economic, or legal significance to the Community; in ordinary cases notifications are be dealt with by a comfort letter, and complaints by national courts or authorities.

The notice, which does not relate to competition rules governing transport, suggests that national courts, before exercising their powers, should ascertain whether the conduct complained of has already been the subject of a decision, opinion or other official statement, such as a comfort letter, and take account of the Commission's powers. If the Commission has initiated a procedure, the courts should stay the matter before them.

The only exception to these principles is that old agreements that, like the Net Book Agreement, were in force before regulation 17 came into existence, or before a Member State joined the Community, remain valid until the Commission has made its decision; this is explained in Case 48/72 *Brasserie de Haecht SA* v. *Wilkin-Janssen* [1973] ECR 77, [1973] CMLR 287. New agreements, although notified to the Commission, do not gain any interim validity and are therefore vulnerable to civil action.

It is anticipated that national courts will find sufficient guidance to assist them in the application of EC competition law from the case law of the European Court, the block exemption regulations, and the various notices issued by the Commission, but if that is not enough they may, within the limits of their national procedural law, ask the Commission for assistance. The Commission can provide the court with procedural information, such as whether the Commission has officially initiated a procedure, can be consulted on points of law, can be asked to give an interim opinion on whether an agreement is eligible for individual exemption, and will provide statistical and other similar information.

The courts of the United Kingdom have yet to determine how this role will be fitted, if at all, to their procedure. In *MTV Europe* v. *BMH Records* [1995] 1 CMLR 437 however, Evans-Lombe J granted a temporary stay of proceedings in a case where the defendants had applied for negative clearance for their agreement (which concerned broadcast rights for music) pending an oral hearing before the Commission. The judge held that a full stay would be granted only if the Commission had not reached a final decision at the setting down of the case for trial.

12.14   *The Competition Act 1998*

The EU competition régime affects intra-Community trade, but purely national arrangements do not concern the Commission. In the UK the Restrictive Trade Practices Acts 1976 and 1977, and the Resale Prices Act 1976 used to regulate conduct at the national level but this legislation was unduly technical. It did not contain sufficient sanctions against anticompetitive conduct and unnecessarily caught many innocuous agreements. It had become a burden to business and cumbersome for the authorities to operate.

The new Competition Act 1998 has repealed the Restrictive Trade Practices Acts 1976 and 1977, the Resale Prices Act 1976, and sections 2 to 10 of the Competition Act 1980. The mergers régime in the Fair Trading Act 1973 remains in place, but the Monopolies and Mergers Commission has been dissolved and replaced by the Competition Commission.

Under the Competition Act 1998 there is a national competition régime based on EU principles. It is applied and enforced by the Director General of Fair Trading and, in relation to the regulated utilities, concurrently with the regulators for telecommunications, gas, electricity, water and sewerage and railway services. Whereas the EU régime extends to agreements affecting intra-Community trade, the Competition Act affects purely domestic agreements and abusive conduct. Thus, for example, a purely domestic distribution agreement comes within the new Act. As a general rule, however, if the parties' combined share of the relevant market does not exceed 25%, the Director General will not consider that an agreement has an appreciable effect on competition. But agreements to fix prices, share markets or impose minimum resale prices are likely to be considered as having an appreciable effect, as are agreements that are part of a network which has a cumulative effect on the market.

There are individual exemptions, and block exemptions modelled on the EU equivalents Block exemptions are made under section 6 of the Act. Under section 50 vertical agreements and land agreements may be excluded or exempted from the effects of the Act. The Competition Act 1998 (Land and Vertical Agreements Exclusion) Order 2000, SI 310/2000, excludes land agreements and vertical agreements from the Chapter I prohibition. A land agreement is an agreement that creates, alters, transfers or terminates an interest in land. This exclusion applies where restrictions arise for the benefit of an undertaking in its capacity as landlord. Where there is an attempt to go beyond this, as for example by requiring the tenant of a petrol station to buy goods only from a particular supplier, or restricting the prices at which he could sell goods, the exclusion will not apply.

The Exclusion Order also deals with vertical agreements arising when undertakings at different levels in the production or distribution chain are involved. The Exclusion Order is intended to follow the treatment of vertical agreements in the European Union so as to minimise the burden on business operating under the two different systems.

Agreements which breach the rules are void and companies are subject to fines of up to 10% of turnover. There are two prohibitions: one of agreements (whether written or not) which prevent, restrict or distort competition and which may affect trade within the United Kingdom (the Chapter I prohibition); the other of conduct by undertakings which amounts to an abuse of a dominant position in a market and which may affect trade within the United Kingdom (the Chapter II prohibition). These correspond with the restrictions under articles 81 [85] and 82 [86] of the EC Treaty, and indeed the Act uses the selfsame words to define the prohibitions.

Section 60 of the Act provides for the United Kingdom authorities to handle cases in such a way as to ensure consistency with Community law. When a national court determines a question under Part I of the Act it must act with a view to securing that there is no inconsistency between the principles applied and decision reached by the court and the principles laid down by the EC Treaty and the European Court in determining any corresponding question arising in Community law. In addition the court must have regard to any relevant statement of the Commission. The Director General of Fair Trading also must have regard to these principles.

There is also a system of parallel exemptions under section 10 of the Act: an agreement is exempt from the Chapter I prohibition if it is exempt from the Community prohibition by virtue of a Regulation, because it has been given exemption by the Commission, or because it has been notified to the Commission under the opposition procedure and the Commission has not objected.

12.14.1 Investigations

The Director General of Fair Trading can conduct an investigation if there are reasonable grounds for suspecting that the prohibitions in Chapters I or II have been infringed. The Office of Fair Trading can obtain documents and information to establish whether an infringement has been committed. This is usually done by means of a written procedure, but section 27 of the Act gives a power to enter premises, on notice, without a warrant and demand the production of documents and computer records. In certain circumstances a warrant may be obtained. An undertaking's legal adviser can be present during an on-site investigation.

By virtue of section 30 of the Act a person cannot be required to produce or disclose privileged communications. A 'privileged communication' means a communication between a professional legal adviser and his client, or made in connection with, or in contemplation of, legal proceedings and for the purpose of those proceedings, which in proceedings in the High Court would be protected from disclosure on grounds of legal professional privilege.

The definition of privileged communications under the Act is wider than that in EU law. In Case 155/79 *AM & S Ltd* v. *EC Commission* [1982] ECR 1575 the European Court said that legal professional privilege extended only to advice given by an independent lawyer, which is interpreted as not including in-house lawyers.

Following an investigation, the Director, if he proposes to make a decision that any prohibition had been infringed, must give notice to any person likely to be affected by his decision and give him an opportunity to make representations. Subject to that, he may make a decision that an agreement infringes the Chapter I prohibition, or that conduct infringes the Chapter II prohibition, and give appropriate directions to bring the infringement to an end. At the same time he can impose a penalty which may not exceed 10% of turnover.

A feature of the Act is a requirement for the Director to publish advice and information, together with guidelines about the appropriate penalties under the Act. These publications are available on the website of the Office of Fair Trading and are of a high standard. The guidance on penalties indicates that there is a five step approach:

- calculation of the starting point by applying a percentage determined by the nature of the infringement to the relevant turnover
- adjustment for duration
- adjustment for other factors
- adjustment for further aggravating or mitigating factors
- adjustment if the maximum penalty of 10% is exceeded and to avoid double jeopardy.

12.14.2   Appeals

Appeals against decisions of the Director lie to the Competition Commission under section 46 of the Act. Third parties can apply to the Director under section 27 asking him to withdraw his decision; they also have a right of appeal. Any appeal is determined by an appeal tribunal. The rules of procedure are set out in the Competition Commission Appeal Tribunal Rules 2000, SI 261/2000. An appeal lies to the Court of Appeal but only with the leave of the Tribunal.

12.15   *State aid*

This chapter has been concerned with the law of competition as it applies to private undertakings. Distortion of competition can also arise as a result of direct state intervention by way of aid to industry. Each year the Commission publishes an Annual Report on Competition Policy; more than half the contents are devoted to state aids. Article 87(1) [92(1)] of the EC Treaty reads as follows:

> 'Save as otherwise provided in this Treaty, any aid granted by a Member State or through State resources in any form whatsoever which distorts or threatens to distort competition by favouring certain undertakings or the production of certain goods shall, in so far as it affects trade between Member States, be incompatible with the Common Market.'

No definition of aid is given in the Treaty but it certainly includes subsidies: Case 30/59 *Steenkolenmijnen* v. *High Authority* [1961] ECR 1. It also includes tax exemptions, preferential interest rates, guarantees of loans on particularly favourable terms, and other similar gratuitous advantages granted through state resources. And in Case 310/85 *Deufil GmbH & Co* v. *EC Commission* ([1987] ECR 901; 1988 3 CMLR 687), in which the applicant claimed that sums paid to a German textile factory were not aid because they were calculated to improve general economic development consistent with article 157 [130] of the Treaty, the Court said that state aid is defined not by its causes but by its effects.

In Case 730/79 *Philip Morris Holland BV* v. *EC Commission* ([1980] ECR 2671; [1981] 2 CMLR 321) a question of whether aid affected trade between Member States arose with regard to aid which the Dutch government proposed to provide towards the enlargement of a cigarette factory. The Court said that when financial aid strengthens the position of an undertaking compared with other undertakings competing in intra-Community trade, the latter must be regarded as affected by that aid. The aid in question was destined for a company organised for international trade, a high proportion of whose production was destined for export to other Member States.

Not all aid is incompatible with the common market. Article 87(2) [92(2)] contains exceptions in the case of aid having a social character, or designed to make good natural disasters, or made to certain areas of Germany to compensate for the economic disadvantage caused by the former division of that country. Aid may be permitted to promote the economic development of areas where the standard of living is low and for certain other purposes and, since Maastricht, to promote culture and heritage conservation where it does not affect trading conditions and competition to an extent that is contrary to the common interest.

Under article 88 [93] of the Treaty the Commission has the duty to keep under review systems of aid in Member States. If, after giving notice to the parties concerned to submit their comments, the Commission finds that aid granted by a Member State is incompatible with the common market or is being misused, it has to decide that the State concerned shall abolish or alter the aid within a time limit fixed by the Commission. If the Member State does not comply the Commission, or any interested State, can refer the matter directly to the Court of Justice.

In Case 6/64 *Costa* v. *ENEL* [1964] ECR 585, [1964] CMLR 425, the question whether articles 87 [92] to 89 [94] of the Treaty were of direct effect was discussed. It was held that none of those articles is of direct effect, except for the final provision of article 88(3) [93(3)]. This is a procedural provision: a Member State may not put its proposed aid into operation until the procedure in paragraph 2 of the article has resulted in a final decision. There is thus the possiblity of challenging in a national court the grant of state aid where article 88(3) [93(3)] is not complied with.

CHAPTER 13
COMPANY LAW

13.1 Introduction

There would be no point in creating a single market if a company operating in the Community was unable to choose where to establish itself, or if a company established in one Member State was not permitted to provide services in another. The right to free movement and freedom of establishment are established by the EC Treaty, but wide variations in the company law of Member States create obstacles to free movement. The *Daily Mail* case, discussed in section 13.3.1, demonstrates the difficulties which can arise when companies choose to move from one Member State to another.

Community legislation in the area of company law is concerned with harmonisation of the laws of Member States. Harmonisation is mostly based on article 44(2)(g) [54(3)(g)] of the EC Treaty, which speaks of

> 'coordinating to the necessary extent the safeguards which ... are required by Member States of companies or firms ... with a view to making such safeguards equivalent throughout the Community.'

Article 48 [58] of the Treaty states that companies or firms are to be treated, for the purposes of the chapter on the right of establishment, in the same way as natural persons who are nationals of a Member State; 'companies or firms' includes cooperative societies, and other legal persons governed by public or private law, save for those which are non-profit making.

Article 94 [100] of the Treaty would appear to be a more appropriate vehicle for the activities of the Commission because it deals with approximation of laws. The difficulty was that under that article, until amendments were inserted by the Single European Act, legislation always required the unanimity of the Council. There

179

are now various derogations contained in article 95 [100a] as expanded by the Amsterdam Treaty.

Under article 293 [220] of the Treaty, Member States can make conventions for

> 'the mutual recognition of companies or firms ... the retention of legal personality in the event of transfer from one country to another, and the possiblity of mergers between companies or firms governed by the laws of different countries'.

There is a Convention on the Mutual Recognition of Companies which was entered into in 1968. No doubt it would be of interest if it was ever ratified, but since this requires unanimity it will probably never happen.

13.2   The harmonisation Directives

Nine Directives on the harmonisation of company law have so far been implemented. Others are languishing as mere proposals; the so-called 'Vredeling Directive' is the most famous of these. It suggests that large companies with a complex structure should regularly provide information to their employees on production plans, management changes, and other matters which might concern them.

The company Directives are important in the interpretation of the corresponding UK legislation. Because they have modified the laws of each Member State so as to achieve the same result there ought not to be any diverging interpretations in different jurisdictions. The European Court has said in Case 14/83 *von Colson* v. *Land Nordrhein-Westfalen* [1984] ECR 1891, [1986] 2 CMLR 430, that, in applying law which implements a Directive, national courts are required to interpret national law in the light of the wording and purpose of the Directive. In *Litster* v. *Forth Dry Dock & Engineering Co Ltd* [1989] 2 WLR 634, [1989] 1 All ER 1134, Lord Templeman said that:

> 'The courts of the United Kingdom are under a duty to follow the practice of the European Court by giving a purposive construction to directives and to regulations issued for the purpose of complying with directives.'

It follows that it is not safe to interpret company legislation without reference to the corresponding European legislation. The main directives on harmonisation are as follows.

13.2.1 First Council Directive of 9 March 1968 (EEC) 68/151 (OJ L65 14.3.68 p8)

This Directive protects third parties dealing with companies by stipulating that basic company documents should be disclosed, restricting the grounds upon which obligations entered into by the company can be held to be invalid, and limiting the circumstances in which nullity can be ordered. In the case of contracts made before a company has acquired legal personality the persons who acted in its name are liable. It was one of the first provisions of Community law to be incorporated into an English statute; it was adopted by means of section 9 of the European Communities Act 1972. Implementing legislation is now to be found in sections 18, 35–35A, 36, 42, 351, 711 and Schedule 22 of the Companies Act 1985.

The Directive has been adopted in all the Member States and it was utilised by the defendant in Case C-106/89 *Marleasing SA* v. *La Comercial* [1990] ECR 4135, [1992] 1 CMLR 305, which established that a national court must not declare that a public company is a nullity on any grounds other than those set out in article 11 of the Directive. For the facts of this case see Chapter 3.

13.2.2 Second Council Directive of 13 December 1976 (EEC) 77/91 (OJ L26 31.1.77 p1)

This Directive safeguards shareholders and creditors of public limited companies in respect of their formation and the maintenance of capital. It supplements the First Directive and was originally implemented by the Companies Act 1980, but is now reflected in Parts IV,V and VIII of the Companies Act 1985. It was amended by Council Directive (EEC) 92/101 (OJ L347 28.11.92 p64).

13.2.3 Third Council Directive of 9 October 1978 (EEC) 78/855 (OJ L295 20.10.78 p36)

The third Directive is concerned with the regulation of mergers. It is complemented by the sixth directive. Implementing legislation is to be found in the Companies (Mergers and Divisions) Regulations 1987, SI 1987 No 1991, and the Insurance Companies (Mergers and Divisions) Regulations 1987, SI 1987 No 2118.

13.2.4 Fourth Council Directive of 25 July 1978 (EEC) 78/660 (OJ L222 14.8.78 p11)

This Directive concerns the layout of accounts and the basis on which they are prepared. Council Directive (EEC) 90/604 (OJ L317 16.11.90 p57) makes amendments designed to simplify the procedures as they apply to small and medium sized enterprises, and Council Directive (EEC) 90/605 (OJ L317 16.11.90 p60) makes amendments so as to include within its scope partnerships with limited liability members. It was first implemented by the Companies Act 1981 which in turn was consolidated in Part VII of the Companies Act 1985. Implementing legislation includes the Companies (Modified Accounts) (Amendment) Regulations 1986, SI 1986/1865, the Companies Act 1985 (Accounts of Small and Medium Sized Enterprises and Publication of Accounts in ECUs) Regulations 1992, SI 1992/2452, the Companies Act 1985 (Accounts of Small to Medium Sized Companies and Minor Accounting Amendments) Regulations 1997, SI 1997/220, and the Partnerships and Unlimited Companies (Accounts) Regulations 1993, SI 1993/1820.

13.2.5 Sixth Council Directive of 17 December 1982 (EEC) 82/891 (OJ L378 31.12.82 p47)

This Directive complements the third Directive and concerns the division of companies where assets are acquired by other companies. The implementing legislation is to be found in the statutory instruments which implement the third Directive (above).

13.2.6 Seventh Council Directive of 13 June 1983 (EEC) 83/394 (OJ L193 18.7.83 p1)

This concerns the preparation of consolidated accounts by parent companies. It was implemented by the Companies Act 1989, Part I. Council Directive (EEC) 90/604 (OJ L317 16.11.90 p57) makes amendments designed to simplify the procedures as they apply to small and medium sized enterprises, and Council Directive (EEC) 90/605 (OJ L317 16.11.90 p60) makes amendments so as to include within its scope partnerships with limited liability members.

13.2.7 Eighth Council Directive of 10 April 1984 (EEC) 84/253 (OJ L126 12.5.84 p20)

This makes provisions for the qualifications of auditors. It was implemented by the Companies Act 1989, Part II, the Company Auditors (Examinations) Regulations 1990, SI 1990 No 1146, and the Companies Act 1989 (Register of Auditors and Information about Audit Firms) Regulations 1991, SI 1991 No 1566.

13.2.8 Eleventh Council Directive of 30 December 1989 (EEC) 89/666 (OJ L395 30.12.89 p36)

This makes disclosure requirements in respect of branches established in Member States by certain foreign companies, including companies not governed by the laws of Member States. Its purpose is to protect persons dealing with foreign companies that carry on business in a Member State. It is implemented by the Companies Act 1985 (Disclosure of Branches and Bank Accounts) Regulations 1992, SI 1992/3178, and the Overseas Companies and Credit and Financial Institutions (Branch Disclosure) Regulations 1992, SI 1992/3179.

13.2.9 Twelfth Council Directive of 21 December 1989 (EEC) 89/667 (OJ L395 30.12.89 p40)

Some Member States, namely Germany, Denmark, France, Belgium and the Netherlands, permit the formation of single-member private limited liability companies. The Twelfth Directive is designed to harmonise laws relating to this kind of company.

13.3 Proposals

There are gaps in the above list. The proposed Fifth Directive (OJ C240 9.9.83 p2) is still a proposal because of the political difficulty that it provides for employee participation in the management of a company. It overlaps with the Draft Vredeling Directive (OJ C217 12.8.83 p3) on procedures for informing and consulting the employees of companies with complex structures. No one ever expects these proposals to be adopted, but Council Directive (EC)

94/45 (OJ L254 30.9.94 p64) lays down requirements for informing and consulting employees in undertakings or groups of undertakings which operate in more than one Member State and employ more than 100 employees within the Community, including at least 100 employees at two establishments in different Member States. Originally the UK objected to this Directive but it was extended to the UK after the Amsterdam Treaty (see Council Directive (EC) 97/74 (OJ L10 16.1.98 p22)).

Future ideas for harmonisation of company law include an informal draft of a ninth Directive concerned with the conduct of groups of companies and a published proposal for a tenth Directive on cross-border mergers (OJ C23 25.1.85 p11). There is a proposal for a thirteenth Directive on takeovers and other general bids (OJ C378 13.12.97 p10), and a draft proposal for a fourteenth Directive to permit the movement of companies from one jurisdiction to another. The reason for the proposal for a fourteenth Directive will become clear on a reading of the *Daily Mail* case.

13.3.1   Moving home – the *Daily Mail* case

In Case 81/87 *R* v. *HM Treasury* ex parte *Daily Mail* [1989] 2 WLR 908, [1989] 1 All ER 328, the *Daily Mail* attempted to take advantage of articles 43 [52] and 48 [58] of the Treaty. Article 43 [52] confers a right to freedom of establishment and article 48 [58] states that companies are to be treated in the same way as natural persons. The applicant, an investment holding company, was resident for tax purposes in the United Kingdom. It discovered that there were certain tax advantages in moving to the Netherlands, whose legislation does not prevent foreign companies from setting up their central management there. The only fly in the ointment is that a company cannot transfer its residence for tax purposes without the consent of the Treasury. After a period of fruitless bargaining with the Treasury the matter came before the European Court on an article 234 [177] reference.

The Court held that the Treaty cannot be interpreted as conferring on Companies a right to transfer to another Member State while retaining their status as companies incorporated under the legislation of the original Member State. The case shows how far real free movement in the Community is dependent upon harmonisation of tax laws.

But, in *R* v. *Inland Revenue Commissioners* ex parte *Commerzbank*

AG [1993] 4 All ER 37, the European Court held that a German bank with a branch in the United Kingdom had suffered from discrimination. The bank claimed a repayment supplement, a sum equivalent to lost interest, on a tax refund, but only a company resident in the United Kingdom was entitled, under English law, to recoup this money. However, the European Court held that this unequal treatment amounted to discrimination contrary to articles 43 [52] and 48 [58] of the Treaty. It follows that sometimes it is possible to gain a tax advantage by relying on article 43 [52].

13.4   *European Economic Interest Groupings*

The Commission has been anxious to encourage cooperative enterprises between European companies. Council Regulation 2137/85 (OJ L199 31.7.85 p1) has introduced a new vehicle for use by companies wishing to set up joint ventures. These entities, known as European Economic Interest Groupings (EEIGs), are not subject to the regulations imposed by national company laws. The relevant United Kingdom legislation is in the European Economic Interest Grouping Regulations 1989, SI 1989 No 638.

The purpose of an EEIG is not to make profits for itself, but to facilitate or develop the economic activities of its members. It cannot exercise management powers over its own members or any other undertaking. It cannot hold the shares of its members. It cannot make loans to directors of companies where that is restricted by the law of a Member State. It can, however, hold the shares of non-member companies

The contract by which an EEIG is founded must include the name and address of the interest grouping, its objects and the names and addresses of its members. From the date of its registration in Britain an EEIG becomes a body corporate under the name in the contract of foundation. The Insolvency Act 1986 has been modified to allow for the winding up of a grouping as if it were an unregistered company under Part V of the Act.

13.5   *Societas Europaea*

The Commission long ago advocated the idea of a new kind of European company, a Societas Europaea formed on Community lines and operating on a Community-wide basis (see [1990] 1 CMLR

120, OJ C263 16.10.89 p41 and OJ C176 8.7.91 p1). From time to time different versions of draft proposals are circulated. It is one of the measures which was listed in the Commission White Paper on completing the internal market, and was first presented as a proposal in 1970, but progress has been slow. The proposal is for a Council Regulation on the Statute for a European Company which will have a minimum capital of €100 000. It will obviate the need for the adoption of the Fifth Directive and the Fourteenth Directive because the advantages of being able to operate on a homogenous European basis will, so it is hoped, compensate for the inconvenience of having to put up with worker participation.

CHAPTER 14
SOCIAL POLICY

14.1 Introduction

The EC Treaty has a profound effect on social policy. The case law in this area has been concerned with the interpretation of the equal treatment provisions of the Treaty, the extent to which those provisions are of direct effect, and conflict with national legislation.

Articles 136 [117] to 145 [122] of the Treaty contain the basic social provisions; these articles are sometimes referred to as the Social Chapter. Articles 146 [123] to 148 [125] provide for the setting up of a European Social Fund which finances vocational training and other schemes to improve employment opportunities. Articles 149 [126] and 150 [127] are a separate chapter devoted to education, vocational training, and youth.

Under article 136 [117] of the Treaty the Community and the Member States, having in mind the 1989 Community Charter of the Fundamental Social Rights of Workers, have as their objectives the promotion of employment and improved living and working conditions, so as to make possible their harmonisation. This is seen as a development which will arise not only from the functioning of the common market, which will favour the harmonisation of social systems, but also from the procedures provided for in the Treaty, and from the approximation of provisions laid down by law, regulation, or administrative action.

Article 138 [118a] was inserted by the Single European Act. It provides for Member States to pay particular attention to encouraging improvements, especially in the working environment, as regards the health and safety of workers.

Article 141 [119] provides for equal pay without discrimination based on sex. It has affected the law of the United Kingdom to a marked extent and the full text is as follows:

Article 141 [119]. 1. Each Member State shall ensure that the principle of equal pay for male and female workers for equal work or work of equal value is applied.

2.   For the purpose of this Article, 'pay' means the ordinary basic or minimum wage or salary and any other consideration, whether in cash or kind, which the worker receives, directly or indirectly, in respect of his employment from his employer.

Equal pay without discrimination based on sex means:

(a)   that pay for the same work at piece rates shall be calculated on the basis of the same unit of measurement;
(b)   that pay for work at time rates shall be the same for the same job.

3.   The Council, acting in accordance with the procedure referred to in article 251 [189b], and after consulting the Economic and Social Committee, shall adopt measures to ensure the application of the principle of equal opportunities and equal treatment of men and women in matters of employment and occupation, including the principle of equal pay for equal work or work of equal value.

4.   With a view to ensuring full equality in practice between men and women in working life, the principle of equal treatment shall not prevent any Member State from maintaining or adopting measures providing for specific advantages in order to make it easier for the under-represented sex to pursue a vocational activity or to prevent or compensate for disadvantages in professional careers.

The last two paragraphs of the above were inserted by the Union Treaty in order to give the Council greater powers to make new legislation and to permit a degree of positive discrimination.

Problems have arisen over whether article 141 [119] is directly applicable, and if so to what extent, whether for example it applies to indirect discrimination, as in the case of part-time workers who predominantly happen to be women. Article 141 [119] is implemented by various directives but the Equal Treatment Directive 76/207 (OJ L39 14.2.76 p40) and the Equal Pay Directive 75/117 (OJ L45 19.2.75 p19) attract the most interest.

14.2   *The Social Charter*

The Community Charter of the Fundamental Social Rights of Workers is simply a solemn declaration that was adopted by the Council in December 1989. It has no legal force, but is supposed to demonstrate the identity of Europe in the social field, and lists a series of rights for workers. The list includes the following:

- a statement on the right to freedom of movement
- protection with regard to living and working conditions
- the right to adequate social benefits
- the right to freedom of association and collective bargaining
- the right to vocational training
- the right to equal treatment
- the right of workers to be consulted and to participate in management decisions
- the right to health and safety at work
- the right to protection of children, the elderly and the disabled.

The right to strike is qualified in that it is made subject to national regulations and collective agreements.

During the Maastricht negotiations for the Union Treaty the United Kingdom opposed the widening of the social scope of the EC Treaty. The other 11 Member States wanted to implement the Social Charter by making changes to the social chapter of the EC Treaty. Because agreement was impossible the text of the social chapter was not changed, but a Protocol on Social Policy was annexed to the Maastricht Treaty which permitted them to form their own club in order to take amongst themselves, and apply as far as they were concerned, the acts and decisions necessary to give effect to an agreement (the Social Agreement) that they had made in order to implement the Social Charter. This arrangement did not last long. The Amsterdam Treaty, which was agreed after a new Labour government had been elected in the UK, made all the necessary amendments so that the Social Chapter is now the same for all Member States. Articles 136 [117] to 143 [120] of the EC Treaty were amended to incorporate the matters which were in the Social Agreement.

14.3 *The* Defrenne *cases*

The development of the law of equal treatment owes much to Miss Defrenne, an air hostess, whose conditions of service with the Belgian national airline SABENA required her to retire at the fatal age of 40. This requirement did not apply to her male colleagues. In proceedings before the Belgian Conseil d'Etat she complained that a decree concerning the pensions payable to air crew, which was issued within the framework of the general state scheme for retirement pensions, was contrary to article 141 [119].

The European Court ruled that a retirement pension which is established within the framework of a social security scheme laid down by legislation does not constitute consideration which the worker receives indirectly in respect of his or her employment within the meaning of the second paragraph of article 141 [119]: Case 80/70 *Gabrielle Defrenne* v. *Belgian State* [1971] ECR 445, [1974] 1 CMLR 494.

Miss Defrenne also brought a second action, this time before the *Tribunal de travail*. In this, Case 43/75 *Gabrielle Defrenne* v. *Société Anonyme Belge de Navigation Aérienne Sabena* [1976] ECR 455, [1976] 2 CMLR 98, she was more successful. Miss Defrenne claimed that the salary paid to her had been less than that to which a male steward would have been entitled. Two questions were referred to the European Court: whether article 141 [119] was directly applicable; and, whether article 141 [119] had become applicable in the internal law of the Member States by virtue of measures adopted by the authorities of the Community, or whether the national legislature alone was to be regarded as competent in the matter.

In answer to the first question the Court replied that, where the discrimination was direct, article 141 [119] can be relied on before national courts. A distinction was drawn between, first, direct and overt discrimination which may be identified solely with the aid of the criteria based on equal work and equal pay referred to by the article, and second, indirect and disguised discrimination which can only be identified by reference to more explicit implementing provisions of Community or national character. This direct dis-crimination can be detected 'on the basis of a purely legal analysis of the situation'. It follows that where one can show direct dis-crimination article 141 [119] can be relied on, both against the State, and against private individuals.

The terminology used to describe those circumstances when article 141 [119] has direct effect is confusing. Advocate General Warner in Case 96/80 *Jenkins* v. *Kingsgate* [1981] ECR 911, [1981] 2 CMLR 24, explains it more clearly:

'Article 141 [119] is, in my opinion, more accurately described as not having direct effect where a court cannot apply its provisions by reference to the simple criteria that those provisions themselves lay down and where, consequently, implementing legislation, either Community or national, is necessary to lay down the relevant criteria.'

The second question, which asked the Court to say who was competent to make measures to implement article 141 [119], was answered in the following way. Although the article was addressed to the Member States, in that it imposed on them a duty to apply the principle of equal pay, that duty did not exclude the competence of the Community. Even in areas where article 141 [119] has no direct effect the national legislature does not have exclusive power to implement the article; implementation may be by a combination of Community and national measures.

Having established that article 141 [119] had direct effect the Court then had to deal with the practical effect of such a judgment; many thousands of women would be filing claims for arrears of pay. The damages would, indeed, be enormous. Fortunately the Court was able to call upon the principle of legal certainty and ruled that the effect of its decision, save for Miss Defrenne herself, was not retrospective. The date of the judgment was 8 April 1976. This is an important date to remember because in some circumstances it is possible for equal pay claims to date back this far.

14.4   *The equality Directives*

Council Directive (EEC) 75/117 (OJ L45 19.2.75 p19) is designed to encourage Member States to apply article 141 [119]. They are required to abolish laws which are contrary to the principle of equal pay, and ensure that wage agreements and contracts containing discriminatory conditions are rendered void. In the *SABENA* case above it was said that Directive 75/117 does not derogate in any way from article 141 [119] and in *Jenkins* v. *Kingsgate* it was said to be designed principally to facilitate the application of the principle of equal pay outlined in article 141. In litigation between private individuals it will not be possible to rely on it directly. It serves, however, to explain article 141 [119] of the Treaty; the principle of equal pay is defined in the directive as meaning

'...for the same work or for work to which equal value is attributed, the elimination of all discrimination on grounds of sex with regard to all aspects and conditions of remuneration'.

Council Directive (EEC) 76/207 (OJ L39 14.2.76 p40) is the Directive which puts into effect the principle of equal treatment with regard to access to employment, vocational training and promotion, and working conditions. Other Directives deal with the following:

- equal treatment in social security (Council Directive (EEC) 79/7 (OJ L6 10.1.79 p24))
- equal treatment in occupational social security schemes (Council Directive (EEC) 86/378 (OJ L225 12.8.86 p40) as amended by Council Directive 96/97/EC (OJ L46 17.2.97 p20))
- equal treatment in self employment (Council Directive (EEC) 86/613 (OJ L359 19.12.86 p56)).

With the aim of ensuring that the measures taken by the Member States to implement the principle of equal treatment are made more effective, Council Directive 97/80/EC (OJ L14 20.1.98 p6) requires Member States to take measures to ensure that when persons who consider themselves wronged because the principle of equal treatment has not been applied to them establish facts from which it may be presumed that there has been direct or indirect discrimination it is for the respondent to prove that there has been no breach of the principle of equal treatment. For the purposes of this Directive the principle of equal treatment means that there shall be no discrimination whatsoever based on sex, either directly or indirectly. Indirect discrimination is defined as existing when an apparently neutral provision, criterion or practice disadvantages a substantially higher proportion of the members of one sex unless that provision, criterion or practice is appropriate and necessary and can be justified by objective factors unrelated to sex.

14.5 Social provisions

A ragbag of Directives seek to regulate working hours, health and safety, transfers, redundancies and other matters. Some of these overlap with the equality Directives. For example Council Directive 92/85/EEC (OJ L348 28.11.92 p1) is a measure to encourage improvements in the safety and health at work of pregnant workers and workers who have recently given birth or are breast feeding. The Directive contains provisions directly related to health and safety, such as prohibitions on exposure to various chemicals, radiation, and biological agents. It also requires Member States to ensure that workers are permitted at least 14 weeks maternity leave. Council Directive 93/104/EC (OJ L307 13.12.93 p18) regulates working time; average working time should not exceed 48 hours in a week. Council Directive 96/34/EC (OJ L145 19.6.96 p4) puts into effect a framework agreement on parental leave made between general cross-industry organisations (UNICE, CEEP and ETUC). The agreement grants men and women workers an individual right to parental leave on grounds of birth or adoption of a child to enable them to take care of that child, for at least three months, until a given age up to 8 years to be defined by Member States and/or management and labour.

14.6   *Transfers, insolvency and redundancy*

Council Directive 98/59/EC (OJ L225 12.8.98 p16), consolidating Council Directive (EEC) 75/129 (OJ L48 22.2.75 p29) on collective redundancies provides for the implementation of procedures for consultation with and notification of workers' representatives in good time. Council Directive (EEC) 80/987 (OJ L283 28.10.80 p23) gives protection to workers on insolvency by requiring Member States to take measures to ensure that guarantee institutions guarantee the payment of workers' outstanding claims.

Council Directive (EEC) 77/187 (OJ L61 5.3.77 p26), as amended by Council Directive (EC) 98/50 (OJ L201 17.7.98 p88) requires Member States to make legislation making the transferee of an undertaking liable for existing contracts of employment. As originally drafted, the Directive posed many problems of interpretation, as to what kinds of undertakings were covered, as to what was meant by a transfer, and as to the concept of an employee. The amendments made by 98/50/EC were for the purpose of clarifying the law in the light of the case law of the European Court of Justice.

The Directive is implemented by the Transfer of Undertakings (Protection of Employment) Regulations SI 1981 No 1794 as amended – known notoriously as TUPE. As originally drafted these regulations defined undertakings as 'commercial ventures' but it is now clear from Council Directive 98/50/EC that they cover private and public undertakings carrying out economic activities, whether or not they operate for gain. An 'employee' is defined as any person who is protected as an employee under national employment law. There is a transfer within the meaning of the Directive where there is a transfer of an economic entity which retains its identity, meaning an organised grouping of resources which has the objective of pursuing an economic activity, whether or not that activity is central or ancillary.

A useful summary of the law is to be found in *Betts* v. *Brintel* [1997] ICR 797 CA, [1997] 2 All ER 840. This was a case in which Brintel Helicopters Ltd, who transported men to and from oil rigs, lost one of their contracts to KLM who then did not take on workers from Brintel but moved the operation to another helicopter base altogether. The problem was whether this amounted to a transfer within the meaning of the Directive. Kennedy LJ referred to two cases where the European Court of Justice had to consider a similar question.

In C-24/85 *Spijkers* v. *Gebr Benedik Abbatoir* [1986] ECR 1119 Mr Spijkers had been employed at an abbatoir at Usbach over Worms that had entirely ceased business when its assets were bought, lock stock and barrel, by a rival. The Court held that in such a case a transfer does not occur merely because the assets are disposed of; it is necessary to consider whether the business was disposed of as a going concern, as might be indicated by the fact that its operation was actually continued or resumed by the new employer with the same or similar activities.

In C-13/95 *Ayse Suzen* v. *Zehnacker Gebandereinigung GmbH* ([1997] ECR I-1259; [1997] 1CMLR 768) Mrs Suzen, a school cleaner, had been dismissed when a new company took over her employer's cleaning contract. The judgment shows that the Directive does not apply where work is merely assigned to a new contractor in place of the one to whom it was previously assigned, as will be the case where the work was contracted out in the first place, with no transfer of significant assets or of a major part, in terms of numbers or skills, of the workforce previously carrying out the work. Accordingly, in the *Brintel* case the Court of Appeal held that there had not been a transfer within the meaning of the Directive.

By contrast, in *ECM (Vehicle Delivery Service) Ltd* v. *Cox* [1999] 4 All ER 669, Axial Ltd, who had a contract to deliver cars from Grimsby docks, lost their contract to ECM, who decided not to take on the drivers. An employment tribunal found that there had been a transfer and the Court of Appeal dismissed the appeal, holding that there was no rule of law that if no staff were taken on there could not be a transfer within the meaning of the Directive.

14.7 Discrimination

Article 141 [119] requires Member States to apply the principle of equal pay for equal work, and the foundation of the European

Court's jurisprudence arising from this is the *Defrenne* case. This case determined that a state pension was not pay within the meaning of article 141 [119]. In *Garland* v. *British Rail* [1981] ECR 359 it was said that pay includes any consideration, whether in cash or in kind, whether immediate or future, provided that the worker receives it, albeit indirectly, in respect of his employment from his employer.

'Equal work' means, as explained by Directive 75/117, the 'same work or work for which an equal value is attributed'. In *Rummler* v. *Dato Druck* [1987] 3 CMLR 127, it was said that physical strength is a criterion, and consequently a job classification system was not discriminatory merely because it was based on characteristics more usually found in men. The comparison must take account of all aspects and conditions of remuneration: *Hayward* v. *Cammell Laird* [1988] IRLR 257 HL.

In *McCarthys* v. *Smith* [1980] ICR 672, the Employment Appeal Tribunal said that the test was entirely qualitative and did not import a requirement of contemporaneity. Here the employers had a man for their stock room at £60 per week. He left and five months later they appointed a woman at £50 per week. She was entitled to equal pay; there was no requirement to be employed on like work at the same time for the comparison to be made.

In C429/96 *Grant* v. *South Western Trains* [1998] All ER (EC) 193, the European Court said that the legislation did not extend to homosexual relationships, but this was before the Amsterdam Treaty came into force, and it may be that article 6 (F) of the Union Treaty, which provides that the Union must respect fundamental rights as guaranteed by the European Convention on Human Rights would make all the difference.

As to what principles apply if there is indirect discrimination there is guidance in C170/84 *Bilka Kaufhaus GmbH* v. *Weber von Hartz* [1986] ECR 1607. Only full-time employees at a store were entitled to a pension. Part-time workers (mainly women) were not. The ECJ followed its judgment in *Jenkins* v. *Kingsgate* [1981] ECR 911, where again a lower rate was paid for part-time work than for full time work, by asking the question whether the difference could be objectively justified. Where there may be indirect discrimination the onus is on the employer to show objective justification for the difference in pay. In C-127/92 *Enderby* v. *Frenchay Health Authority* [1993] ECR I-5535, [1994] 1 CMLR 8, [1994] 1 All ER 495, a woman speech therapist claimed parity of pay with pharmacists and clinical psychologists. It so happens that speech therapists generally happen to be women, whereas pharmacists and psychologists, for no particular politically correct reason, tend to be men. The European Court held that the fact of the difference in pay having been reached by a collective bargaining process was not sufficient objective justification, but it was for the national court to determine, applying proportionality if necessary, whether and to what extent need to attract candidates to the job constituted objectively justifiable reason for difference in pay.

14.8   *The* **Barber** *case*

After the *Defrenne* case it was generally assumed that a pension was not pay. Indeed Council Directive 79/7/EEC (OJ L6 10.1.79 p24) on the progressive implementation of the principle of equal treatment for men and women in matters of social security, authorised Member States to defer compulsory implementation of the principle of equal treatment, with regard to the determination of pensionable age for the purpose of granting old age pensions. That exception was incorporated in Council Directive 86/378/EEC (OJ L225 12.8.86 p40) on the implementation of the principle of equal treatment for men and women in occupational social security schemes. In the light of those provisions it never occurred to anyone to think about contracted-out pension schemes and how they might come within article 141 [119].

Mr Barber thought about it. He had a company pension, a contracted-out scheme entirely financed by his employer. At the age of 52 he was made redundant. When he got over the shock he discovered that a woman in his position was entitled to an immediate pension, but he was not. Under the terms of the scheme the normal retirement age for women was 57, and for men it was 62; but, in the case of a redundancy an immediate pension was payable for a woman at the age of 50, and for a man at 55. He went to the Employment Appeal Tribunal complaining of discrimination contrary to article 141 [119] of the Treaty. His complaint about the breach of Directives 75/117 on equal treatment, and 76/207 on equal pay, could not succeed because they were not directly effective, nor could he rely upon the Sex Discrimination Act 1975, because that contained an exception in the case of arrangements relating to death or retirement. The Employment Appeal Tribunal said that he could not rely on article 141 [119] either, because access to pensions benefits was a question of equal treatment and therefore nothing to do with article 141 [119]. He appealed to the European Court.

In Case 262/88 *Barber* v. *Guardian Royal Exchange Assurance Group* [1990] ECR I-1889, [1990] 2 CMLR 513, the Court ruled that money paid under a contracted-out scheme *was* pay within article 141 [119]; it did, however, concede that its judgment was so unexpected that it should not be retrospective, except in the case of Mr Barber himself. In case the Court had not made itself sufficiently clear, the second protocol to the Maastricht Treaty states that benefits under occupational social security schemes are not considered as pay within article 141 [119], in so far as they are attributable to periods before 17 May 1990, the date of the judgment; this is another important date to remember.

But, the time limitation in the *Barber* decision only applies to discrimination which might have been thought to be justified on the basis of the transitional derogations in Council Directive 79/7 and 86/378. In C-246/96 *Magorrian* v. *Eastern Health and Social Services Board* [1997] ECR I-7153, [1998] All ER (EC) 38, two nurses were members of pension schemes which stipulated that those who had worked full time for 20 years were entitled to have their time counted double for benefit purposes. Because the applicants were women who necessarily had worked part time they were not entitled to come within this arrangement at all. They were not barred by the *Barber* decision from backdating their claims to 8 April 1976 (the date of *Defrenne*). The decision of the European Court does not affect the requirement to make a contribution to the scheme in order to acquire the relevant benefit and this is a disincentive to most backdated claims.

The time limits as to the period of employment needed to qualify to bring a claim, or as to the limitation period for bringing a claim before an employment tribunal have been the subject of challenge. In *Preston* v. *Wolverhampton Health Care Trust* [1998] 1 WLR 280, Mrs Preston brought a claim to an employment tribunal that she had been excluded from a pension scheme because membership was dependent on her working a minimum number of hours. What is more, she had been employed on a series of short-term contracts. The tribunal rejected the application because under the Equal Pay Act 1970 she had to bring it while still in employment, or at least within six months of its termination; it was not like the *Magorrian* case where the only issue was the question of entitlement to be in the scheme. She countered by saying that these limits made it impossible or excessively difficult to enforce her rights under the

Treaty, and as we know from C-271/91 *Marshall* v. *Southampton Health Authority* [1994] QB 126 the means of enforcement should be as effective as they would be for analogous rights under national law.

In C-78/98 *Preston* v. *Wolverhampton Healthcare Trust* (2000) *The Times*, 19 May, the European Court said that a six months time limit for bringing her claim was reasonable, as within the legal certainty principle. But, under section 2(5) of the Equal Pay Act 1970 only two years' service could be taken into account and this was incompatible with the principle of effectiveness.

In C-326/96 *Levez* v. *T H Jennings Ltd* [1999] All ER (EC) 1, [1999] ICR 521, the European Court said that such a limitation was not lawful, at least where the delay in bringing a claim was attributable to a misrepresentation by the employer about the remuneration of employees of the opposite sex. The application of the ruling was left to the Employment Appeal Tribunal who then decided to make a declaration that section 2(5) was no bar to recovery of money due over a period of six years. This ruling applies whether or not there is a misrepresentation: see *Levez* v. *T H Jennings Ltd* (1999) *The Times*, 10 November.

In *EOC* v. *Secretary of State for Employment* [1995] 1 AC 1, [1994] 2 WLR 409, [1994] 1 All ER 910, the Equal Opportunities Commission brought proceedings for judicial review, seeking a declaration that the United Kingdom was in breach of its obligations under article 141 [119] and Council Directives 75/117 and 76/207. At that time full-time workers (most of whom were men) had to be employed for two years before they could bring a claim for unfair dismissal or claim redundancy pay, whereas part-time workers (most of whom were women) had to wait for five years. The House of Lords granted the declaration.

It makes a difference whether an equal treatment claim is made within Directive 75/117 and under article 141 [119], rather than within Directive 76/207. This is because the Directives do not have direct effect. In C-167/97 *R* v. *Secretary of State for Employment* ex parte *Nicole Seymour-Smith* [1999] 2 CMLR 273, [1999] All ER (EC) 97, an estate agent, driven to economies, asked his secretary do the cleaning because it was 'woman's work'; the usual altercation ensued. It was said that since she had not been employed for two years she could not bring a claim for unfair dismissal, to which she replied that women generally are employed for short periods and found it more difficult than men to acquire the necessary years of service. In the European Court it was said that her claim could constitute pay within 75/117 and under article 119, but the remedy of reinstatement was governed by 76/207.

As to the requirement for two years of employment, it was said that if a Member State proved that a measure reflected a necessary aim of social policy which was unrelated to discrimination based on sex, and was proportionate to this aim, the fact that it affected more women than men was not a breach of article 141 [119]. In reaction to these cases the Unfair Dismissal and Statement of Reasons for Dismissal (Variation of Qualifying Period) Order 1999, SI 1999/1436, reduced the qualifying period to one year, but it is a wonder any time limits are left.

14.9   *Affirmative action*

The question somtimes arises whether affirmative action is lawful. In C-450/93 *Kalanke* v. *Freie Hansestadt Bremen* [1995] ECR I-3051, [1996] 1 CMLR 175, an affirmative action programme which gave women unconditional priority was held to be unlawful. But in C-409/95 *Marschall* v. *Land Nordrhein-Westfalen* [1997] ECR I-6363, [1998] 1 CMLR 547, Mr Marschall, a teacher, was overlooked in favour of an equally qualified female candidate; there was a scheme for promotion of women in circumstances where there were too few in higher grades. The European Court, in a less than pellucid judgment, held that where there are fewer women than men at the level of the relevant post it was not unlawful to give priority to women, provided that the male candidate was subject to an objective assessment which took account of all criteria specific to the candidates, and which would override the priority accorded to female candidates where one or more of those criteria tilted the balance in favour of the male candidate, but such criteria were not to discriminate against female candidates.

CHAPTER 15
THE COMMON AGRICULTURAL POLICY

15.1 Introduction

The common agricultural policy (CAP) is best understood by those who have read Genesis. It will be recalled that it was Joseph who originally thought of the idea. Pharoah, having had serious differences with the food processing industry, arrested the head baker and the chief butler. While they were on remand, their cell mate Joseph demonstrated a talent for the interpretation of dreams, predicting that the chief baker would be hanged.

The butler was happily acquitted and reinstated. One day he heard that Pharoah had had a bad night dreaming about food shortages, and put in a word for Joseph. The latter, having foreseen seven years of plenty and seven years of famine, was asked to formulate a plan to deal with the problem.

Joseph proposed that commissioners should be appointed to buy up the corn of Egypt during the years of plenty. This meant that the price of grain would be maintained in times of surplus. When there were shortages Pharoah would be able to guarantee supplies. So impressed was Pharoah that he took up the idea, grew immensely rich, and bought up all the land in Egypt.

15.2 Article 33 [39]

The objectives of the Common Agricultural Policy are set out in article 33 [39] of the Treaty and may be summarised as follows:

(a) to increase agricultural productivity and efficiency
(b) to ensure a fair standard of living for the agricultural community
(c) to stabilise agricultural markets
(d) to assure the availability of food supplies
(e) to ensure that supplies reach consumers at reasonable prices.

In order to attain the above objectives article 34 [40] of the Treaty requires Member States to develop a common organisation of agricultural markets. The financial arrangements for this are contained in article 34(3) [40(4)] which, in order to enable the common organisation to attain its objectives, provides for one or more agricultural guidance and guarantee funds to be set up. The European Agricultural Guidance and Guarantee Fund (EAGGF), often referred to by its French initials FEOGA, is divided into two parts: a Guidance Section which finances structural policy; and, a Guarantee Section concerned with expenditure relating to refunds on exports and intervention measures. The Commission is reponsible for the administration of the fund.

A common organisation of agricultural markets could have been achieved under article 34 [40] by means of common rules on competition, or the compulsory coordination of national market organisations; in practice it has been achieved by means of a European market organisation, that is to say the replacement of individual arrangements for marketing produce by a system which applies throughout the Community. This European market organisation has been constructed from a series of Council Regulations. There is a regulation for each kind of product affected: Council Regulation (EEC) 1766/92 (OJ L181 1.7.92 p21) deals with cereals; Council Regulation (EC) 1255/99 (OJ L160 26.6.99 p48) deals with milk products; Council Regulation (EC) 1493/99 (OJ L179 14.7.99 p1) deals with wine; Council Regulation (EC) 2200/96 (OJ L297 21.11.96 p1) deals with fruit and vegetables, Council Regulation (EC) 1254/99 (OJ L160 26.6.99 p21) deals with beef and veal, and so on. Nearly every agricultural product has its own regulation setting out its régime. There are some 20 of these main regulations. The main Council regulations have sprouted a number of ancillary and implementing regulations.

Some regulations, for example Commission Regulation 3665/87 (OJ L351 14.12.87 p1) on export refunds, are common to all régimes and are therefore referred to as 'horizontal'. The main regulations are themselves amended frequently, but there is little consolidating legislation to aid reference.

The system differs for each régime but the salient features are as follows. An *intervention price* is fixed at which intervention agencies in Member States are obliged to buy in products; this ensures that the farmer will receive a proper price for his crop. A *threshold price* is fixed above which goods can be imported from outside the Community; this protects the internal market and is achieved by means of a variable levy.

Depending on prices on world markets, it will sometimes be advantageous to encourage exports: at other times it may be necessary to discourage them. This balance is adjusted by means of export refunds or levies.

The system involves fixing each year a *target price* for each product. The target price is the level which the Community wishes to rule in the wholesale market. It will thus act as a guide to producers when they plan production.

Other terms are used in the regulations. The target price may sometimes be referred to as the *base price, reference price* or *guide price*. The intervention price may also be referred to as the *floor price* or *purchase price*.

The cereal market, which has the support of this system to the full, is the archetypal market organisation. By contrast the fruit and vegetable market concentrates on quality control: common standards are set for products and producers' organisations have the power to fix a withdrawal price below which they will not offer for sale products supplied by their members.

In the United Kingdom the body responsible for intervention purchases is the Intervention Board for Agricultural Produce. This body was created by section 6 of the European Communities Act 1972. In practice its powers are delegated to other agencies in the industries concerned.

15.2.1 Disaster

Like Pharoah the founders of the common agriculture policy feared shortages. They bought up the harvest so as to maintain high prices and guarantee an income for farmers, but the seven years of famine did not arrive and consequently mountains of butter and lakes of wine grew up. The Commission could not maintain high prices for the farmer and low prices for the consumer because these aims were incompatible. Various so-called co-responsibility levies, schemes for turning wine into alcohol, set aside, and quotas were introduced in an effort to curb overproduction.

There was no true free movement of goods in this common market. The Community continuously fixes intervention prices and the other guide prices for agricultural produce, but Member States have not been willing to accept the consequences for farm prices that would follow if the market rate of exchange were used. Instead, an artificial rate of exchange was used which became known as *green money*. Since green money would not necessarily correspond with the market rate there were still differences in the price of agricultural products between Member States that had to be evened out in some way. A system whereby monetary compensatory amounts (MCAs) were paid either as a levy (negative MCA) or a subsidy (positive MCA) on exports and imports was developed. The system meant that you could, for example, collect money simply for exporting your pig. If you could find a way of getting your pig back without paying a levy you could collect your compensatory amount again. This gave rise to constantly circulating pigs, a situation which brought the system into disrepute.

In order to cut down on milk production, farmers in Italy were offered payments for slaughtering their cows. As evidence of the demise an ear of the deceased animal was supposed to be produced. Whether it was the right or the left ear was not said, and perhaps the farmers mistook it for the method of slaughter, because many earless cows were to be seen in the fields.

Even without fraud the system was expensive. The UK Ministry of Agriculture estimated that in 1996 the cost to consumers and taxpayers for paying subsidies and supporting prices (the resource costs) of the common agricultural policy amounted to some €20 000 per farm (see *Europe's Agriculture, The Case for Change*, MAFF 1999). For many farmers this sum was more than their income from farming.

15.3   The 1992 reforms

In 1992 a series of reforms were initiated. Intervention prices were reduced and compensatory payments to farmers were substituted. Various accompanying measures were introduced such as an early retirement scheme, grants to encourage the protection of the environment, and aid for afforestation. Monetary compensatory amounts were eliminated because they could not survive the elimination of border controls. Council Regulation (EEC) 3813/92 (OJ L387 31.12 92 p1) substituted new arrangements which included direct compensatory aid to the farmer.

Council Regulation (EEC) 1766/92 (OJ L181 1.7.92 p21), as amended by 1253/1999 (OJ L160 26.6.99 p18) applies to cereals and illustrates the nature of the reforms. It is both a consolidating and a reforming measure. The preamble states that the support provided by the market organisation should be reorientated in such a way that it no longer depends solely on guaranteed prices. Target, threshold and intervention prices were fixed at gradually reducing levels. A management committee for cereals was created which must be consulted before detailed rules can be made by the Council or the Commission to determine standards and qualities and the intervention centres. Imports to and exports from the Community are subject to the submission of a licence. A levy is charged on imports, and there is a system of refunds on exports.

Council Regulation 1765/92 (OJ L181 1.7.92 p2), which is replaced by Council Regulation 1251/1999 (OJ L160 26.6.99 p1) from the 2000/2001 marketing year onwards, set up a system of support for cereal farmers, whereby they are compensated for the loss of income they will suffer because of the reduction in intervention prices. Payment is fixed by the hectare. In order to qualify the farmer has to set land aside from production.

15.4   *Agenda 2000*

Agenda 2000 is the name given to a series of reforms to modernise Community policies in the light of the coming enlargement of the Union. The agricultural reforms consolidate the reforms of 1992. Arable crops and milk will see gradual reductions in their intervention prices. In the case of beef and veal the intervention price will be maintained but the basic price will be reduced. The reduction in prices will be partly offset by direct aids to farmers. The market in wine will be controlled by a ban on new plantings until 2010.

The reform measure for cereals is Council Regulation (EC) 1253/ 1999 of 17 May 1999 (OJ L160 26.6.99 p18); it amends Council Regulation 1766/92 (OJ L181 1.7.92 p21), setting new intervention prices for the two marketing years from 2000 to 2002. Council Regulation (EC) 1255/99 (OJ L160 26.6.99 p48) sets up the new milk régime; it repeals, consolidates and replaces Council Regulation 804/68 (OJ L148 17.6.68 p13) and its subsidiary regulations. Council Regulation (EC) 1254/1999 (OJ L160 26.6.99 p21) on beef and veal repeals, consolidates and amends Council Regulation (EEC) 805/68; it contains measures to improve stock breeding, to organise marketing better, to improve quality, to provide aid for storage, and to make direct payments to producers. All the reforming measures so far mentioned in this paragraph came into effect on 1 January 2000.

The new organisation of the market for wine is contained in Council Regulation (EC) 1492/99 (OJ L170 14.7.99 p1). This applies from 1 August 2000. The regulation repeals amends and con-solidates a confusing array of earlier legislation. It contains measures to restrict the planting of vines, to pay premiums for the abandonment of wine growing, to restructure and convert vine-yards, to pay aid for the storage of wine, to restrict over pressing of grapes, to regulate labelling and marketing, and to regulate trade with third countries.

15.5 Structural reforms

Council Regulation (EC) 1257/99 (OJ L160 26.6.99 p80) is a serious attempt to make structural reforms. Some efforts were made towards modernisation as long ago as 1975 when Member States were authorised to introduce a system of aid for hill farmers by Council Directive (EEC) 75/268 (OJ L128 19.5.75 p1). Council Regulation (EEC) 2328/91 (OJ L218 6.8.91 p1) was a consolidating measure on improving agricultural structures. It required Member States to introduce an aid system to encourage set-aside of arable land and the conversion of production to non-surplus products. It also includes specific measures to assist farming in less favoured areas. Directive 75/268 and Regulation 2328/91 were repealed, amended and incorporated in Council Regulation (EC) 950/97 (OJ L142 2.6.97 p1). Council Regulation (EC) 1257/99 (OJ L160 26.6.99 p80) contains a series of accompanying measures, funded by the European Agricultural Guidance and Guarantee Fund, to comple-ment the price reforms with the object of establishing a system of support for rural development. It includes measures on support for investment in agricultural holdings, establishing young farmers, training, early retirement, support for less favoured areas, support for environmentally friendly agriculture, and forestry.

15.6 Competition

Article 36 [42] of the Treaty states that the provisions of the chapter relating to the rules on competition apply to production and trade in agricultural products only to the extent determined by the Council. This exception is now of little practical effect. Council Regulation 26 (OJ 1962 p993, OJ Sp edn 1959–62 p129) has brought into effect articles 81 to 86 [85 to 90] of the Treaty in the relation to agriculture. Articles 81 to 86 [85 to 90] of the Treaty now apply to all agreements decisions and practices referred to in articles 81(1) and 82 [85(1) and 86] of the Treaty which relate to production of or trade in agricultural products. Regulation 26 does not, however, include article 87 [92] which deals with state aids.

Council Regulation 26 is designed to afford some limited shelter from the competition rules as they apply to national marketing organisations. Article 2 of Regulation 26 states that 81(1) [85(1)] does not apply to

> 'agreements, decisions and practices of farmers, farmers' associations or associations of such associations belonging to a single state which concern the production or sale of agricultural products or the use of joint facilities for the storage treatment or processing of agricultural products and under which there is no obligation to charge identical prices, unless the Commission finds that competition is thereby excluded or that the objectives of article 33 [39] are jeopardised'.

The Commission has the sole power, subject to review by the ECJ, to determine by decision which agreements fulfil these conditions.

The kind of problem that can arise over the application of competition law in the area of agriculture is illustrated by the following case. In C319/93 *Dijkstra* v. *Friesland (Frico Domo) Cooperatie BA* v. *De Cooperatie Vereniging Zuivelcooperatie Campina Melkunie BA* [1995] ECR I-4471, [1996] 5 CMLR 178, a Dutch farmer was expelled from his cooperative for failing to deliver all his milk production to it, and was required to pay a resignation fee under the rules of the organisation. His contention was that article 81 [85] made the rules void in this respect.

The European Court stated that if an agreement or decision falls within the scope of article 81(1) [85(1)] and the criteria in Regulation 26 are not met, and if it does not qualify for exemption under article 81(3) [85(3)], it is automatically void and the nullity is retroactive.

The difficulty was that the Commission has exclusive jurisdiction to decide whether an agreement fulfils the conditions set out in article 2(1) of Regulation 26. So a question arose as to what the national court was to do if the Commission had not made a decision. The European Court accepted that there was a division of power between the national court and the Commission. If the position was clear – taking into account the case law and practice of the Commission – the local court should rule that the agreement was void. If, on the other hand, it was considered that the agreement might fall within the exemption in article 2 of Regulation 26 it should stay the proceedings and allow the parties to approach the Commission for a decision.

15.7 Interaction with other areas of the Treaty

15.7.1 Piggies going to market

Case 83/78 *Pig Marketing Board* v. *Redmond* [1978] ECR 2347, [1979] 1 CMLR 177, is a useful case to illustrate the relationship between Community provisions on agriculture and other areas of the Treaty. It explains the nature of common organisations of the agricultural market.

In Northern Ireland the marketing of pigs was controlled by the Pig Marketing Board, which had a monopoly. The law compelled farmers to sell their pigs to the Board. Regulations prohibited any transport of pigs otherwise than to one of the Board's processing centres, and by a person in possession of a permit. Mr Redmond's lorry was stopped in Armagh and discovered to contain 75 pigs; there was no permit. He protested that the prosecution was contrary to the Treaty and the rules on the common organisation of the market in pigs, as set out in Council Regulation (EEC) 2759/75 (OJ L282 1.11.75 p1).

The European Court said that the common organisations of the agricultural markets are based on an open market. Every producer has free access to this market which is regulated solely by the instruments provided for by those common organisations. National practices or laws which might prevent producers from taking advantage of intervention measures or any other measures regulating the market were not compatible with the principles of such organisations.

It followed from article 32 [38] that where there was a discrepancy between the Treaty articles relating to the Common Agricultural Policy and the rules relating to the Common Market it was the former that had precedence. Once the Community had legislated for the establishment of the common organisation of the market Member States could not undermine or create exceptions to it.

15.7.2 Milk quotas

Milk quotas can give rise to litigation, and present curious problems to conveyancers. They are a Community invention which can perhaps be described as a kind of quasi-interest in land. Land with a quota is worth more than land without a quota, but the quota cannot be sold without a land transaction; except that it is possible temporarily to transfer quota to another producer. When part of a holding is sold an apportionment of quota must be made, and Community rules provide that unused quota must be added to a national reserve of quota.

With such market protection the result was overproduction, and the chosen method of tackling the problem was to introduce a levy, payable by every milk producer, on the quantities of milk sold for direct consumption which exceed a certain reference quantity. It is this 'reference quantity' which is usually referred to as the quota. The system was originally created by Regulation (EEC) 856/84 (OJ L90 1.4.84 p10), which inserted a new article 5c into the original milk régime regulation 804/68 (OJ L148 28.6.68 p13, Sp edn 1968 (I) p176); other regulations by the Council and Commission made detailed rules for its application. Eventually the system was simplified and codified by Council Regulation 3950/92 (OJ L405 31.12.92 p1), which extended the quota for a further seven years from April 1993. Detailed rules for the application of the quota were set out in Commission Regulation 536/93 (OJ L57 20.3.1983 p12). Regulation 3950/92 was amended and extended for a further eight years from 1 April 2000 by Council Regulation (EC) 1256/1999 (OJ L160 26.6.99 p73).

In the United Kingdom the system is implemented by the Dairy Produce Quotas Regulations 1997. The Agriculture Act 1986 contains provisions relating to compensation to tenants for loss of milk quotas where a tenancy has ended, or been assigned. Certain questions arising under this legislation are dealt with by a Dairy Produce Quota Tribunal.

The development of the system is described by the Advocate General Sir Gordon Slynn, as he then was, in Case 120/86 *Mulder* v. *Minister van Landbouw en Visserij* [1989] 2 CMLR 1. The case arose because Mr Mulder had given up milk farming for a period because of a Community measure designed to encourage farmers to suspend production in return for a special premium (see article 8 of Council Regulation (EEC) 3950/92, as amended by (EC) 1256/1999 for the present system). He found, to his dismay, that when the milk quota scheme was introduced the reference year, upon which his quota depended, fell during the very period in which he had temporarily given up dairy farming. The Court ruled, however, that he had a legitimate expectation that he would receive a quota. The

Council was therefore bound to protect that expectation, and the relevant measure was held to be invalid in so far as it did not allow him to receive a quota.

Mr Mulder was then able to bring a direct action for compensation under article 235 [178] of the Treaty against the Council and the Commission, and was awarded damages in a sum equivalent to the difference between what he earned and what he would have earned had he been awarded a quota (see Case C104/89 and C37/90 *Mulder v. EC Council and EC Commission* [1992] ECR I-3061.

The organisation of the market for milk products is now set out in Council Regulation (EC) 1255/99 (OJ L160 26.6.99 p48). The regulation sets a target price for milk, which will reduce over a period from July 2000 to July 2007, and an intervention price for butter. There is a system of aid for skimmed milk and powder for feeding stuffs. Producers qualify for a dairy premium. The CCT applies but there is an additional import duty for certain products and a system of export refunds.

BIBLIOGRAPHY

EU Law (Text, Cases and Materials)
Paul Craig and Grainne d Burca
2nd edition
Oxford University Press
1998

European Community Law in the English Court
Edited by Mads Adena and Francis Jacobs
Clarendon Press
Oxford
1998

Remedies in EC Law
Mark Brealey and Mark Hoskins
Sweet & Maxwell
1998

EC Company Law
Vanessa Edwards
Clarendon Press
Oxford
1999

The EC Law of Competition
Edited by Jonathan Faull and Ali Nikpay
Oxford University Press
1999

Constitutional Law of the European Union
Koen Lenaerts and Piet Van Nuffel
London
Sweet & Maxwell
1999

European Union Law
Margot Horspool
2nd edition
Butterworths
2000

Bibliography

Introduction to the Law of the European Community
3rd edition
Edited by L Gormley
Kluwer Law International
1998

Textbook on EC Law
Josephine Steiner and Lorna Woods
7th edition
Blackstone Press Limited
2000

Wyatt & Dashwood's European Union Law
A Dashwood, D Wyatt
4th edition
Sweet & Maxwell
2000

INDEX

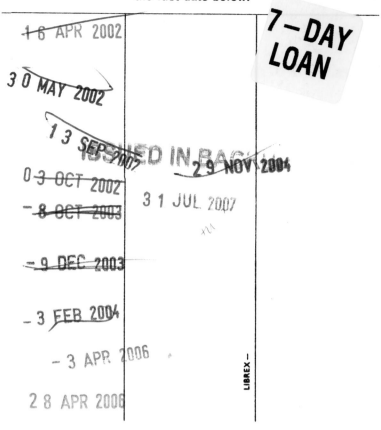

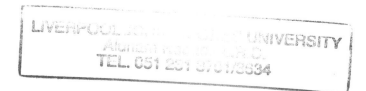

Also by
David Medhurst

EU Public Procurement Law
0-632-03813-6